January 2012

Ex Libris

van

MERKENSTEIJN

NIXON'S DARKEST SECRETS

ALSO BY DON FULSOM

The Billary Quiz

NIXON'S DARKEST SECRETS

THE INSIDE STORY OF AMERICA'S
MOST TROUBLED PRESIDENT

DON FULSOM

Thomas Dunne Books
St. Martin's Press New York

THOMAS DUNNE BOOKS.
An imprint of St. Martin's Press.

NIXON'S DARKEST SECRETS: THE INSIDE STORY OF AMERICA'S MOST TROUBLED
PRESIDENT. Copyright © 2012 by Don Fulsom. All rights reserved.
Printed in the United States of America. For information, address St. Martin's Press,
175 Fifth Avenue, New York, N.Y. 10010.

www.thomasdunnebooks.com

www.stmartins.com

Library of Congress Cataloging-in-Publication Data

Fulsom, Don.
Nixon's darkest secrets : the inside story of America's most troubled president /
Don Fulsom.—1st ed.
    p. cm.
Includes bibliographical references.
ISBN 978-0-312-66296-7 (hardcover)
ISBN 978-1-4299-4136-5 (e-book)
  1. Nixon, Richard M. (Richard Milhous), 1913–1994—Psychology. 2. Nixon,
Richard M. (Richard Milhous), 1913–1994—Friends and associates. 3. United
States—Politics and government—1969–1974. 4. Political corruption—United
States—History—20th century. 5. Misconduct in office—United States.
6. Watergate Affair, 1972–1974. 7. Presidents—United States—Biography.
I. Title.
    E856.F85 2012
    973.924092—dc23   2011035849

First Edition: February 2012

10 9 8 7 6 5 4 3 2 1

TO MY FAMILY,
FRIENDS AND STUDENTS

Contents

Acknowledgments

This book was a long time in the making, and therefore I have many people to thank who have encouraged me in the varying stages that led up to publication.

I first want to thank my agent, Jane Dystel, who took my project on so enthusiastically, and Thomas Dunne of Thomas Dunne Books, who considered the book worthy of his imprint. My editor at Thomas Dunne, Rob Kirkpatrick, offered extremely helpful suggestions and encouragement as we went along, as did Rob's talented assistant, Nicole Sohl.

I also want to thank those who have helped me think through the manuscript and mold it over the years. I am grateful to Linda Cashdan and her savvy book doctoring skills; Pat O'Connor, Editor of CrimeMagazine.com; and several of my former students at American University—Madeline Cohen, Austin Trantham, Mary Jane Egan, and Tara Fircak.

I have spent a lot of time at the National Archives gathering the latest data, and archivists at the Nixon Project at the National

Archives at College Park, Maryland, were very helpful, especially Steve Greene, Dick O'Neill, and Allen Rice.

I want to thank my family members who offered continuous support and encouragement, led by my daughter, Beth Willett, and my sister, Deanna Nowicki, and their spouses—my son-in-law, James Willett, and brother-in-law, Frank Nowicki.

And then there were many others who made suggestions, helped with the subject matter, looked over chapters, and added their knowledge. These include: Jay Bell; Tom Foty, Tom DeLach, and Rob Thaler; Roger Gittines and Jane Berger; Bob Frishman and Jeanne Schinto; Mike Magor and Katherine Lenard; Keith Koffler; Greg Clugston; Tina Rafalovich; Larry Webb; Neal Augenstein; Jimmy Minichello; Craig Smith; Warren Corbett; Kenneth Williams; Joe Gomez; Jonnie and Jerry Mitchell; Penny Pagano; Mitch Kominsky; Patti and David Victorson; Pat Sloyan; Dan Moldea; Stanley Kutler; Rick Boardman; Robert Enelow; Devra Marcus; Glenn Fuchs; Frank Sciortino; William Klein; Bob and Nancy Sloan; Sid Davis; Muriel Dobbin; Jim McManus; Luke Nichter; Michael Hussey; Maya O'Connor and Joel Tomlinson; Marc Borbely; Lee Edel; Bill McCloskey; Janette Alsford; Nicole Hollander; Dusty Rhodes; Steve and Dave Toth; Denise Gamino; Roxi Slemp; Mary Belcher; Dan and Elaine Mackolin; Candice Nelson; Bonnie Angelo; Bob Moore; Bill Scott; Dave Rosso; Charlotte Astor; Elias Demetracopoulos; Pye Chamberlayne, Maureen Kelly, and Marilyn Z. Tomlins; Ted and Cornelia McDonald; Carol Camelio; Gordon MacDougall and Linda Geurkink; Kelly Lux, Tom Gauger, Howard Dicus, and Philomena Jurey.

NIXON'S DARKEST SECRETS

Introduction

At 8 A.M. on June 18, 1972, I was at the Key Biscayne Hotel, covering President Nixon on one of his frequent weekends in the Florida and Bahamas sunshine with Charles "Bebe" Rebozo, when I got a call from Washington. The caller was Tom Girard, a close buddy and former radio reporter who had gone on to become the deputy press secretary for CREEP (the Committee to Re-elect the President).

Tom was every inch a Nixon man, but he was also a straight shooter with a solid grounding in the difference between what is ethically and legally right and wrong. Tom had just read the early edition of *The Washington Post* in which there had been a photo of the five Watergate burglars, along with their names.

"The guy they're identifying as 'Edward Martin' is not 'Edward Martin,'" Tom told me. "That's James McCord!" Normally laid back, Tom was really riled up. "McCord is the top security man for CREEP and he is a former CIA agent who was in charge of security for the CIA. McCord was always a nut about security at CREEP headquarters—instructing staffers how to thwart possible spies and such."

Tom, who had totally soured on Nixon's campaign tactics, wanted to get out the news about "Edward Martin's" true identify and its significance as soon as possible—without, of course, in any way implicating himself.

My story linking CREEP to the Watergate burglary was broadcast to UPI Audio's 1,200 radio clients at 10:10 A.M. It was one of those "reliable source" stories that would be very hard to trace. Since most people in the White House press operation knew Tom and I were good friends and might have put two and two together, rather than use my own voice and a Key Biscayne dateline on the forty-five-second spot, I dictated my piece to our weekend reporter in Washington, Charles Van Dyke, who then voiced my words and signed off with his own name. And with that, I became the first reporter to link the Watergate burglary to Nixon's re-election committee.

I covered the White House during the Johnson and Nixon presidencies, and although I went on to continue covering the White House during the Ford, Reagan and Clinton administrations, I never quite got over Richard Nixon. I was one of the few White House reporters who took a highly skeptical view of Nixon's Watergate denials from the very beginning, grilling Nixon's eventually discredited spokesman, Ron Ziegler, as hard as I could. My outrage at the dishonesty being fed to the press fueled me to score a number of significant scoops during the Nixon presidency.

I have now spent more than three decades pursuing the shadowy details of Richard Nixon's deeds, and the links to illicit activities keep coming, thanks to the extensive research I've done and the staggered release of Nixon's White House tapes and documents. The new revelations give us both insight into the character of the thirty-seventh President of the United States, and an understanding of why Nixon spent an estimated $20 million in legal fees to try to keep the incriminating information private.

Nixon's Darkest Secrets is about the portrait that is emerging. It is about Nixon the trickster, who burglarized the campaign office of his competitor in his first political campaign, and hired people posing as communists to hand out the opponent's political literature, who secretly ordered aides to supply reporters with false information that the man who shot and crippled Alabama governor George Wallace was a left winger, and that the 1972 Democratic vice presidential candidate, Sargent Shriver, had slaveholding ancestors.

It is a book about Nixon the assassination planner. As vice president, he headed supersecret CIA/Mafia efforts to kill Cuban leader Fidel Castro, and he approved a plan to assassinate Greek shipping tycoon Aristotle Onassis ("If it turns out we have to kill the bastard," he admonished an aide, "just don't do it on American soil."). As president he authorized the assassination of Chilean president Salvador Allende, and made it clear to Vietnamese president Nguyen Van Thieu, in 1972, that if he kept resisting a political settlement of the Vietnam War, he might not be around long. He concocted a plan to assassinate Panamanian strongman Omar Torrijos, and only at the last moment reportedly canceled a plan to kill columnist Jack Anderson, his nemesis in the press.

It is no wonder his vice president, Spiro Agnew, feared that when Nixon asked him to resign there was an "or else" implied. And it's no wonder star Watergate reporters Bob Woodward and Carl Bernstein feared for their lives after being warned by "Deep

Throat," who was revealed in recent years to have been the FBI's No. 2 agent, Mark Felt.

It is a book about Nixon's hidden Mafia ties—from two early campaigns, which were financed by money rounded up by Los Angeles mobster Mickey Cohen, to the payoff he took to pardon Jimmy Hoffa, to his best buddy Bebe Rebozo—who, FBI reports contend, was an associate of organized crime figures, and through whom Nixon reportedly did business for years with people in Florida godfather Santos Trafficante's family.

Relying on exhaustive research into recently declassified government documents and tape recordings, previously published accounts, little-known historical facts and fresh interviews, *Nixon's Darkest Secrets* paints a picture of a racist, anti-Semitic, homophobic chief executive who dwelled in a world of dishonesty, paranoia and secrecy, a president whose darkest clandestine maneuvers are only now coming to light, more than fifteen years after his death, and—ironically—through his own words.

ONE

TREASON WINS THE
WHITE HOUSE

Treason is the highest crime an American can commit against his country. And that's what one president accused his successor of committing.

Richard Nixon's secret sabotaging of President Lyndon Johnson's 1968 Paris peace talks—much more than Watergate or his longtime ties to the Mafia—should stand as our thirty-seventh president's greatest sin. There are no better words than "despicable" and "sordid" and "treason" (used by LBJ in this context) to describe Nixon's betrayal of his country for his own political gain. In a newly released Johnson phone call to Senator Everett Dirksen, just before the November 1968 election, the Senate GOP leader readily agreed with the president's treason conclusion about Nixon, and pledged to call his party's presidential candidate on the carpet on it.

Johnson himself—a number of times earlier, and later—scolded Nixon, who repeatedly denied knowing anything about the meddling with the Paris negotiations and pledged to do nothing to hurt President Johnson's efforts to end the war. (When the phone was hung up after at least one of these lies, Nixon and his cohorts reportedly burst into loud and sustained laughter.)[1]

The newest LBJ Library tapes tell the dramatic story of how Johnson blew his stack and nearly the whistle on Nixon's treachery: On November 2, 1968, three days before the election, Johnson let Dirksen peek at Johnson's self-described "hole cards" in his unbeatable poker hand in a high-stakes showdown against Nixon.[2]

Alluding to NSA intercepts, FBI wiretaps and CIA bugs, Johnson says on the tape that he knows—because South Vietnamese president Nguyen Van Thieu's offices are bugged—that China Lobby stalwart Anna Chennault went to Thieu on Nixon's behalf and told Thieu he should hold out on the peace talks until after the election. "They oughtn't be doing this," Johnson tells Dirksen. "This is treason." Dirksen agrees.

Johnson says he doesn't want to go public with the information, but he wants Nixon to know that he is aware of what Nixon's doing and to whom he and his emissaries have been talking. "They're contacting a foreign power in the middle of a war!" Johnson tells Dirksen on the tape. "It's a damn bad mistake. You just tell them that their people are messing around in this thing, and if they don't want it on the front pages, they better quit it." Dirksen vows on the tape to get in touch with Nixon and call him off.

Later, as president in mid-1971, Nixon got word—apparently from his chief of staff, H. R. "Bob" Haldeman—that President Johnson's Vietnam files were being housed at the left-leaning

Brookings Institution in Washington, D.C. These files included not only the decision behind LBJ's pre-election bombing halt (which Nixon erroneously thought was timed to help Democratic candidate Hubert Humphrey), but also evidence of Nixon's interference with the Paris peace talks. "You can blackmail Johnson on this stuff," Haldeman excitedly asserted about the bombing halt material.[3] (Haldeman thought that perhaps Johnson could be blackmailed into supporting Nixon's Vietnam policies.) Nixon biographer Anthony Summers noted that Nixon had another reason for wanting to get the Vietnam files. "[Nixon] had actively worked to sabotage the 1968 peace talks, and the record in question might actually prove more damaging to him than to President Johnson."[4]

So President Richard Nixon endorsed a wild scheme, shockingly wild: the firebombing of, and theft of files from, the Brookings Institution in Washington. The documents were well worth the risk, he figured, if they held evidence of his deliberate subversion. He also thought they might offer proof that his own 1968 campaign plane was bugged; it wasn't. Without specifically mentioning his Brookings break-in demand in his 1975 memoirs, Nixon did admit he had told his staff he wanted the Vietnam files he believed were in Brookings' possession delivered to him, "even if it meant having to get it surreptitiously."[5]

The Brookings plan was bizarre. "Masterminded" by G. Gordon Liddy of later Watergate infamy, it would have featured an old fire truck repainted with the markings of the District of Columbia's Fire Department. Operated by a group of pro-Nixon Cubans from Miami, disguised as a fire crew, the fake fire engine would make its way to Brookings. While ostensibly there to battle their own Molotov cocktail–caused blaze, the break-in experts from Miami would enter the building, crack open the vaults, make off with the Vietnam files, and then quickly ditch the slow-moving fire engine—after transferring the files and themselves to a nearby waiting van.

In his autobiography, Liddy surmised that a successful Brookings caper might have prompted some guessing games about the identities of the miscreants "in the liberal press," but that "because nothing could be proved, the matter would lapse into the unsolved-mystery category."[6]

John Dean, President Nixon's White House lawyer, had a far more sensible take on the contemplated firebombing. Dean claims he was able to shut down the operation (the "joint" had already been "cased"—in Dean's words—by Nixon agents, who were turned away by an alert security guard). Dean convinced presidential aide John Ehrlichman that if anyone died in the blast, it would be a capital crime that might be traced back to the White House. Ehrlichman later acknowledged calling off the plan— and confirmed that Nixon knew of it in advance.[7]

Just think: Had Dean not prevailed with Ehrlichman, had this break-in actually occurred, had it involved a death, and had it been botched as badly as Watergate, then murder and domestic terrorism might well have been added to Nixon's list of impeachable offenses.

In addition, just ordering the Brookings break-in "would be an impeachable offense," according to Terry Lenzner, who was a top official on the Senate Watergate committee. "It is the President ordering a felony to obtain information."[8]

And don't forget treason—had DC police recovered the 1968 campaign files from the phony firemen or fake DC fire engine.

What would have been found? Piles of evidence of Nixon's treachery, including this "smoking gun" intercept of a back-door message from Nixon to Thieu: "Hold on. We're gonna win." The message was plain, according to Nixon's go-between Anna Chennault: "Stay away from the peace talks."[9]

In 1968, Vietnam was the No. 1 issue in the campaign. Nixon was generally viewed as the dovish candidate because he promised to implement a secret plan to "end the war and win the peace." Humphrey was viewed as a candidate who would continue President Lyndon Johnson's unpopular hawkish war policies.

LBJ had dropped out of the presidential race to devote the remainder of his tenure to peace in Vietnam. He'd hoped, since quitting, to bring the fighting to an end through three-way (Hanoi, Saigon and Washington) peace talks in Paris. Nixon feared that if Johnson succeeded, Humphrey would win the November election. It was the kind of "October Surprise" the paranoid GOP nominee feared most.

Shortly before voters went to the polls, to ensure that Hanoi would attend the Paris talks, President Johnson announced a halt in the U.S. bombing of the North. Nixon learned of this important development through Henry Kissinger—an informal LBJ advisor to the peace talks. In *Nixonland*, Rick Perlstein observes, "The Johnson team trusted [Kissinger] implicitly. They shouldn't have. Kissinger was a double agent feeding the intelligence to Nixon that let him scotch the peace deal before the election."[10]

Johnson's bombing halt announcement, just days before the election, briefly gave Humphrey a slight lead in public-opinion polls—though he would go on to lose to Nixon by about 500,000 votes.

All during the 1968 campaign, working through a separate

secret agent—one even more secret than Kissinger—Nixon had been telling South Vietnam's president Nguyen Van Thieu to boycott any LBJ-sponsored talks and hold out for a better deal under a Nixon presidency. Thieu obliged, wrecking the talks and any chance for peace during the final months of Johnson's presidency.

Nixon's back channel in his contacts with Thieu was Anna Chennault, aka the Dragon Lady. The gorgeous forty-three-year-old widow of World War II U.S. "Flying Tigers" hero General Claire Chennault had moved from Taiwan to the United States in 1960. Anna was co-chairman of Women for Nixon-Agnew.

At Nixon's request, Chennault established contacts with the South Vietnamese ambassador to Washington, Bui Diem. In July 1968, Chennault introduced the ambassador to the GOP presidential hopeful at a hush-hush meeting at Nixon's New York apartment. According to Chennault, Nixon told Bui Diem he could "rest assured" that, if elected, "I will have a meeting with [Thieu] and find a solution to winning the war." He added that Chennault was to be "the only contact between myself and your government."[11]

Anna Chennault also had some dealings, face-to-face and on the telephone, with Nixon's campaign manager, John Mitchell. Unless he was speaking on a secure phone line, however, Mitchell kept most of his thoughts to himself. He strongly suspected that government agents were monitoring the Dragon Lady's activities.

Mitchell's suspicions were spot-on. And a furious Johnson didn't hesitate to let Mitchell's boss himself know what he knew about Nixon's underhanded antipeace maneuverings.

On a number of occasions, President Johnson talked directly to Nixon about the sabotage. In one conversation, after filling

Nixon in on his campaign's dealings with Thieu, LBJ added, "I'm not trying to trick you." It was a not-so-subtle dig at Nixon for his well-deserved nickname: Tricky Dick. Of course, Nixon denied knowing anything about the sabotage. And he reassured the president he would do nothing to undercut the peace process.

Even after the election, Johnson kept pressing the issue with Nixon:

> **LBJ:** These people [the South Vietnamese] are proceeding on the assumption that folks close to you tell them to do nothing 'til January the 20th.
> **Nixon:** I know who they're talking about too. Is it John Tower?
> **LBJ:** Well, he's one of several. Miss Chennault is very much in there.
> **Nixon:** Well, she's very close to John Tower.

In this discussion, Nixon not only threw loyal Texas Republican senator John Tower under the bus, but he also stressed the words "very close." What Nixon was apparently alluding to was a not-so-secret affair Senator Tower was having with the fabled Dragon Lady.

The supposed lovers were both right-wingers and heavy partiers on the Washington cocktail circuit. Tower had replaced Lyndon Johnson in the Senate. The two men were bitter enemies. So Nixon probably had that in mind when he ratted out Tower to LBJ.

A former Tower associate says the senator, long after his second failed marriage, freely admitted having a long-term liaison with Chennault. Tower was very fond of Anna, and, the source added, after they broke up, Tower claimed Chennault went on to "a torrid fling" with Thomas McIntyre, a left-wing Democratic Senator from New Hampshire and a "heavy foreign policy hitter."

Perhaps Chennault became soured on Republicans after Nixon quickly proceeded to betray her and the South Vietnamese government. Her "boss," as she referred to Nixon in her clandestine communications, was soon publicly voicing the LBJ line on Vietnam. Chennault and Thieu rightly concluded they had been duped by the soon-to-be thirty-seventh president of the United States.

In a 2002 interview with the *Shanghai Star*, a bitter Mrs. Chennault declared: "To end the war was my only demand. But after [Nixon] became president, he decided to continue the war. Politicians are never honest."[12]

In the phone call in which he falsely fingered John Tower as a possible traitor, Nixon promised Johnson he would contact Ambassador Bui Diem and urge South Vietnam to take part in the Paris negotiations. He didn't say exactly how he would do this, but Nixon pretended to know little about the ambassador, even asking LBJ at one point, "Does he speak English?" After all, Nixon had conferred with Bui Diem—who spoke perfect English—just months before.

So, no wonder when President Nixon heard that LBJ's files on Nixon's 1968 "treason" might be at Brookings—he repeatedly insisted that the liberal think tank be raided.

At a Nixon meeting with National Security Advisor Henry Kissinger and chief of staff Bob Haldeman, Kissinger observed: "I wouldn't be surprised if Brookings had the files."

> **Haldeman:** The bombing halt is in the same file, or in some of the same hands.

Nixon: Do we have it? I've asked for it. You said you don't
have it?

Kissinger: We have nothing here, Mr. President.

Nixon: Damn it! I asked for that [unintelligible]. Get in
there and get those files![13]

In a later conversation with Haldeman, Nixon asked: "Did they
get the Brookings Institute (sic) raided last night? No? Get it
done. I want it done. I want the Brookings Institute's safe cleaned
out and have it cleaned out in a way that it makes somebody else
responsible."[14]

Freshly declassified documents make it evident that Nixon had
unsuccessfully tried even earlier to find out what the CIA's files
contained about possible connections among LBJ's bombing
halt, the Paris peace negotiations, and the 1968 U.S. presidential
campaign. At first, he approached CIA director Richard Helms
through NSC Advisor Henry Kissinger.

In response, on March 19, 1970, Helms sent Kissinger
a three-page "secret" document outlining some of the intelligence data the agency collected in Vietnam in October
and November of 1968. Several sections of the document are
still classified, but Helms told Kissinger that, because of
the sensitivity of the Paris peace talks, President Johnson had
put a "freeze" on the distribution of such intelligence during
that time period, allowing only a small number of people to
see it.

"The President personally had to approve every reader of this
material . . . No one at the agency saw it except myself and even

I read the documents down at the White House," the CIA chief declared.

Helms's memo to Kissinger continues: "In compliance with President Johnson's explicit instructions, all of the field intelligence on matters germane to the subject of your request was shortstopped by my office. The only dissemination of this data," he added, was "sent on an EYES ONLY basis to Secretary [of State Dean] Rusk and Mr. [Walt] Rostow. For this reason, we cannot give you a list of [SEVERAL WORDS CENSORED] during October of 1968 because there were none until the 'freeze' ended on 1 November." In other words: No, you can't have those particular CIA records.

Nixon didn't give up hounding the agency for the files. On October 21, 1971, White House chief of staff Bob Haldeman sent a "secret/sensitive" memo to John Ehrlichman, the White House go-to guy on CIA matters.

An exasperated Haldeman asks Ehrlichman to try his hand at persuading Helms to fork over the documents: "I tried once before to get the information from the CIA through Henry Kissinger's office. Director Helms claims that this information is not available in their files because it was forwarded directly to the White House. I can't help but believe that the CIA would keep a copy of all intelligence reports even if they were only 'bootleg' copies."

Ehrlichman wasted no time in getting on Helms's case. On the same day, in a "secret/sensitive" memo to Helms, the White House aide cited the CIA boss's earlier refusal to provide the requested material to Kissinger. And then Ehrlichman bluntly stated: "It has been requested that these documents be obtained despite prior restrictions on their distribution. Would you please forward copies of the requested documents?"

The Helms, Haldeman and Ehrlichman memos were declassified in December 2010. There is no indication that Helms ever shared with Nixon or any of his aides any of the Vietnam intelligence data from October of 1968 that the president was so eager to obtain.

Why didn't President Johnson blow the whistle on Nixon's sabotaging of the Paris peace talks? He explained his thinking in a newly released phone chat with Senator George Smathers of Florida—a good friend of Nixon's: "I didn't expose it because I just couldn't use those sources [CIA, NSA and FBI] and I didn't want to make it impossible for [Nixon] to govern."[15]

LBJ had also been listening to the good advice of aide Clark Clifford, who counseled: "Some elements of the story are so shocking in their nature that I'm wondering whether it would be good for the country to disclose the story and then possibly have a certain individual [Nixon] elected."

"It could cast his whole administration under such doubt that I think it would be inimical to our country's interests," according to investigative reporter Robert Parry.[16]

On the other hand, LBJ did not listen to a young White House aide named Richard Holbrooke, who went on to become a top State Department official. Holbrooke later charged that Nixon and his co-conspirators "massively, directly and covertly interfered in a major diplomatic negotiation ... probably one of the most important negotiations in American diplomatic history."[17]

President Johnson's attitude toward a top political adversary and toward his country could possibly rank as one of the noblest gestures in modern American political history. He'd caught a political opponent undermining sensitive negotiations that might have ended the fighting in Indochina and brought 500,000 U.S. troops home immediately.

As president, Richard Nixon went on to order the dropping of more bombs than any other commander-in-chief. He even secretly bombed neutral Cambodia for more than four years. Nixon double-crossed Thieu time and time again—and eventually even issued a thinly veiled threat on the South Vietnamese president's life.

Some 20,000 American troops died during Nixon's White House years, and the Vietnam War was still going on, when— faced with impeachment and conviction for a wide range of corrupt and illegal domestic conspiracies and cover-ups—the president was forced from office in disgrace in 1974. When Saigon fell to communist troops in 1975, the United States lost its first war. Yet Richard Nixon's gravestone reads: "The greatest honor history can bestow is the title of peacemaker."

TWO

TIES THAT BIND: THE MOB'S PRESIDENT

The dark, deceitful side of Richard Nixon—brought to light by Watergate and reinforced by the tapes and records that have been released since—actually goes all the way back to the very beginning of his political career. By the time he became president in 1969, in fact, Richard Nixon had been on the giving and receiving end of major Mob favors for more than two decades. Nixon's earliest campaign manager, Murray Chotiner, had several Mob figures as legal clients—and was particularly close to mobbed-up Teamsters union chief Jimmy Hoffa and to New Orleans Mafia boss Carlos Marcello. Working through Chotiner, Mickey Cohen—one of the most notorious mobsters in Los Angeles—rounded up Mafia money for two early Nixon campaigns.

In his first political foray—a successful 1946 race for Congress as a strong anticommunist Republican from southern California—Nixon was on the receiving end of a $5,000 contribution from Cohen. The gangster also provided the candidate with free office space for a "Nixon for Congress" headquarters in one of his buildings. And there was more to come.

In 1950, at Chotiner's request, Cohen set up a fund-raising dinner for Nixon at the Knickerbocker Hotel in Los Angeles. The affair took in $75,000 to help Nixon go on and defeat Democratic Representative Helen Gahagan Douglas in a race for the U.S. Senate. Nixon had portrayed Douglas as a Communist sympathizer—"pink right down to her underwear."

When Nixon went on to the White House, both as vice president and later as president, he took Chotiner with him as a key behind-the-scenes advisor despite (or because of) his ties to the Mob, even when the press tried to expose Nixon's shady associations. For example, in the fall of 1968, columnist Jack Anderson had gotten a signed statement from the imprisoned Cohen linking the presidential candidate to the Mob. But according to Pearson biographer Mark Feldstein, that column "was largely dismissed . . . and lost amid the end-of-the-campaign hoopla."[1]

Even Cohen, from his jail cell, looked down on Nixon. After Nixon barely won the election that year, Cohen wrote a private letter to Anderson: "In my wildest dreams (never) could I ever have visualized or imagined 17 or 18 years ago that the likes of Richard Nixon could possibly become the President of the United States . . . Let's hope that he isn't the same guy that I knew: A rough hustler (when he was) a goddamn small-time ward politician. Let's hope this guy's thinking has changed, and let's hope it's for the betterment of our country."[2] This from a mobster who controlled the Syndicate's drug and gambling operations in California; and who had been arrested more than thirty times—once for murder.

Later, of the Nixon dinner at the Knickerbocker, Cohen himself recalled, "Everyone from around here that was on the pad naturally had to go . . . It was all gamblers from Vegas, all gambling money. There wasn't a legitimate person in the room."[3] The mobster said Nixon addressed the dinner after Cohen told the crowd the exits would be closed until the whole $75,000 quota was met. They were. And it was.

Cohen has said his support of Nixon was ordered by "the proper persons from back east," meaning the founders of the national syndicate, Frank Costello and Meyer Lansky.[4]

Lansky was considered the Mafia's financial genius. Known as "The Little Man" because he was barely five feet tall, Lansky developed Cuba for the Mob during the dictatorship of Fulgencio Batista; and reportedly put out a $1-million hit on Cuban leader Fidel Castro. During the Batista era, Havana was "the Las Vegas of the Caribbean." Under its swaying palms, gambling, prostitution and drug trafficking netted the Syndicate more than $100 million a year—even after handsome payoffs to Batista.

In the mid-'50s, Batista (who was awarded a medal of honor by Vice President Nixon) designated Lansky the czar of gambling in Havana. This was so Batista could stop some Mob-run casinos from using doctored games of chance to cheat tourists. A shrewd, master manipulator whose specialty was gambling, Lansky was also known among mobsters as honest. It wasn't necessary to rig the gambling tables to make boatloads of bucks. Lansky directed all casino operators to "clean up."[5]

Like Nixon, Lansky was very generous with the Cuban dictator. As former Lansky associate Joseph Varon told The History Channel: "I know every time Meyer went to Cuba he would bring a briefcase with at least $100,000 [for Batista]. So Batista welcomed him with open arms, and the two men really developed such an affection for each other. Batista really loved him. I guess I'd love him too if he gave me $100,000 every time I saw him."[6] Lansky also took money—in the form of a "skim" from the casinos—from Cuba back to the United States. In a September 1958 search of Lansky when he arrived in Miami, Customs agents found $200,000 in cash and $50,000 in checks. Mob experts Robert Blakey and Richard Billings say "the inference was inescapable: the $200,000 represented skim."[7] Three Syndicate gamblers from Cleveland—including Bebe Rebozo's friend Morris "Moe" Dalitz—were part owners of Lansky's Hotel Nacional. In fact, during the Batista regime, as recalled by Mafia hit man Angelo DeCarlo, "The Mob had a piece of every joint down there. There wasn't one joint they didn't have a piece of."[8]

Senate crime investigator Walter Sheridan once offered this opinion on why Lansky was such a big fan of Richard Nixon: "If you were Meyer, who would you invest your money in? Some politician named Clams Linguini? Or a nice Protestant boy from Whittier, California?"[9]

Miami police department records from that era show that Rebozo was "very close" to Lansky—and was involved in Lansky's gambling operations. Another Rebozo associate, Tampa godfather Santos Trafficante, was the undisputed gambling king of Havana. Trafficante owned substantial interests in the San Souci—a nightclub and casino where fellow gangster Johnny Roselli had a management role.[10]

The CIA eventually learned of Lansky's $1-million bounty for Castro's assassination. In the fall of 1960, there were high-level CIA talks—which included CIA Director Allen Dulles—about joining the Mafia in plotting Castro's murder. The agency picked former Nixon aide Robert Maheu—then working as billionaire Howard Hughes's chief aide—to act as the main go-between with the Mob. Hughes had approved of Maheu's assignment.

In September 1960, Maheu met with two top mobsters: Sam Giancana and Roselli. The meeting took place in the Boom Boom Room at Miami's lavish Fontainebleau Hotel. As a result of that session, a CIA "support chief" soon met with Gianacana and Santos Trafficante to discuss Castro's murder. The CIA eagerly awaited the results of its co-conspiracy with the Mafia, but nothing happened. All the efforts—including one to poison Castro's food at his favorite restaurant—failed.[11]

The tight relationship between Nixon and Rebozo began in Cuba in the early fifties, according to historian Anthony Summers, when Nixon was gambling very heavily, and Bebe covered Nixon's losses—possibly as much as $50,000. Most of Nixon's gambling took place at the Lansky-owned Hotel Nacional in Havana. The hotel rolled out the royal treatment for Nixon, who stayed in the Presidential Suite on the owner's tab.[12]

Rebozo was short, swarthy, well dressed and glib. The American-born Cuban had risen from airline steward to wealthy Florida banker and land speculator. Nixon's No. 1 pal was there to lend moral as well as financial support to his idol through Nixon's many political ups and downs. Rebozo came in and out of the White House as he pleased, without being logged in by the Secret Service. Though he had no government job, Rebozo had his own private office and phone number in the executive mansion.

Rebozo had solid organized crime connections. For one, he had both legal and financial ties with "Big Al" Polizzi, a Cleveland gangster and drug kingpin. Rebozo built an elaborate shopping center in Miami, to be leased to members of the right-wing Cuban exile community, and he let out the contracting bid to Big Al—a convicted black marketeer described by the Federal Bureau of Narcotics as "one of the most influential members of the underworld in the United States."[13]

Nixon and Rebozo were both prominent in the anti-Castro movement. Nixon, while vice president, was the White House action officer for the Bay of Pigs invasion. Rebozo was heavily involved with Cuban exiles in Mafia-sponsored activities against Castro. Both men had a number of shady financial entanglements in the Bahamas and Florida—including deals assisted by the Keyes Realty Company, a Mob-linked business whose vice president was Watergate burglar Eugenio Martinez.

Nixon and Rebozo bought Florida lots on upscale Key Biscayne, getting bargain rates from Donald Berg, a Mafia-connected Rebozo business partner.[14] The Secret Service eventually advised Nixon to stop associating with Berg. The lender for one of Nixon's properties was Arthur Desser, who consorted with both Teamsters President Jimmy Hoffa and mobster Meyer Lansky.

Nixon and Rebozo were friends of James Crosby, the chairman of a firm repeatedly linked to top mobsters, and Rebozo's Key Biscayne Bank was a suspected pipeline for Mob money skimmed from Crosby's casino in the Bahamas. By the 1960s, FBI agents keeping track of the Mafia had identified Nixon's Cuban-American pal as a "non-member associate of organized crime figures."[15]

Former Mafia consigliere Bill Bonanno—the son of legendary New York godfather Joe Bonanno—asserts that Nixon "would never have gotten anywhere" without his old Mob allegiances.

And he reports that, through Rebozo, Nixon "did business for years with people in [Florida Mafia boss Santos] Trafficante's Family, profiting from real estate deals, arranging for casino licensing, covert funding for anti-Castro activities, and so forth."[16]

Teamsters union leader Jimmy Hoffa hated John and Robert Kennedy as much as Nixon did. Robert Kennedy had been trying to put Hoffa in jail since 1956, when RFK was staff counsel for a Senate probe into the Mob's influence on the labor movement. In a 1960 book, Kennedy said, "No group better fits the prototype of the old Al Capone syndicate than Jimmy Hoffa and some of his Lieutenants."[17]

Because he shared a common enemy with Nixon, Hoffa and his two-million-member union backed Vice President Nixon against Senator John Kennedy in the 1960 election, and did so with more than just a get-out-the-vote campaign. Edward Partin, a Louisiana Teamster official and later government informant, revealed that Hoffa met with New Orleans godfather Carlos Marcello to secretly fund the Nixon campaign. Partin told Mob expert Dan Moldea: "I was right there, listening to the conversation. Marcello had a suitcase filled with $500,000 cash which was going to Nixon . . . [Another half-million dollar contribution] was coming from mob boys in New Jersey and Florida."[18] The Hoffa-Marcello meeting took place in New Orleans on September 26, 1960, and has been verified by William Sullivan, a former top FBI official.[19]

Nixon lost the 1960 election, and Hoffa—thanks to Attorney General Robert Kennedy—soon wound up in prison for jury tampering and looting the union's pension funds of almost $2 million. But the Nixon-Hoffa connection was strong enough to last at least until December 23, 1971, when Nixon gave Hoffa an executive grant of clemency and sprung him from the slammer. The action allowed Hoffa to serve just five years of a thirteen-year sentence.

Hoffa evidently bought his way out. In 1996, Teamsters expert William Bastone disclosed that James P. ("Junior") Hoffa and racketeer Allen Dorfman "delivered $300,000 'in a black valise' to a Washington hotel to help secure the release of Hoffa's father" from the pen. The name of the bagman on the receiving end of the transaction is redacted from legal documents filed in a court case.[20] Bastone said the claim is based on "FBI reports reflecting contacts with [former Teamster boss Jackie] Presser in 1971."[21] In a recently released FBI memo apparently confirming this, an informant details a $300,000 Mob payoff to the Nixon White House "to guarantee the release of Jimmy Hoffa from the Federal penitentiary."[22] Breaking from clemency custom, Nixon did not consult the judge who had sentenced Hoffa. Nor did he pay any mind to the U.S. Parole Board, which had unanimously voted three times in two years to reject Hoffa's appeals for release. The board had been warned by the Justice Department that Hoffa was Mob-connected. Longtime Nixon operative Chotiner eventually admitted interceding to get Hoffa paroled. "I did it," he told columnist Jack Anderson in 1973. "I make no apologies for it. And frankly I'm proud of it."[23]

At the time, the *New York Times* called the clemency a "pivotal element in the strange love affair between the [Nixon] administration and the two-million-member truck union, ousted from the rest of the labor movement in 1957 for racketeer domination."[24]

As one example of President Nixon's "strange love affair"

5

orders from BILL BUFFILLINO. Source advised that BILL
BUFFILLINO has been double dipping with regard to union
funds. Source advised that BUFFILLINO is traveling all
over the country and charging his expenses to his local
in Detroit, Michigan, collecting the monies for these
expenses; but in reality, BUFFILLINO has been charging the
expenses on his union credit card, thus collecting twice.
Source further advised that BUFFILLINO is also collecting
monies from TONY PROVENZANO for acting as his attorney in
criminal actions being taken against him. Source advised
that it is possible, although not known by the source, that
PROVENZANO is obtaining these legal fees from funds within
IBT Local 560.

THE ABOVE INFORMATION SHOULD NOT BE DISSEMINATED
OUTSIDE THE BUREAU AND SHOULD BE HANDLED WITH EXTREME CARE
IN THAT THE INFORMATION WAS OBTAINED BY THE SOURCE AND IS
SINGULAR IN NATURE.

RE: ▓▓▓▓▓▓

Source advised that all contacts made by the source
in the recent past have revealed that there was no $500,000
payoff by FRANK FITZSIMMONS to ▓▓▓▓▓▓▓▓ Source,
however, advised that there may have been a payoff from someone else, but to the best of the source's knowledge,
FITZSIMMONS had no knowledge of it.

Source advised that approximately one to two weeks
before the Christmas before HOFFA was released from prison,
ALAN DORFMAN and JIMMY HOFFA, JR. delivered $300,000 in
cash to the Mayflower Hotel, Washington, D.C. in a black
valise and turned this money over to ▓▓▓▓▓▓
▓▓▓▓▓▓ The purpose of this money was to guarantee
the release of JIMMY HOFFA from the Federal Penitentiary.

Source advised with regard to the bombing of
DICK FITZSIMMONS' car in Detroit, Michigan, as follows:

Source advised that prior to this bombing, as
previously reported by the source, HOFFA was attempting to
obtain loans through the Central States Pension Fund and
was continually being turned down by ALAN DORFMAN.

*Newly released memo cites FBI informant saying the Mob paid $300,000 to get
Nixon to grant clemency to ex-Teamsters President Jimmy Hoffa.* COURTESY
OF FBI/SMOKINGGUN.COM

with the Teamsters, in a May 5, 1971 Oval Office conversation,
Nixon and his chief of staff Bob Haldeman pondered a little favor they knew the union would be happy to carry out against antiwar demonstrators:

Haldeman: What [Nixon aide Charles] Colson's gonna do on it, and I suggested he do, and I think they can get a, away with this . . . do it with the Teamsters. Just ask them to dig up those, their eight thugs.

Nixon: Yeah.

Haldeman: Just call, call, uh, what's his name.

Nixon: Fitzsimmons.

Haldeman: Is trying to get, play our game anyway. Is just, just tell Fitzsimmons . . .

Nixon: They, they've got guys who'll go in and knock their heads off.

Haldeman: Sure. Murderers![25]

Veteran Mafia bigwig Bonanno describes Nixon's clemency for Hoffa as "a gesture, if ever there was one, of the national power [the Mob] once enjoyed."[26]

President Nixon did put one restriction on Hoffa's freedom: Hoffa could never again, directly or indirectly, manage any union. This decision, too, was the result of a financial incentive. The restriction was reputedly bought by a $500,000 contribution to the Nixon campaign by New Jersey Teamster leader Anthony "Tony Pro" Provenzano, the head of the notorious Provenzano family, which, a House panel found in 1999, had for years dominated Teamsters New Jersey Local 560.[27]

During the Nixon administration, pressure from Washington eased off on other Mafia leaders, too, like Chicago godfather Sam Giancana. And long-standing deportation proceedings against CIA-connected mobster Johnny Roselli were dropped. Without going into specifics, government lawyers explained in court that

Roselli had performed "valuable services to the national security."[28] A Giancana henchman, Roselli, as previously noted, was an important contact man in the CIA-Mafia assassination plots against Cuban leader Fidel Castro. (Roselli and Dallas gangster Jack Ruby—the killer of JFK assassination suspect Lee Harvey Oswald—are reported to have met in hotels in Miami during the months before the JFK assassination.)[29]

Roselli was also apparently acquainted with longtime Nixon associate CIA agent E. Howard Hunt. Nixon and Hunt were secretly top planners of the assassination plots on Castro when Nixon was vice president. And later, Roselli and Hunt are reported to have been co-conspirators in the 1961 assassination-by-ambush of Rafael Trujillo, dictator of the Dominican Republic.[30] In the '70s, a Senate committee established that the CIA had supplied the weapons used against Trujillo. In 1976, *Cygne*, a Paris publication, quoted former Trujillo bodyguard L. Gonzalez-Mata as saying that Roselli and Hunt arrived in the Dominican Republic in March, 1971 to assist in plots against Trujillo. Gonzalez-Mata described Hunt as "a specialist" with the CIA and Roselli as "a friend of Batista" who was operating on orders from both the CIA and the Mafia.[31]

The Nixon administration intervened on the side of Mafia figures in at least twenty trials, mostly for the ostensible purpose of protecting CIA "sources and methods." Nixon even went so far as to order the Justice Department, in July 1970, to halt using the words "Mafia" and "La Cosa Nostra" to describe organized crime because they were demeaning to Italian-Americans. The president was roundly applauded when he boasted about his order at a private 1971 Oval Office meeting with some forty members of the

Supreme Council of the Sons of Italy. The group's Supreme Venerable, Americo Cortese, thanked Nixon for his moral leadership, declaring, "You are our terrestrial god."[32]

As president, Nixon also pardoned Angelo "Gyp" DeCarlo, described by the FBI as a "methodical gangland executioner."[33] Supposedly terminally ill, DeCarlo was freed after serving less than two years of a twelve-year sentence for extortion. Soon afterward, *Newsweek* reported the mobster was not too ill to be "back at his old rackets, boasting that his connections with [singer Frank] Sinatra freed him." Sinatra had been ousted from JFK's social circle when the Kennedy Justice Department reported to the president that the singer had wide-ranging dealings and friendships with major mobsters. But the Nixon White House disregarded similar reports, and Sinatra went on to become fast friends with both Nixon and his corrupt vice president, Spiro Agnew.

In April 1973, at Nixon's request, Sinatra came out of retirement to sing at a White House dinner for Italian President Giulio Andreotti. On the night of the dinner, the president compared Sinatra to the Washington Monument—"The Top." That summer, the *New York Times* reported that Nixon pardoned DeCarlo as a result of Sinatra's intervention with Agnew. The newspaper said the details were worked out by Agnew aide Peter Malatesta and Nixon counsel John Dean. The release reportedly followed an "unrecorded contribution" of $100,000 in cash and another contribution of $50,000 forwarded by Sinatra to an unnamed Nixon campaign official. FBI files released after Sinatra's 1998 death seem to confirm this and provide fresh details. An internal bureau memo of May 24, 1973, describes Sinatra as "a close friend of Angelo DeCarlo of long standing." It says that in April 1972,

DeCarlo asked singer Frankie Valli of "My Eyes Adored You" and "Big Girls Don't Cry" fame (when Valli was performing at the Atlanta Federal Penitentiary) to contact Sinatra and have him intercede with Agnew for DeCarlo's release.

Eventually, the memo continues, Sinatra "allegedly turned over $100,000 cash to [Nixon campaign finance chairman] Maurice Stans as an unrecorded contribution." Vice presidential aide Peter Malatesta "allegedly contacted former presidential counsel John Dean and got him to make the necessary arrangements to forward the request [for a presidential pardon] to the Justice Department." Sinatra is said to have then made a $50,000 contribution to the president's campaign fund. And, the memo reports, "DeCarlo's release followed."[34]

Frank Sinatra's Mob ties go back at least as far as Nixon's. In 1947, the singer was photographed with Lucky Luciano and other mobsters in Cuba. The photo led syndicated columnist Robert Ruark to write three columns about Sinatra and the Mafia. The first was titled "Shame, Sinatra!"[35]

The Kennedy administration's war on organized crime was highly effective. Indictments against mobsters rose from zero to 683 and the number of defendants convicted went from zero to 619.[36]

While the Kennedys made war, however, the Nixon Administration made peace with organized crime, showing remarkable generosity toward top Mob and Teamsters officials. Nixon had first met Teamsters president Frank Fitzsimmons when Jimmy Hoffa was still in jail and Fitzsimmons was in line to succeed him as Teamsters boss. The president and Fitz quickly colluded on a plan for Hoffa's release, and they started an alliance that was sealed

with cold cash—huge payments involving the Mob in return for
White House kindness. A few months after trouncing Senator
George McGovern in 1972, Nixon secretly entertained Fitzsim-
mons in a private room at the White House. Attorney General
Richard Kliendienst was summoned to the session and ordered by
Nixon to "make sure that government investigators of the Team-
sters then in progress did not harm Fitzsimmons or his allies," ac-
cording to a 1981 investigation by *Time*.[37]

A year and a half later when the *New York Times* disclosed
that FBI wiretaps had uncovered a massive scheme to establish a
national health plan for the Teamsters, with pension fund members and top mobsters playing crucial roles and getting lucrative
kickbacks, Kleindienst again came to the rescue, rejecting the
FBI's plan to continue taps related to the scheme. The chief
schemers behind the proposed rip-off had included Fitzsimmons and Teamsters pension fund consultant Allen Dorfman.

From 1969 through 1973, more than one half of the Justice
Department's 1,600 indictments in organized crime cases were
tossed out because of "improper procedures" followed by Attorney General John Mitchell in obtaining court-approved authori-
zation for wiretaps, and the Treasury Department declared a
moratorium on $1.3 million in back taxes owed by former Team-
sters president Dave Beck.

Mitchell was the first person since the FBI was established in
1908 to hold the office of attorney general without undergoing
an FBI investigation, thanks to a special request made by Nixon
to his ever-loyal crony J. Edgar Hoover. In 1975, Mitchell himself was found guilty of conspiracy, obstruction of justice, and
perjury and sentenced to two and a half to eight years in prison

RICHARD NIXON

May 3, 1984

EXHIBIT
II
ALL-STATE LEGAL SUPPLY CO.

2G FEDERAL PLAZA
NEW YORK CITY

Dear Mr. President,

I am pleased to learn that Pan East·International and its associates, Colonel John V. Brennan and the Honorable John Mitchell, both of whom served in my Administration, are working with your Ministry of Light Industries.

I trust that this relationship which involves the production of military uniforms and accessories, will be a very successful and long-lasting one.

I can assure you that Colonel Brennan and former Attorney General John Mitchell will be responsible and constructive in working on this project with your representatives.

Mrs. Nixon joins me in·sending our warm personal regards to you and Mrs. Ceausescu.

Sincerely,

His Excellency
Nicolae Ceausescu

In retirement, Nixon puts in a good word for his former attorney general, ex-Watergate felon John Mitchell, who is making army uniforms for Romanian dictator Nicolae Ceausescu. COURTESY OF NIXON LIBRARY/NATIONAL ARCHIVES.

for his role in the Watergate break-in and cover-up. The first attorney general to be imprisoned, Mitchell served only nineteen months at Maxwell Air Force Base in Montgomery, Alabama, a minimum security prison, before being paroled for medical reasons.

In May 1973, the *Oakland Tribune* reported that Nixon aide Murray Chotiner had interceded in a federal probe of Teamsters involvement in a major Beverly Hills real estate scandal. As a result, the investigation ended with the indictment of only three men. One of the three, Leonard Bursten, a former director of the disreputable Miami National Bank, and a close friend of Jimmy Hoffa, had his fifteen-year prison sentence reduced to probation.[38] One month later, ex–Nixon aide John Dean revealed to the Senate Watergate Committee that leading Florida Teamsters official Cal Kovens had won an early release from federal prison in 1972 through the efforts of Nixon aide Charles Colson, Bebe Rebozo, and former Florida Senator George Smathers. Shortly after his release, Kovens contributed $50,000 to Nixon's re-election effort.[39]

Of course, none of the "good deeds" Nixon performed for his Mafia friends were done for free. Debts that weren't called in as campaign contributions were merely postponed until a later date. At the same time, there were widespread rumors Teamsters funds helped buy the silence of E. Howard Hunt and his Watergate cohorts.

Furthermore, records reveal that FBI agents suspected the Nixon White House of soliciting $1 million from the Teamsters to pay hush money to the burglars. In fact, in early 1973 when the Watergate cover-up was coming apart at the seams, John Dean told the president that $1 million might be needed to keep the burglary team silent. Nixon responded, "We could get that . . . you could get a million dollars. You could get it in cash, I know where it could be gotten." When Dean observed that money laundering "is the type of thing Mafia people can do," Nixon calmly answered: "Maybe it takes a gang to do that."[40]

• • •

It is suspected that most of the Watergate "hush money" distributed to E. Howard Hunt—who, during Watergate, was Nixon's secret chief spy—and other members of the burglary team came from Rebozo and other Mob-linked Nixon pals like Tony Provenzano, Jimmy Hoffa, Howard Hughes, Carlos Marcello, Santos Trafficante, Meyer Lansky, and Lansky buddy John Alessio. The gambling king of San Diego, Alessio donated $26,000 to the Nixon campaign in 1968 and went on to attend Nixon's inaugural ball.[41] He also went on to serve two years in Federal prison in the 1970s for tax evasion. Alessio was convicted of skimming millions of dollars from San Diego racetrack revenues. *Life* magazine reported that evidence from a police inquiry indicated Alessio had paid off the police department's intelligence chief in 1967.[42]

On June 20, 1972, an anxious Richard Nixon picked up the Oval Office phone and called Anthony Provenzano's top henchman, Joseph Trerotola—a key Teamsters union power broker in his own right. Perhaps the president had some laundered cash in mind to help keep the Watergate burglars quiet about their White House ties. We will never know for sure why Tony Pro's right-hand man was one of the first people Nixon called after the burglary. Scholars who try to listen to that recently released one-minute-long conversation at the National Archives will find that the tape has been totally erased.[43]

A short time before phoning Trerotola, Nixon had an Oval Office conversation about Watergate with his chief of staff, Bob Haldeman. This is the famous tape that contains an eighteen-and-one-half minute erasure. The president's secretary, Rose Mary

Woods, publicly took the fall for the "gap" in the Nixon-Haldeman tape, saying she might have accidentally made the erasure. Many historians suspect the president was the Eraser-in-Chief. Back then, the strangest explanation of all came from Nixon aide Alexander Haig, who publicly blamed a "Sinister Force." Behind closed doors, however, Haig told Watergate Special Prosecutor Leon Jaworski that the tape in question had been "screwed with." At first, Nixon went along with this "the secretary did it" story. But he later blamed one of his Watergate lawyers, Fred Buzhardt—after Buzhardt's death.

After Nixon left office in August 1974 to avoid being impeached by Congress for the illegal activities he supervised and concealed during the Watergate scandal, he spent more than a year brooding in self-exile at his walled estate in San Clemente, California. The very first post-resignation invitation the disgraced ex-president accepted was from his Teamsters buddies. On October 9, 1975, he played golf at a Mob-linked California resort with Teamsters chief Frank Fitzsimmons and other top union officials. Among those who attended a post–golf game party for Nixon were Provenzano, Dorfman, and the union's executive secretary, Murray "Dusty" Miller.[44] Tony Pro would later die in prison, a convicted killer. Key Mob-Teamster financial coordinator Dorfman was later murdered gangland-style. Murray "Dusty" Miller was the man, records show, whom Jack Ruby had telephoned several days before Ruby murdered alleged JFK assassin Lee Harvey Oswald in Dallas.

In July 1975, Jimmy Hoffa vanished in a Detroit suburb, and his body has never been found. Some federal investigators believe he was shot to death after being lured to a reconciliation meeting with Provenzano, who never showed up. On at least two occasions, Tony Pro had threatened to kill Hoffa and kidnap his children.[45] Investigators theorize Hoffa's body was then taken away by truck, stuffed into a fifty-gallon drum, then crushed and smelted.[46] Jimmy Hoffa was declared legally dead in 1982.

Newly released FBI documents show that, in 1978, federal investigators sought to force former president Nixon and Teamster boss Fitzsimmons to testify about events surrounding Hoffa's disappearance. The investigators concluded that such testimony offered the last, best chance of solving the Hoffa mystery. But they accused top Justice Department officials of derailing their efforts to call the two men before a Detroit grand jury.

The records also reveal that FBI agents suspected the Nixon White House of soliciting $1 million from the Teamsters to keep the Watergate burglars silent.[47] The disclosures are detailed in more than 2,000 pages of previously secret FBI documents, obtained by the *Detroit Free Press* through a Freedom of Information lawsuit. They show that Fitzsimmons had actually been a government informant on an unspecified matter from 1972 to 1974.

Could Fitzsimmons's cooperation in that case have persuaded the Justice Department to turn thumbs-down on the grand jury idea? The records don't say. But they do show that the Detroit FBI office sent a number of memos to Washington stressing that Nixon and Fitzsimmons could hold the answers to the Hoffa case.

Robert Stewart, a former assistant U.S. attorney in Buffalo, NY, who helped lead the investigation into just how Hoffa vanished, said in another memo: "The one individual who could prove the matter beyond a doubt is Richard Nixon." Stewart wasn't sure whether Nixon would cooperate, given that he had been pardoned by successor Gerald Ford for his involvement in the Watergate scandal. But the investigator added that Nixon "must certainly appreciate that while the pardon may protect him as to whatever happened in the White House, a fresh perjury committed in a current grand jury would place him in dire jeopardy."[48]

In a separate memo to headquarters, Detroit FBI agents concluded, "It would be a gross understatement to state that Fitzsimmons is the key to the solution of this case, and yet he represents the major problem encountered with the Department of Justice . . . Fitzsimmons should have appeared long ago before the federal grand jury in Detroit to answer questions about his association with Hoffa and any possible involvement he had in dealings leading up to Hoffa's disappearance. To date, the Department of Justice has refused to allow Fitzsimmons to testify."[49]

Fitzsimmons died three years later, never appearing before the grand jury. Of course, Nixon—who died in 1994—never appeared either.

In 1997, a former Fitzsimmons crony named Harry Hall told historian Anthony Summers: "Fitzsimmons figured he'd found an ally in Nixon. The Teamsters would help him financially, and Nixon ate that up . . . I was told they gave money to Chotiner that was to go to Nixon. I think it was close to $500,000."[50] Hall added that the half million was intended for Nixon's personal use, and that a similar amount was donated to the president's re-election campaign.

Nixon privately praised the union's members to Fitzsimmons as "stand-up guys."[51] And the president did a big personal favor for the Teamsters chief—he had the Justice Department stop a probe of Fitz's son, Richard, who was accused of allowing his wife and children to use a union credit card to buy $1,500 worth of gas for their cars.[52] One federal investigator said the case against Richard Fitzsimmons was dropped because of the "love affair" between Nixon and Fitz.[53]

In a smaller favor, but one that meant a great deal to the golf-addicted Fitzimmons, Nixon ordered aide Charles Colson to try to get Fitz into a prestigious Washington country club. Colson wrote a memo to his assistant, George Bell: "Fitz wants Columbia because that's where [AFL-CIO union president George] Meany belongs. But if [Fitz] got into Burning Tree [where the president golfed] he could be one up on Meany, which would appeal to him—any way you have to, but do it somehow, whatever needs to be done. I suspect the president would write a letter [on Fitz's behalf] if needed."[54]

Colson wore horn-rimmed glasses and was a tall, heavy-set, tough-talking ex-Marine who was ruthless with Nixon's enemies—he had a motto above his bar: "Once you have them by the balls, their hearts and minds will follow." Yet Chuck showed an amiable, even pliable side, when doling out favors to the president's mobbed-up labor allies.

A January 19, 1972 Justice Department memo predicted that a reputed Fitzsimmons Teamsters associate named Daniel Gagliardi would be indicted for extortion "sometime next month." But Gagliardi knew whom to phone for help in the Nixon White House: Chuck Colson. He actually spoke with Colson's aide George Bell, who later told his boss in a memo: "I talked to Gagliardi, who maintained complete ignorance and innocence regarding the Teamsters. [He] asked that he be gotten off the hook." Colson wrote back to Bell: "Watch for this. Do all possible." Bell obviously carried out his assignment: Gagliardi was never indicted.[55]

Nixon's and Colson's courting of Fitzsimmons paid off big time at a July 17, 1972 meeting of Teamster leaders at a country club near San Diego. The union's seventeen-member executive board enthusiastically endorsed Nixon for re-election. Afterward, the entire board traveled thirty-five miles up the California coast to the Western White House in San Clemente. There they delivered the good news to President Nixon and posed for individual pictures with him.

In October, Fitzsimmons issued a statement saying, "The biggest weapon the American worker has to protect himself and his country is the ballot. This year we are going to use it to reject the extremism of [Democratic nominee Senator] George McGovern, and to re-elect a great American—President Richard Nixon."[56]

In November, Nixon scored a landslide victory over McGovern—who won only Massachusetts and the District of Columbia—and prepared to give the nation "four more years" of his rather peculiar brand of law and order.

THREE

NIXON'S FAVORITE GODFATHER: CARLOS MARCELLO

At the start of the 1920s, marijuana use in America was concentrated in New Orleans, and its intoxicating vapors were mainly inhaled by migrant workers from Mexico, by blacks, and by a growing number of "low-class" whites. Sailors and immigrants from the Caribbean brought this "new" (its known uses go back to 7,000 B.C.) drug into major southern U.S. ports—above all into the Crescent City.

Along with jazz, pot traveled north to Chicago, and then east to Harlem, where it soon became an indispensable part of the music scene, even entering the language of the black hits of the day—Louis Armstrong's "Muggles," Cab Calloway's "That Funny Reefer Man," and Fats Waller's "Viper's Drag."

A squat but muscular fireplug of a man, rising New Orleans mobster Carlos Marcello was perfectly placed to make boatloads of money from illegal marijuana shipped into his territory. In 1938, though, Marcello sold twenty-three pounds of pot to an undercover agent. Convicted and sentenced to one year in the

Atlanta Federal Penitentiary, Marcello was also fined more than $75,000. Using his political influence, that particular "Reefer Man" was able to get, the fine reduced to just $400. And he was out of prison in nine months. With Louisiana Mafia boss Silvestro "Silver Dollar Sam" Carolla pulling the strings, Governor O. K. Allen, a former stooge of assassinated Senator Huey Long, provided the leniency. Legend has it that Marcello eventually had a tailor sew a foot-long pocket into the left leg of his trousers, "which he would stuff with cash as he made his rounds through [Jefferson] Parish paying off the police one by one."

From pot-dealing, police- and politician-corrupting street thug, Marcello graduated to godfather of New Orleans (and Dallas), governing a vast and violent criminal empire that brought in an estimated $2 billion a year. He succeeded Sam Carolla, who was deported to Sicily in 1947. Marcello quickly became a generous financial supporter of Richard Nixon—and, eventually, a suspect in the Dallas murder of Nixon's nemesis, President John F. Kennedy. Marcello's first dealings with Vice President Dick Nixon involved the CIA-Mafia plots to murder Fidel Castro. The entire plan, which included an invasion of Cuba by CIA-trained exiles, was placed under Nixon's supervision. Marcello later admitted to an FBI undercover agent that he was part of the conspiracy to kill Castro, according to Marcello expert John Davis in his book *Mafia Kingfish*.[1] In 2007, the CIA finally confirmed that it worked hand-in-glove with the Mob in trying to rub out Castro.[2]

In 1961, Marcello had been deported to Guatemala by Attorney General Bobby Kennedy, but the Louisiana godfather quietly returned in a small plane piloted by an associate named David Ferrie. Ferrie is by far the oddest character in the Kennedy assassination saga. He was bald from head to toe, but sported part of a red floor rug as a hairpiece, and drew brows over his eyes with stage greasepaint. A rumored pedophile who had been fired by Eastern Airlines after his arrest on morals charges, he had both Mafia and CIA connections and was a friend of Lee Harvey Oswald's. Photographic evidence demonstrates that Ferrie knew Oswald back as far as 1955.[3] Six witnesses saw Ferrie and Oswald together in Louisiana in the summer of 1963.[4]

In his book *First Hand Knowledge: How I Participated in the CIA-Mafia Murder of President Kennedy*, former CIA Operative Robert Morrow claims David Ferrie planned the Kennedy assassination, with help from a prominent New Orleans businessman named Clay Shaw. According to Morrow, the Mob-CIA conspiracy involved Mob leaders Sam "Mooney" Giancana, New Orleans boss Carlos Marcello and Florida chieftain Santos Trafficante. He also maintains that he bought three rifles used in the Dallas shooting from Sunny's Surplus in Baltimore.

In 1967, just as New Orleans district attorney Jim Garrison prepared to indict him, Ferrie was found dead in his apartment. He was lying on a sofa with a sheet pulled over his head. Two typed "suicide" notes were found. Ferrie's name was typed, not signed, on each note. New Orleans Metro Crime Commission director Aaron Kohn believed Ferrie was murdered, but the New Orleans coroner officially reported that the cause of death was a cerebral hemorrhage.[5] At the time D.A. Garrison publicly speculated that the CIA had deliberately silenced Ferrie. Ferrie pal Eladio Del Valle, a Cuban exile leader, was murdered at about the same time, the victim of a gunshot to the heart and an apparent machete chop to his skullcap.[6]

Garrison's investigators had learned that Ferrie, shortly before the JFK assassination, had deposited $7,000 in his bank accounts and had taken over a profitable gas station—a gift from Marcello.[7]

Jack Ruby, too, had concrete connections to the Marcello crime family. According to a 1979 report by House assassination investigators Ruby was a friend and business associate of Joseph Civello, Marcello's top deputy in Dallas, and was also very close to Joe Campisi, the No. 2 man in the Dallas Mafia hierarchy who was on such good terms with Marcello that he sent the Marcello family 260 pounds of homemade sausage every Christmas.

Joe Campisi, the owner of Dallas's Egyptian Lounge, dined with Ruby at the lounge the evening before Kennedy was murdered and visited Ruby in the Dallas County Jail six days after Ruby murdered Oswald. Ruby met with four New Orleans nightclub operators and Marcello associates in June and October 1963 and made a telephone call on October 30, 1963 to the New Orleans office of Marcello gang member Nofio Pecora, whose associate, Emile Bruneau, had bailed Lee Harvey Oswald out of jail that summer.[8]

Ruby also made pre-assassination phone calls to Irwin Weiner, described as "a frontman for organized crime"; Robert "Barney" Baker, a Hoffa associate; Murray "Dusty" Miller, a close ally of Hoffa and the Mafia; and Lewis McWillie, who had ties to Syndicate bosses Santos Trafficante and Meyer Lansky.[9]

Identified by the Warren Commission as the lone killer of President Kennedy, Lee Harvey Oswald had his own ties to Carlos Marcello. In New Orleans, where Oswald spent significant portions of his life, Oswald's uncle and substitute father was Charles "Dutz" Murret, an important bookie in Marcello's gambling operations. Oswald's mom, Marguerite, dated some of Marcello's wise guys. According to *The Encyclopedia of the JFK*

Assassination, an FBI plant later reported that Marcello paid Lee Harvey Oswald for serving as a gofer for his betting ring. Payoffs to Oswald were reportedly made by Marcello lieutenant Joe Poretto and took place at the Town and Country, a New Orleans restaurant run by Marcello's brother Anthony.[10]

Marcello was so devoted to the Mafia's code of secrecy, "omerta," he had a mortifying motto hanging in his office: "Three can keep a secret if two are dead." Yet even the most secretive of people occasionally let the cat out of the bag. In 1979, according to JFK assassination authority Anthony Summers, Marcello told an FBI informant that he had known both Murret and Oswald, and that Oswald had worked as a runner in Marcello's gambling operation during 1963. In *Not in Your Lifetime,* Summers asserts "there is compelling circumstantial evidence indicating Marcello's possible involvement in the Kennedy assassination. To say otherwise is to reject at least nineteen witnesses and informants as fabricators, and to reject the web of interconnections between the Marcello apparatus and Oswald and Ruby."[11] Summers says his conclusion jibes with that of the House Select Committee on Assassinations, which found, in 1979, "that the most likely family bosses of organized crime to have participated in such a unilateral assassination plan were Carlos Marcello and Santos Trafficante." The panel said both godfathers had "motive, means and opportunity," adding that "it was unable to establish direct evidence of Marcello's complicity."[12]

Shortly after entering the White House in 1969, Richard Nixon moved to solidify his close favor-trading friendship with Carlos Marcello, known in the underworld as "the Big Daddy in the Big Easy." Their main go-between was old Nixon loyalist and Mob lawyer Murray Chotiner. The pinky ring–wearing Chotiner and his brother were responsible for defending 221 organized crime figures in California.[13]

Chotiner had a White House office and an official government job from which to trade on his powerful behind-the-scenes influence. He had served Nixon since the Navy vet's very first campaign for Congress in 1946. In fact, it was Chotiner who introduced Nixon to L.A.'s top hoodlum, Mickey Cohen, and pressured Cohen to contribute to the Nixon campaign. Chotiner was associated with scores of other leading gangsters, including Meyer Lansky and Ben "Bugsy" Siegel. When Chotiner, on behalf of President Nixon, sought to aid Marcello, the godfather was facing a two-year prison term for his 1968 conviction of assaulting a federal official.

Throughout Nixon's first two years in office, Marcello and his lawyers used all the clout they could muster with the administration to get Marcello's sentence cut. Nixon's attorney general, John Mitchell, finally put the squeeze on a federal judge to slice Marcello's prison term to six months—and arranged for him to spend that time at the medical center for federal prisoners in Springfield, Missouri.

Carlos Marcello emerged from his term at Springfield in March 1971, just in time to aid Chotiner's efforts to spring Jimmy Hoffa from prison. By now, Marcello was possibly the most powerful godfather in the country. His only rival to this title may have been Carlo Gambino, the elderly don who ran a big Brooklyn-based family. The House Select Committee on Organized Crime declared in 1972, "We believe Carlos Marcello has become a formidable menace to the institution of government and the people of the United States."[14]

At about the same time, President Nixon—perhaps, in part, to aid Marcello's illegal drug trafficking business—ignored a call by a blue-ribbon presidential commission to decriminalize marijuana. That decision has had startling repercussions: an estimated 15 million Americans have since been arrested on pot charges.

Nixon's main motive, of course, was political: A Republican "law and order" president could not turn his back on his conservative, antidrug constituents. But, as Gore Vidal pointed out in the *New York Times* in 1970, "The [government] has a vested interest in playing cops and robbers. Both the Bureau of Narcotics and the Mafia want strong laws against the sale and use of drugs because if drugs are sold at cost there would be no money in it for anyone."[15]

Though Nixon reintroduced Jimmy Hoffa to a world without bars, Hoffa wouldn't stay in it for long. Fantasizing about the restoration of his old powers, despite a clemency ban on that, Hoffa openly plotted to unseat his successor as Teamsters president, Frank Fitzsimmons. More amiable and pliable than Hoffa, Fitz was now backed by the Syndicate—and he had established an ultra-chummy relationship with President Nixon.

The ban on Hoffa's return to his old job cost the Mob an additional $500,000 in bribes to Nixon. The money reputedly came from another wing of the Mafia, one run by New Jersey Teamster leader Anthony Provenzano. When Hoffa was killed in 1975, his corpse was reportedly crushed in a steel compactor used for junk cars. Mafia expert Dan Moldea smilingly opined in a TV interview that Hoffa possibly became "someone's hubcap."

. . .

In 1962, Hoffa associate Ed Partin told the FBI that Hoffa said JFK would be shot while riding in an open convertible. That same year, according to Cuban exile leader Jose Aleman, Trafficante told him JFK was "going to be hit." And in 1989, while serving a sentence in a Texarkana prison, Marcello became delusional and talked to his attendants at the prison's hospital as though they were his trusted underlings. Several times the godfather shouted, "That Kennedy, that smiling motherfucker, we'll fix him in Dallas . . . we are going to get that Kennedy in Dallas."[16]

In 1979, the House Select Committee on Assassinations concluded that at least two shooters were likely involved in the JFK assassination, and that the most likely conspirators were Hoffa, Marcello, Trafficante and Chicago godfather Sam Giancana.[17] Two top committee staffers, Robert Blakey and Richard Billings, later wrote of their conviction that "Oswald was acting on behalf of members of the Mob, who wanted relief from the pressure of the Kennedy administration's war on crime led by Attorney General Robert F. Kennedy." It is a viewpoint that is also endorsed in a recent book by former Mafia consigliere Bill Bonanno, the son of legendary New York godfather Joe Bonanno, who maintains that Hoffa, Marcello, Trafficante, and Giancana were involved in the JFK assassination.[18]

Blakey wishes he knew—back when he was leading the House probe—what he has since learned about the CIA's possible role in the assassination. He recently confessed that he had trusted the CIA too much in the mid-'70s.[19] Blakey is one of a diverse group of authors and legal experts who have announced their support of a lawsuit that demands the release of secret CIA records related to the assassination. Authors supporting the suit include anticonspiracist Gerald Posner and proconspiracist Anthony Summers. Experts include John Tunheim, a federal judge who chaired the Assassination Records Review Board of the mid-1990s.

Robert Blakey's new suspicions seem to mesh with the assertions of President Nixon's chief of staff Bob Haldeman, who flatly declared in a 1978 book that the CIA pulled off a "fantastic cover-up" that "literally erased any connection between the Kennedy assassination and the CIA."[20] Dozens of other investigators and assassination experts now believe the CIA was somehow involved. And the CIA and the Mafia have often been known as two sides of the same coin.[21]

Meantime, one of Bobby Kennedy's top Mob fighters, Ron Goldfarb, now concludes that the JFK assassination was the work of Hoffa, Trafficante and Marcello. "Oswald was, as he claimed, a patsy. Neither I, nor anyone, knew how the Mob recruited Oswald. But it was a Mob touch to use someone to carry out its deadly assignments and then to kill that person to avoid detection. The case was circumstantial, but compelling."[22]

Marcello spent some time at Texarkana Prison during his final years of life. In 1989, he became ill and was taken to Texarkana's medical facility. Following that final prison stint, Carlos Marcello died a free man in one his mansions in Metairie, Louisiana, in March 1993. At the time of his death, he had Alzheimer's and had regressed to his infancy.

FOUR

MOBSTER IN THE WHITE HOUSE: BEBE REBOZO

When Richard Nixon was president, a disreputable character named Charles Gregory "Bebe" Rebozo (aka Charles Gregory) all but lived in the White House. Not known beyond the executive mansion at that time—or to most people even now—Rebozo had working and sleeping quarters there. He was even plugged into the White House switchboard, which knew how to reach him anywhere at any time.

Rebozo was not a high-ranking government employee who deserved or required such free space or services. In fact, the only government entity that knew much about Bebe was the FBI, which said he was cozy with Mafia biggies, especially Tampa godfather Santos Trafficante and Alfred "Big Al" Polizzi of Cleveland. Big Al was a drug trafficker associated with the Syndicate's financial genius, Meyer Lansky. In 1964, the Bureau of Narcotics branded Polizzi "one of the most influential members of the underworld in the United States."[1]

Rebozo and Polizzi were partners in developing a Cuban shopping center in Miami. Bebe purchased land in Florida with a reputed front man for Lansky, Robert Fincher. Telephone records show Fincher was in regular contact with Trafficante and New Orleans godfather Carlos Marcello. Fincher once boasted, "Bebe is a very close friend of mine."[2]

Investigative journalist Anthony Summers notes that, by the 1960s, there was no doubt among G-men that Bebe was pals with a who's who of the country's major gangsters. A former FBI agent who specialized in organized crime in the Miami area, Charles Stanley, identified Rebozo as a "non-member associate of organized crime figures."[3] This designation applied to individuals determined to have significant, witting association with "made members" of La Cosa Nostra.

In later years, Summers got further confirmation. Vincent "Jimmy Blue Eyes" Alo, a close cohort of Meyer Lansky, told Summers in 1997: "Everyone knew Rebozo would take a hot stove . . . He was the one who picked up the money for Nixon."[4] This was backed up by Vincent Teresa, a high-ranking Mafioso who became a government informant: "I understood [Rebozo] would take a hot stove, too, if you gave it to him."[5]

Indeed, Rebozo was Nixon's No. 1 bagman for payoffs from not only the Mafia, but from mobbed-up loopy billionaire Howard Hughes, a longtime "Daddy Warbucks" to Nixon. Rebozo came under investigation during Watergate for accepting a $100,000 bribe from Hughes for Nixon, but the Watergate Special Prosecution Force went out of business before completing its Rebozo probe. The bribe from Hughes, delivered in two installments, was turned over to the president's best buddy under the most secure of circumstances—behind the walls of the Secret Service–guarded Florida and California White Houses. Bebe Rebozo was profoundly more important to the president than the way one of Nixon's ex-aides recently described him: "He was just the guy who mixed the martinis."

The real Bebe, an American-born Cuban land speculator and banker, was not only Nixon's chief ambassador to the Mafia and Hughes. He'd also been a principal secret Mob-CIA go-between in the assassination plots hatched against Fidel Castro. He was a big deal in the Cuban exile community in Miami.

Bebe did business in Florida with at least two of the Watergate burglars, Bernard Barker and Eugenio Martinez. And Rebozo arranged for Nixon's chief spy and Watergate supervisor E. Howard Hunt to investigate Hoke Maroon, a former partner of Rebozo, who had inside information on Nixon's early business investments in Cuba. Maroon also claimed Nixon was once the part owner of Rebozo's Coral Gables Motel.[6]

High school grad Rebozo's first big job was as a steward with Pan-American Airways. He served patrons on flying boats that shuttled between Miami, the Caribbean and Panama. Later he owned a gas station; got into retreading old tires for a time; and then purchased a coin laundry, from which he allegedly ran a numbers racket. Eventually Bebe opened a bank near his home on upscale Key Biscayne, a small island just South of Miami.

Richard Nixon led 1964 dedication ceremonies for the bank and held Savings Account No. 1. The bank reputedly laundered Mob money—mostly the "skim" from gambling casinos in the Bahamas. Vincent Teresa, a high-ranking Mafioso, admitted using Rebozo's bank to launder stolen money.[7]

• • •

Nixon and Rebozo first met in Florida in 1947. Miamian Richard Danner, an ex-FBI agent who had fallen under Mob control and was a Nixon friend and close to both Rebozo and Mafia boss Santos Trafficante, made the introductions. Danner was City Manager of Miami from 1946 until 1948, when he was fired after a dispute involving the underworld's control over the local police department. Big-time crime and gambling were well entrenched in Miami then, and Danner and Rebozo and a third Florida boating companion of Nixon, Chubby Wofford, were working hand-in-glove with major mobsters.[8]

The Senate's Kefauver Committee—actually named the Special Committee to Investigate Crime in Interstate Commerce, but referred to by the name of its chairman, Senator Estes Kefauver—heard testimony that Wofford's hotel was the headquarters for crime figures from New York; and that Abe Allenberg, the Syndicate's Miami representative, was a friend and former employer of Dick Danner.[9] In 1952, Nixon and Danner secretly visited Havana and gambled at a Syndicate-run casino. Danner later credited Nixon for using his clout with the Mafia to ultimately land him a cushy job at a Las Vegas casino.[10] During Nixon's presidency, Danner was the payoff man for bribes from Howard Hughes to Nixon, through Rebozo.

Rebozo and Congressman Nixon didn't hit it off immediately when they met in Florida. "I don't want to say that Bebe's level of liking Nixon increased as Nixon's [political] position increased,"

Rebozo friend Senator George Smathers put it, "but it had a lot to do with it."[11]

Within months of their first Florida cruise aboard Bebe's $18,000 houseboat, the *Cocolobo,* the two men became almost inseparable, with Rebozo lending both moral and financial support through Nixon's many political highs and lows. He was there in Key Biscayne in 1952 when Nixon celebrated his election to the vice presidency; he was in Los Angeles in 1960 when Nixon learned that Senator John Kennedy had edged him out for the presidency; he comforted Nixon after his crushing 1962 loss to incumbent Edmund "Pat" Brown for California governor; and Rebozo and Nixon drank and sunbathed together in Key Biscayne after Nixon narrowly defeated Vice President Hubert Humphrey in the 1968 presidential election.

Known as "Uncle Bebe" to Nixon's two children, Trisha and Julie, Rebozo frequently bought the girls—and Nixon's wife, Pat—expensive gifts. "Beeb," as Nixon referred to Rebozo (who always called Nixon "Mr. President") purchased a $100,000 house in the suburbs for Julie after she married David Eisenhower. Rebozo paid for bowling alleys to be put in the White House and Camp David.

In pre-presidential times on Key Biscayne, Nixon and Rebozo were always given their special spot at their favorite restaurant, the Jamaica Inn. They were seated at a cozy, dark out-of-the-way booth near a waterfall. A martini or two usually preceded chopped steaks, medium rare. Bebe always picked up the tab and left a big tip. After all, the fancy eatery with the British décor was owned by their old friend Donald Berg—who gave Nixon a cut-rate deal on the land for his Key Biscayne vacation home as a favor for posing for a promotional picture with Berg in 1967.

Like Rebozo, Berg had been indicted in stolen stock deals but never prosecuted. The Secret Service eventually asked the president to find a more suitable restaurant after uncovering Berg's ties to the Mafia. But, for some reason, the president's protectors issued no similar warning about socializing with Rebozo. Both Nixon and Rebozo had close ties to Keyes Realty—an "investment funnel for the hundreds of millions of dollars that Syndicate figures and freebooting Cuban politicians hauled out of Batista's Cuba."[12]

Bebe Rebozo came in and out of the White House as he pleased, without being logged in by the Secret Service. Though, as noted, he had no official government position, Rebozo had his own private office with a telephone and a designated bedroom always at his disposal at 1600 Pennsylvania Avenue.

In Florida, his home was right next door to Nixon's. It was equipped with free worldwide telephone service through the White House Office of Communications, as was Rebozo's private villa on the grounds of the San Clemente White House.

Behind the scenes, Rebozo was "deeply involved" with expensive government-funded remodeling plans at both of the president's vacation homes, according to White House aide John Ehrlichman in *Witness to Power:*

> He flew to Los Angeles for meetings with the General Services Administration official in charge of the [San Clemente] project. Over the months, he so successfully co-opted the GSA project manager, that the GSA began carrying out Rebozo's instructions without

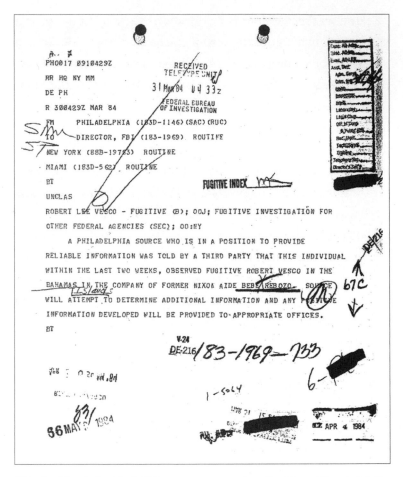

This freshly declassified FBI memo reports that President Nixon's Mafia-connected buddy Bebe Rebozo has been consorting with one of the FBI's Most Wanted criminals, fugitive financier and Nixon benefactor and Mob-linked Robert Vesco. COURTESY OF THE FBI.

question. If there was undue government expenditure, at either the San Clemente or the Key Biscayne house, Mr. Rebozo should be given full credit for his persuasive involvement.[13]

Bebe was secretly put in charge of a reconstruction project at the presidential retreat at Camp David, where he also had his own cabin. He purchased most of the president's suits and sports clothes, and even picked the movies Nixon would watch. Bebe was frequently sneaked in and out of Nixon's suite when the president was traveling abroad. On one such occasion, Nixon's chief foreign policy advisor Henry Kissinger cursed a blue streak and nearly threw a fit. Rebozo's presence was always a major distraction to the foreign policy issues Kissinger hoped to discuss with the president.

Kissinger was sometimes the target of late night drunken crank phone calls from the president offering Bebe's foreign policy suggestions. In one of these calls, Nixon warned Kissinger that if he didn't take Bebe's advice about the invasion of Cambodia, "It'll be your ass, Henry."[14]

Kissinger got particularly perturbed when Rebozo flew on Air Force One, which was frequently. On such flights, Bebe, like Kissinger, donned a blue Navy flight jacket bearing the Presidential Seal with his name stitched onto it. (Nixon's own flight jacket was inscribed "The President," as though no one would recognize that fact by just looking at him.) And Bebe was far more likely to be granted an airborne audience with the president than Henry.

The thirty-seventh president's intimate relationship with a mafia-crony like Rebozo raises serious questions about just how deeply the country's biggest and most profitable illegal business—the blood-soaked Mob—had gotten its sinister hooks into Nixon.

In the 1960s, crooked gambling operations alone brought in an estimated $50 billion a year. There were many additional billions the Mafia made through prostitution, narcotics trafficking, extortion, labor racketeering and political corruption. Attorney General Robert Kennedy reckoned that—by the sixties—the Mob had donned a disguise and greatly expanded its power. He told a congressional committee in 1963 that organized crime had become a big business "resting on a base of human suffering and moral corrosion"—and corrupting business, labor, politics, and government. He added that the modern-day racketeer was no longer "someone dressed in a black shirt, white tie, and diamond stickpin" with influence only in underworld circles. Today's mobster, Kennedy asserted, is more likely to be attired "in a grey flannel suit and his influence is more likely to be as far-reaching as that of an important industrialist.[15]

In April 1969, President Nixon put out a printed message describing the Mafia's influence as "more secure than ever before" and warning that it "had deeply penetrated broad segments of American life." Nixon stated, "The organized criminal relies on physical terror and psychological intimidation, on economic retaliation, on political bribery, on citizen indifference and governmental acquiescence. He corrupts our governing institutions and subverts our democratic processes."[16]

Unfortunately, that printed presidential condemnation of the Mafia was a leftover boilerplate pronouncement from the Johnson administration and a one-time call to arms at that. Nixon never again issued a report on the dangers of the Mob.

Nixon's final White House chief of staff, Alexander Haig, was suspicious enough of his boss's mob connections to order an old military buddy to conduct a supersecret probe of the president's darkest, most secretive side. Most specifically, Haig wanted to know whether Nixon's spies and bagmen Jack Caufield and Tony

Ulasewicz had traveled to the Far East and brought back huge stacks of cash to Nixon.

Second, Haig wanted to know if the president was beholden to organized crime. Haig's secret sleuth on the Army's Criminal Investigations Command, Russell Bintliff, reported back that Caufield and Ulasewicz "probably had gone to Vietnam, and I considered there were strong indications of a history of Nixon connections with money from organized crime."

This bizarre and overlooked tale of the president's top aide mounting a secret criminal investigation against his boss didn't surface until 1976, when it was disclosed by Jerry O'Leary, a *Washington Star* reporter with tight ties to U.S. intelligence.[17]

And just what role did Nixon's constant companion and chief link to the Syndicate, Bebe Rebozo, play in the president's "history of connections with money from organized crime"? From all the circumstantial evidence, a major one.

FIVE

NIXON'S SEXUALITY

Was Bebe Rebozo's relationship with Nixon more than just friendship? Veteran Nixon-watcher George Reedy, who reported for *United Press* on Nixon's years as a senator and vice president, once provided the most likely answer. Nixon's tightness with Rebozo, he said, was "the most important unsolved mystery in Nixon's life."[1] Reedy, who went on to serve as President Lyndon Johnson's press secretary, was by no means the only person with an opinion on the subject.

Newsday investigative reporter Robert Greene has said, "My own particular thought was that [Rebozo] was one of those guys who has an extremely low sex drive. He had a tendency to keep the company of whiskey-drinking, fishing, rather masculine-type men, with the exception of Nixon. Nixon studied the part, but he really wasn't."[2]

Bobby Baker, a top aide to Senator Lyndon Johnson, said Nixon and Rebozo were "close like lovers."[3] Rebozo's friend Jake

Jernigan is quoted as saying that Bebe "loved Nixon more than he loved anybody. He worshipped Nixon. Nixon was his God . . . his Little Jesus."[4]

And then there were the hand-holding sightings. After Nixon's 1962 loss in the California governor's race, Nixon and Rebozo "held hands and pledged eternal friendship no matter what happened." Anthony Summers, author of the best, most comprehensive book about Nixon, *The Arrogance of Power*, is the source for that hand-holding story, as well as for this one: "Once, at a Washington dinner party, a woman journalist who sat near them bent below table level to retrieve a dropped fork and was astounded to see that Nixon and Rebozo were clasping hands, an intimacy rare indeed in males in the Western World."[5]

In 1972, shortly after President Nixon's resounding re-election victory, *Time*'s Bonnie Angelo was covering Nixon at Key Biscayne for a special issue her magazine would soon run about the second Nixon administration. On December 1, 1972, she was allowed to accompany the press travel pool when Nixon went out to dinner in Miami with Bebe Rebozo and Charles Colson.

Angelo says the threesome was screened off from other diners during dinner, but that Nixon was in a "very rosy" and "celebratory mood"—"almost jovial"—when he walked through the main dining room to exit the restaurant. He'd obviously had a few drinks, she recalls. And she thought he might be saying to himself, "I've now got a lock on the next four years."

Nixon started shaking hands with diners, and then pulled Bebe, who had been standing behind him, forward by the hand so his best friend could get into some of the photos being snapped of Nixon. But the hand-holding continued. "They were so tight!" Angelo reports.

She says she's never seen two men hold hands for as long and as fondly as Nixon and Rebozo proceeded to do. Surprisingly, she says, they were still holding hands outside the restaurant while waiting for the presidential limousine to pull up. In stark contrast, Nixon seldom, if ever, held hands with his wife—as recounted by Nixon biographer Anthony Summers:

> Evlyn Dorn, his longtime secretary, saw her boss reach out to touch his wife only once—and then merely to steady her as they stood in the back of a car. "He had a way of ignoring her," she said. "I never saw him touch Pat's hand," recalled Tom Dixon, a broadcaster who acted as an aide during elections in the late forties. "I have never seen quite so cold an arrangement."[6]

Angelo says one member of the press pool, A.P.'s Fran Lewin, also observed the Nixon-Rebozo hand-holding scene at the Miami restaurant. She says she and Fran rolled their eyes at each other at what they were viewing.

Neither the A.P. nor *Time* decided to run the story that so amazed these two top-flight veteran reporters. Angelo says she hasn't used it in print herself, just saved it as a great insider's story she can use to raise the eyebrows of her closest friends.

Angelo thinks the Nixon-Rebozo relationship was a one of "repressed homosexuality. Because they were both such uptight guys, I don't think they'd engage in it [a homosexual act]. But their longings and devotion were so obvious. Nixon loved being with Bebe. And Bebe would do anything for Nixon. He'd lie in front of a train for him."

Angelo, now in her eighties, believes it was particularly curious that when Nixon and Rebozo would spend time at the private Bahamian island of Robert Abplanalp, the wealthy businessman would disappear to another island—leaving his own island, mansion and swimming pool exclusively to Dick and Bebe.[7]

Jim McManus, then a White House reporter for Westinghouse Broadcasting, was on the same 1972 Nixon trip to Florida as Bonnie Angelo. He vividly recalls her reaction to the odd presidential behavior she and Fran Lewin had witnessed:

> The first evening of this trip, Press Secretary Ron Ziegler assigned Bonnie as the magazine representative in a press pool that would accompany the president and Mr. Rebozo to their favorite restaurant, the Hasta, on Miami's Miracle Mile. It was Ms. Angelo's first opportunity to observe the president relaxing in public.
>
> The next morning, Bonnie came to me in a state of at least mild agitation, drew me aside, and asked if I would help her understand something she had seen the night before. She told me the story she has iterated to you. In detail. She asked how she should regard the event, how did it fit into my own observations of the president.
>
> It was still the era of never straying into the personal habits and customs of the president. Facts and

suspicions, especially in the matter of sex life, were muttered among reporters and some politicians. But, that was the extent of it. "I told Bonnie . . . she should not try to start a confirming conversation."

Wait until we go home and then tell your boss, I said. Maybe even write a memo to the record and keep it among her notes. And most especially, tell [Sim] Fentress, her colleague [at *Time*], so that he would not be blindsided if the story leaked.

And so, for [about] 40 years, the story has lain there, unpublicized.

What does it tell us? That, at the very least, the president and his friend were extraordinarily close at a time when that sort of relationship was suggestive of more than a teenage buddyship. Beyond that, who knows? We know that the president could not "hold" his liquor and that his buttoned-down personality became unguarded according to rumors among other politicians.

As one who observed Mr. Nixon up close for six years, I have my own opinion. For now, I can only confirm Bonnie Angelo's story.[8]

A UPI radio reporter at the time, Roger Gittines, says McManus told him, back then, what Bonnie saw—but did not report. As Gittines recently recalled: "Nixon went to a restaurant, had a few pops, and worked the room schmoozing people with his arm around Bebe the way you'd cuddle your senior prom date. Something was fishy there."[9]

Nixon and Rebozo were certainly quite playful together, especially when loaded. One White House aide recalls seeing the two grown men playing a child's game called "King of the Pool" at Key Biscayne. "It was late at night," according to Watergate authority, J. Anthony Lukas. "The two men had been drinking. Nixon mounted a rubber raft in the pool while Rebozo tried to turn it over. Then, laughing and shouting, they'd change places and Nixon tried to upset Rebozo."[10]

And they were just about always together. During Nixon's White House years, rough estimates show Rebozo was at Nixon's side one out of every ten days. The president made fifty trips to Key Biscayne—most of them without family members—to be with Bebe. Nixon took his top aides along on most of these jaunts, which were billed as working vacations. But the aides were there mainly as decoys, as almost no meetings ever occurred and very little work was done. As aide John Ehrlichman later recalled: "Haldeman, Kissinger, and I were often taken to Florida and, from time to time were reported to have worked with Nixon on affairs of state. If such staff meetings at the house next to Nixon's took place they were rare."[11]

Rebozo seldom talked to the press without the president's permission. So let's assume the following story, told by Rebozo, was approved by Nixon—perhaps as a horribly misguided effort to show the president's manliness and humor (neither of which he actually possessed).

Rebozo made his only network TV appearance, an interview on CBS, at about the same time Nixon's press secretary, Ron Ziegler, was whispering to reporters that Nixon was a "with-it" individual who even wore hippie-inspired bell-bottoms while strolling the grounds of Camp David. Presidential photographer Ollie Atkins snapped a staged photo of Nixon with a foot up on a log fence at Camp David. For the shoot, the president decked himself out in a rather incongruous black leather motorcycle jacket . . . along with black dress shoes. The photo was so bizarre, the White House never released it.

In the CBS interview on December 19, 1973, Rebozo claimed that Nixon had a secret comedic side. Bebe was asked to provide an example. Without hesitation, Rebozo recounted a practical joke he and Nixon allegedly played on Robert Abplanalp, their drinking buddy, while the trio was vacationing by themselves in the Bahamas.

Bebe said he and the president set up a pair of inflated fake female legs "skin-colored and all" so the legs would protrude from the bottom of the sheets on Bob's bed. While Bebe hid in a corner, the president led Bob into the bedroom. Bebe then jumped out and snapped a flash-bulb photo of Bob gaping in surprise at the results of Dick and Bebe's ribald trick, the president's best friend stated. Rebozo cited the incident as showing that Nixon "really has a rare and quick sense of humor, very quick."

A top psychiatrist with expertise on Nixon's thinking had a completely different take on this so-called practical joke. Dr. David Abrahamsen, author of *Nixon Vs. Nixon*, called it "exceedingly immature sexually, the kind of thing eight- or nine-year-old boys would do."[12]

Bebe had an even more salacious off-camera version of the story. He revealed that the legs really belonged to a full-sized inflatable doll, complete with a vagina.[13]

. . .

Before he met Nixon, Rebozo had three very brief marriages (twice to the same woman), and was reportedly active in Miami's homosexual community. He was said to have had a longtime affair with an airline steward and was known for throwing male-only barbecues at his Key Biscayne home.[14]

A recently published exchange of early 1970s letters between Rebozo and Richard Danner, the Mafia-connected Miamian who introduced Bebe to Nixon and went to Havana with Nixon in 1952, is more than just curious. At one point Danner refers to "constant invitations" from Rebozo to stay at his Key Biscayne home, and to Rebozo himself as a "man-eating tiger." For his part, during a quarrel, the short and compact Rebozo says to the tall and thin Danner: "Frankly, you are not my type."

In another letter, however, a more affectionate Bebe apologizes for fading off too early during one of Danner's overnight stays at Bebe's place. "Sorry father time has sort of caught up with me, and I was unable to get through the entire evening. Some day when you reach my age you'll know what I mean." Bebe then promises Danner that, when he next visits, he'll get to stay in " 'the queen for a day' room."[15]

Nixon was a vociferous homophobe. He once protested that Northern California had become so "faggy" that "I won't shake hands with anybody from San Francisco." He also declared that homosexuality "destroyed" ancient Greece, adding, "Aristotle was a homo, we all know that. So was Socrates."[16] On being told of

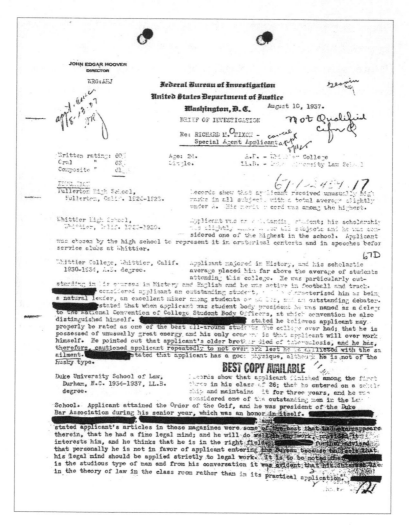

JOHN EDGAR HOOVER
DIRECTOR

Federal Bureau of Investigation
United States Department of Justice
Washington, D. C. August 10, 1937.

BRIEF OF INVESTIGATION

Re: RICHARD M. NIXON -
Special Agent Applicant

Written rating: 60%
Oral   "   63%
Composite "   61%

Age: 24.
Single.

A.B. - Whittier College
LL.B. - Duke University Law School

FULLERTON
Fullerton High School,
Fullerton, Calif. 1920-1923.

Records show that applicant received unusually high marks in all subjects, with a total average slightly under A. His merit record was among the highest.

Whittier High School,
Whittier, Calif. 1926-1930.

Applicant was an outstanding student; his scholarship was slightly above average in all subjects and he was considered one of the highest in the school. Applicant was chosen by the high school to represent it in oratorical contests and in speeches before service clubs at Whittier.

Whittier College, Whittier, Calif.
1930-1934, A.B. degree.

Applicant majored in History, and his scholastic average placed him far above the average of students attending this college. He was particularly outstanding in his courses in History and English and he was active in football and track. _____ considered applicant an outstanding student, _____ characterized him as being a natural leader, an excellent mixer among students of all ages, and an outstanding debater. _____ stated that when applicant was student body president he was named as a delegate to the National Convention of College Student Body Officers, at which convention he also distinguished himself. _____ stated he believes applicant may properly be rated as one of the best all-around students the college ever had; that he is possessed of unusually great energy and his only concern is that applicant will over work himself. He pointed out that applicant's older brother died of tuberculosis, and he has, therefore, cautioned applicant repeatedly to not over work lest he be afflicted with the same ailment. _____ stated that applicant has a good physique, although he is not of the husky type.

Duke University School of Law,
Durham, N.C. 1934-1937, LL.B.
degree.

Records show that applicant finished among the first three in his class of 26; that he entered on a scholarship and maintained it for three years, provided he was considered one of the outstanding men in the Law

School. Applicant attained the Order of the Coif, and he was president of the Duke Bar Association during his senior year, which was an honor in itself. _____ and _____ stated applicant's articles in these magazines were some of the finest that had ever appeared therein, that he had a fine legal mind; and he will do well in any work, provided it interests him, and he thinks that he is in the right field. _____ further advised that personally he is not in favor of applicant entering the Bureau because he feels that his legal mind should be applied strictly to legal work. It is to be noted that is the studious type of man and from his conversation it was evident that his interest lies in the theory of law in the class room rather than in its practical application.

BEST COPY AVAILABLE

the death of his reputedly gay friend, FBI Director J. Edgar Hoover, the president declared, "Jesus Christ! That old cocksucker!"

Was Nixon's tough-guy attitude toward gays just a cover for his own homosexuality, bisexuality or asexuality? Was he shrouding some kind of subliminal or "unaddressed" issue? Well, he isn't still called "Tricky Dick" for nothing.

Nixon certainly never showed his wife, Pat, the affection he showed Bebe Rebozo—in public or in private. Few realize that Nixon's marriage to Pat was extremely unhappy. A recently released May 4, 1970 memo reviewing a presidential trip to Houston urged Nixon to display a little on-stage fondness for, or at least awareness of, his wife. The memo, from TV consultant Roger Ailes (now head of Fox News) to top White House aide Bob Haldeman, stresses the importance of the women's vote:

> I think it is important for the President to show a little more concern for Mrs. Nixon as he moves through the crowd. At one point he walked off in a different direction. Mrs. Nixon wasn't looking and had to run to catch up. From time to time he should talk to her and smile at her. Women voters are particularly sensitive to how a man treats his wife in public. The more attention she gets, the happier they are.

A relatively recent book and a TV documentary of the same name—partly based on the accounts of several of Nixon's Secret Service agents—contend that Nixon even beat his wife before,

PRODUCTIONS INC. 888 Eighth Avenue. Suite 7F New York, New York 10019

New York 212-765-3022 Washington 202-544-6449

MEMORANDUM

TO: H. R. Haldeman   cc: Dwight Chapin

FROM: Roger E. Ailes

DATE: May 4, 1970

SUBJECT: WHITE HOUSE TELEVISION

- -

HOUSTON

(1) Arrival of cars in Houston was good, exciting, but a little long. Nixon's entrance through crowd looked good.

(2) There was an audio lag after the announcer introduced President and Mrs. Nixon. The networks don't seem to mike for crowd reaction so it might be good to ask the director to do a cut-away shot in these instances.

that's why we should be inside

(3) At any outdoor event the President must assume that he is on camera at all times. There was one bad shot of him sneaking a look at his notes after he got to the platform in Houston.

— you tell him

(4) I think it is important for the President to show a little more concern for Mrs. Nixon as he moves through the crowd. At one point he walked off in a different direction. Mrs. Nixon wasn't looking and had to run to catch up. From time to time he should talk to her and smile at her. Women voters are particularly sensitive to how a man treats his wife in public. The more attention she gets, the happier they are.

√

The first page of a memo from TV advisor Roger Ailes urging President Nixon show more affection toward Pat in public, released in 2007. (Nixon reportedly beat Pat before, during, and after their White House years.) COURTESY OF NIXON LIBRARY/NATIONAL ARCHIVES.

during, and after his presidency. In *Arrogance of Power,* Anthony Summers portrays Nixon as an ugly drunk who sometimes roughed up Pat while under the influence.

Investigative reporter Seymour Hersh developed similar evidence, saying in 1998: "There was a serious empirical basis for believing [Nixon] was a wife-beater, and had done so—at least hospitalized her a number of times . . . I'm talking about trauma, and three distinct cases."[17]

Nixon had a long history of violent behavior; and no wonder: he was whipped, pushed, kicked, punched—and worse—by an abusive father, Frank Nixon. His mother, Hanna, was cold and often absent. Frank verbally, and possibly physically, abused Hanna.

Young Dick favored his mom ("My mother was a saint," he tearfully asserted, in his farewell speech to his White House staff) while, for unknown reasons, his siblings did not. "[This] must have given rise within him to significant feelings of uncertainty about himself as a person, and more specifically, as a male," according to psycho-historian Eli Chesen in *President Nixon's Psychiatric Profile*.[18]

Dick and Pat Nixon had separate bedrooms at the White House, as well as at Nixon's retreats in Florida, California, and Camp David. When Pat, Julie and Trisha Nixon accompanied the president to Florida, the females even stayed in a separate house on Key Biscayne—while the president stayed in one next door to Rebozo.

Pat once confided to one of her White House physicians that "she and her husband had not really been close since the early 1960s."[19] The pair even occupied separate compartments on Air Force One. The president's military aide Jack Brennan used to privately joke that his secret job was to teach the president how to kiss his wife.

Nixon foreign policy advisor Henry Kissinger was fond of

regaling colleagues with a tale that strongly suggested that Pat, too, was far from thrilled with her marriage. At his first meeting with Mrs. Nixon, Kissinger said he started heaping extravagant praise on the president, but that Pat leaned over and interrupted him by saying, "Haven't you seen through him yet?" Former Kissinger aide Roger Morris says Henry also used that anecdote to reinforce his view to his staff that, "This man is not stable."[20]

Shortly after the president took office, Muriel Dobbin of the *Baltimore Sun* got a close-up look at Dick and Pat Nixon's relationship—which she terms "one of the strangest" she'd ever encountered. Dobbin was seated at the First Couple's table at El Adobe, a Mexican restaurant in San Juan Capistrano, California. The Nixons were treating the White House press corps to a very rare dinner. When the ill-at-ease president ran out of other small talk, he began praising the restaurant's decorations, including its flowers. "But Dick," Pat interrupted, "they're plastic."

To be made light of by his wife in public, and in front of reporters, to boot, had clearly galled Nixon, so much that he was not able to hide his deep displeasure. Dobbin saw the president's "face darken," the first time she'd ever seen that cliché actually occur. It was obviously a "terrible moment" for him, she recalls.

Aside from his facial response, Nixon completely ignored his wife's comment, which Dobbin describes as "a devastating putdown for no particular reason." Once his face returned to its normal color, however, the president wore a kind of "What can I expect from her?" expression, according to the reporter.

Overall, Dobbin feels Nixon was a "sociopath" with what she terms "a strange artificiality about him. Whatever was inside him never came out." And she believes Nixon behaved in an "appalling" way toward Pat: "He drained her, and there was nothing she could do to help." At the end of the Nixon presidency, according to Dobbin, Pat had "totally empty eyes. She was simply someone who wasn't there."[21] California journalist Frank McCullough is another longtime close observer of Nixon who had great disdain for him and the way he related to his wife. McCullough, as well as Dobbin, are more than a dozen people—including yours truly— who'd heard rumors from credible sources that Dick, as Dobbin puts it, "physically mistreated" Pat.

Over his many years of covering the Nixons, McCullough witnessed no violence between Dick and Pat, but did accidentally overhear Nixon belittling Pat in 1950, when Nixon was running for the Senate against Representative Helen Gahagan Douglas. Then a reporter with *Time*, Frank was a little early to arrive at Nixon's Whittier home, so Dick, clad in a bathrobe, asked him to wait in the living room. Soon, the Nixons' guest began to hear a loud and angry dispute from behind the closed kitchen door.

Though he doesn't recall just what the shout-fest was about, McCullough will never forget Dick ending the exchange by screaming, at Pat: "You're a dumb fucking bitch!"

When he returned to the living room and determined that McCullough had heard the verbal climax to this domestic dispute, the candidate asked, "Are you going to put that in your magazine?" Dick was greatly relieved when Frank explained that Nixon was speaking in the privacy of his own home, and assured him that the anti-Pat vulgarity would never see print.[22]

Dick showed a sadly similar attitude toward his wife, this time in public, during a 1962 plane trip. As usual, Pat was sitting apart from her husband. On this flight, he was conferring with aides when Pat asked if she could join the group for a drink. Dick reportedly snarled in response: "Keep your fucking mouth shut."[23]

CBS White House reporter Bob Pierpoint knew Pat back in high school, when he was a student, she his teacher. He said Dick and Pat "tried to play the game of being the perfect husband and wife, but it came through as transparent. It looked so phony, so unrealistic."[24]

Westinghouse radio reporter Sid Davis, who covered the Nixon campaign in 1960, agrees. After carefully observing the couple's on-stage behavior, he strongly suspected they were just putting on a show. "I thought to myself at almost every campaign stop . . . 'I wonder what really goes on between them.'"[25]

"She gave so much and got so little of what was really meaningful to a woman—attention, companionship, consideration," Kandy Stroud, who worked on Pat Nixon's staff, observed. "Sometimes [the president] was so brutally indifferent I wept for her."[26]

In *First Families*, correspondent Bonnie Angelo voiced sorrow that, "as First Lady, Pat Nixon was never given the chance to be all that Patricia Ryan could be."

Patricia Ryan had been an attractive and popular young woman, her students' favorite teacher at Whittier High School, and a talented aspiring stage actress and film extra. Yet, in the White House, as Angelo observes, "The men around the President—and the President himself?—saw her only as an appendage to make him look better."[27]

In her book, Angelo recounts the time that Nixon ignored Pat when she returned from a grueling overseas goodwill trip to South America. The First Lady "joined the President at the Grand

Ole Opry in Nashville, only to have him forget to introduce her at what was planned as her birthday celebration." Great performer Roy Acuff smoothly covered the blunder.

The president made up for his slight by playing "Happy Birthday" to Pat on an old upright piano that was wheeled onstage. When Nixon finished playing, however, another blunder ensued when "he perfunctorily brushed [Pat] aside as she came toward him with outstretched arms, and resumed his ceremonial duties."[28]

The *Washington Post*'s Myra MacPherson also wrote of the Nixons' strangely aloof and cold relationship: "The press corps used to look in vain for some sort of emotion to pass between Pat and Dick Nixon; observers looked for anything that spoke of warmth."[29]

Only rarely did the president and the first lady dine alone in the White House. When they did, the waiters and chefs sped up their pace. As one butler explained to reporters Bob Woodward and Carl Bernstein: "A minute is a long time when you're not talking."[30] A study of Nixon's presidential diaries by reporter Jimmy Breslin "showed he spent a half-hour, at the most up to an hour, a day with his wife."[31]

In *Inside the White House*, investigative reporter Ronald Kessler said the Secret Service found Nixon and his family to be the strangest they covered, and that "Nixon seemed to have no relationship with his wife ... and he barely spoke with his two daughters, Tricia and Julie." Kessler quotes one agent as saying that Nixon, after his resignation, once "walked a nine-hole golf course [in San Clemente] with his wife and daughters, and not a word was spoken among the four of them. It was an hour and a half, and he never said a word."[32]

. . .

Nixon seemingly despised women in general, once flatly declaring, "I don't even think women should be educated."[33] Onetime Nixon aide Jim Bassett observed that Nixon had "a total scorn for female mentality."[34]

In his lone political run against a woman, Nixon went to great lengths to inject gender into the race. This was in 1950, in the era before the women's rights movement took hold, when he was running against Helen Gahagan Douglas for the U.S. Senate in California. Douglas biographer Sally Denton reported that Nixon was "always referring to Helen as his *female* or *woman* opponent, making crass sexual remarks if he was in an all-male gathering—even smirking and hinting that [Helen] was sexually involved with [President] Truman—and using every opportunity to dismiss her intellectual attributes with a reference to her sex."[35]

Nixon's problem with women and establishing his own sexual identity as a male apparently went back to his childhood, according to historian James David Barber, who says Nixon's brothers and playmates teased him about being a mama's boy. His general reaction, especially in school, was to be antigirl. "Oh, he used to dislike us girls so!" a classmate remembered. "He would make horrible faces at us. As a debater, his main theme in grammar school and the first years of high school was why he hated girls." Barber also notes that in school plays, Nixon was, as one female classmate put it, "a little stiff in the romantic scenes."[36]

The question remains: Was Bebe Rebozo's relationship with Richard Nixon more than a close friendship? Nixon biographer Fawn

Brodie points out that after President Johnson's right-hand man, Walter Jenkins, was arrested while administering sexual favors to a retired soldier in a staked-out YMCA restroom in Washington, Nixon publicly pounced on the scandal, saying that Jenkins "was ill. But people with this kind of illness cannot be in places of high trust."[37]

In another comment on the Jenkins scandal, Nixon said: "A cloud hangs over the White House this morning because of Lyndon Johnson and his selection of men." In *Nixonland*, Rick Perlstein observes that the construction of that particular Nixon statement suggested Johnson "might as well have been right there in that men's room with Jenkins."[38]

Brodie also observes that "Nixon seems to have been willing to risk the kind of gossip that frequently accompanies close friendship with a perennial bachelor, this despite his known public aversion to homosexuals, and his acute sensitivity to the damage that the label of homosexual on a friend could bring to a public man."[39]

The ever-faithful Bebe was at Nixon's bedside when the former president died in 1994. When Rebozo died in 1998, he left $19 million to the Nixon Library in Yorba Linda, California.

SIX

NIXON'S WOOING OF
FRANK SINATRA

Newly released tapes and documents show President Nixon assiduously courted Frank Sinatra because Nixon thought the
singer's connections in the entertainment industry and the Syndicate could produce an abundance of political endorsements
and campaign funds. Sinatra eventually succumbed—hanging
around so much with Nixon and Vice President Spiro Agnew
that Sinatra even acquired a Secret Service code name: Napo-
leon. Sinatra, the greatest popular singer of the twentieth century, was a high-strung alcoholic whose ties to organized crime
were "woven into the fabric of his life and career by 1948," according to Sinatra biographer Anthony Summers, who adds that
"the Mafia had a continuing interest in every aspect" of Frank's
life.[1] Sinatra usually carried a pistol in a shoulder holster.[2]

Initially Sinatra was a Democrat, entranced by John F. Kennedy's star power. In fact, he hooked his favorite presidential
candidate up with Mob mistress Judith Campbell Exner (whose

other lovers included Sinatra, Mafia figure Johnny Roselli and Chicago godfather Sam Giancana) and also introduced JFK to Hollywood sex goddess Marilyn Monroe. But once he was elected president, JFK wisely moved away from the crooner with Mafia ties. The distancing was politically understandable.

Sam Giancana, the dapper don of Chicago, was so tight with Sinatra that he always wore Sinatra's gift to him, a star sapphire pinky ring, and Sinatra had such great affection for Giancana, he ended every personal performance singing "My Kind of Town, Chicago" as a tribute to Sam.

By the time Kennedy entered the White House, however, Giancana had been arrested some seventy times and had reportedly ordered some 200 torture-murders of men who had done him wrong. Sinatra's friend, movie actor Peter Lawford— President Kennedy's brother-in-law—told Sinatra biographer Kitty Kelley that "when the word got out around [Hollywood] that Frank was a pal of Sam Giancana, nobody but nobody ever messed with Frank Sinatra. They were too scared. Concrete boots were no joke with [Giancana]. He was a killer."[3]

For his part, however, Giancana, who felt he had used his financial and political clout to secure the election for Kennedy in Illinois, was furious that while his campaign help had been accepted, he was getting nothing in return for his contributions, and worse yet, the president's younger brother, Attorney General Robert Kennedy, was going all out against organized crime.

Early in the new administration, an FBI wiretap picked up a conversation between the Chicago gangland boss and fellow mobster Johnny Roselli in which Giancana said he'd instead anticipated that, "one of these days, the guy will do me a favor . . ."

Roselli empathized: "If I ever got a speeding ticket, not one of those fuckers would know me."

Giancana's reply: "You told that right, buddy."[4]

In fact, Giancana blamed Sinatra for failing to persuade the Kennedys to turn a blind eye toward the Mafia in exchange for the election victory he had helped swing, and was so incensed that at one point he considered having Sinatra bumped off. But Sinatra never got more than a chilling warning.

Early in JFK's presidency, the singer received a traditional Mafia death threat, according to Summers. When a silver dome was lifted off a silver room service dinner tray in Sinatra's Miami Beach hotel suite, the skinned head of a lamb was displayed as the main course.

The frightened Sinatra reportedly canceled all his engagements and, for a time, hid out in the basement of a Catholic church (later donating $50,000 to the church for the priest's help). Frank had heard through the Mob grapevine that Giancana was gunning for him.[5]

Giancana was angry at Ol' Blue Eyes for more than just the entertainer's inability to turn the Kennedys away from their war on the underworld, according to the daughter of the Syndicate's financial genius, Meyer Lanksy. In 2010, Sandi Lansky Lombardo, then seventy-two, claimed Giancana was upset that Sinatra was becoming too arrogant and careless, and was pushing around members of Sam's gang. She says Sinatra called Lansky in tears, saying he would do anything—even playing a million gigs in all of Giancana's joints—if Lansky would ask Sam to call off the plot on Sinatra's life. What Sinatra didn't know, according to Lombardo, was that Giancana was listening in on the other line, and that Lansky quietly hung up just as Giancana was about to burst out laughing.[6]

Frank's plea to Lansky apparently worked: "According to a member of [Giancana's] family, only the intercession of East Coast associates persuaded Giancana not to have Frank killed in 1963. 'That motherf****r,' he said when Frank arrived unexpectedly at the Armory Lounge [in Chicago], 'is lucky to be alive.'"[7]

If Sinatra's Mafia connections banned him from Camelot, however, they most certainly didn't keep President Richard Nixon from trying to lure the popular crooner. In fact, in a conversation with his daughter, Tricia, Nixon speculates that JFK's rejection of Sinatra turned out to be his good luck:

Nixon: "[Sammy Davis Jr.] had never appeared at the White House before. I would have thought that he would have during the Kennedy period because he was very close to Kennedy. But Kennedy never invited him.

Tricia: He dropped him like hot potatoes after the election [of 1960].

Nixon: Kennedy was one of those guys who just thought Sammy Davis and Frank Sinatra were not useful to him, and he just dropped them!

Tricia: Was he really like that? Did he just use people as long as [garbled]?

Nixon: Absolutely! Oh, sure. None at all.

Tricia: That's fascinating! I think that's one of the reasons Frank Sinatra came over . . .

Nixon: I think so too![8]

The courtship of Frank Sinatra actually started with Nixon's unsavory vice president, Spiro Agnew, who first got together with Sinatra during the Thanksgiving holiday in 1970. They enjoyed each other's company so much that "Agnew became a regular houseguest at Frank's [Palm Springs] place, and made eighteen visits in the months that followed. The two men played golf together, dined out, talked through the night in Frank's den, and on one occasion watched the porn movie *Deep Throat* together. Frank's guest quarters, previously remodeled for John F. Kennedy, were eventually renamed 'Agnew House,'" according to Anthony Summers.[9]

The president himself evinced a keen interest in Sinatra's possible endorsement during a September 13, 1971 Oval Office meeting with top aide Bob Haldeman. Nixon was in the middle of a rant against the IRS for investigating some of his friends— including preacher Billy Graham, movie actor John Wayne, and close friends Bebe Rebozo and Robert Abplanalp—when he worried aloud over whether he could obtain Sinatra's support.

Nixon ordered Haldeman to look into Sinatra's possible ties to Democratic presidential hopeful Sen. Edmund Muskie: "[The IRS is] after, you know, every one of our people. Goddamnit, they were after me . . . Somebody told me that Muskie used Frank Sinatra's plane in California. Did you hear that? Maybe we should investigate that."

Haldeman was hot on the case the next day. In a September 14 memo, he sought a secret White House probe to discover "whether this is true. If so, check with the Vice President's office and find out how this jibes with the reports that Sinatra wants to support the President . . . As you probably know, we've received reports from a number of directions that Sinatra was on our side. His supplying a plane to Muskie would not seem to be evidence of that." The Haldeman memo, sent to key assistants and stamped "Administratively Confidential," was declassified in 2010.

In another newly released confidential memo of September 16, Haldeman staffer Gordon Strachan cites the probe's main findings: Edmund Muskie had indeed used a plane jointly owned by Sinatra and Danny Schwartz, a San Francisco Democrat and supporter of Hubert Humphrey. Schwartz okayed Muskie's use of the plane. But most important, Strachan reported, "The Vice President's Office [Roy Goodearle] reports that 'Sinatra is still with us.' "

Strachan's investigation also determined that aide Chuck Colson was pressing "very hard to have Sinatra introduced to the president quietly," but that Attorney General John Mitchell opposed the idea—though, possibly, Mitchell's mind could be changed. The Strachan memo ends brightly for those favoring a solid Nixon-Sinatra alliance: "The net result is that Sinatra is still with us and could be brought into full endorsement if he met the President, if this were deemed appropriate."

On October 25, 1971, Chuck Colson, Nixon's top political advisor, sent out a "Confidential/Eyes Only" memo to Haldeman. Also released in 2010, the Colson memo recommends an informal "one-on-one" White House meeting, over drinks, between the president and the Mob-tainted singer. Colson suggests that if such a session was held and a number of other steps were taken "we are relatively certain to have completed our seduction of Frank Sinatra."

In the memo, Colson concludes that a personal relationship between the president and Sinatra could yield major campaign contributions because "[Sinatra] has a great deal of control over what we understand to be massive financial resources." The

Colson memo does not contain a single cautionary word about Sinatra's longtime Mafia affiliations . . . or the fact that "massive financial resources" he mentions could refer to Mob money. But the proposed one-on-one meeting apparently never took place.

The apparent main reason: strong objections by Haldeman, who proudly called himself "Nixon's S.O.B." Haldeman knew of Sinatra's multiple ties to the underworld and, as a result, his P.R. man's good judgment kept the entertainer at arm's length from the president.

Evidence of that comes in a newly declassified November 9, 1971 memo to Haldeman from Nixon aide Dwight Chapin. Haldeman penned a series of bold capital NOs next to each of Chapin's suggestions for "the breakthrough we're after, in terms of getting the President together with Sinatra." The rejected ideas included a Sinatra-hosted dinner for the president, Vice President Agnew, Governor Ronald Reagan and comedian Bob Hope at Sinatra's home in Palm Springs, California, or a dinner with the same people hosted by the president at the Western White House. Despite Haldeman's veto of these ideas, pro-Sinatra aide Colson wrote at the bottom of the Chapin memo: "Sinatra has purchased a table at tonight's LA fundraiser—and is going!"[10]

In 1972, when a House committee sought to question Sinatra about his Mob ties, Agnew unsuccessfully tried to delay the service of a subpoena. When Sinatra did testify, he was surly and defiant. President Nixon personally phoned Sinatra afterward to congratulate him for stonewalling the panel. At least Nixon had the good political sense to reject Agnew's attempt to get a top government post for Sinatra: director of the American Revolution Bicentennial Administration. Nixon aide John Ehrlichman said he "gulped" when Agnew phoned him with that suggestion. Agnew, in his "high sing-songy voice," pitched the crooner for the job because Sinatra was what Agnew called a "world-renowned figure, an ethnic, an Italian and an able executive," Ehrlichman remembered.

Ehrlichman promised the vice president he'd pass the suggestion on to Nixon. "But," he added, "I'd seen Sinatra's thick FBI package, full of innuendos about connections with organized crime. I couldn't imagine trying to get him through a Senate confirmation."[11]

Sinatra's FBI file ran to 1,275 pages, thirty-six pages more than mobster Carlo Gambino's. After all, Sinatra's Mob ties went all the way back to at least 1947, when he was photographed with the notorious Lucky Luciano on a balcony of the Hotel Nacional in Havana. Luciano, who headed the world's largest illegal drug cartel, was in Havana for a convention of about one dozen American crime bosses, including Trafficante, Marcello, and the owner of the Nacional, Meyer Lansky. Sinatra used the occasion to give Luciano a gold cigarette case that was inscribed, TO MY DEAR PAL LUCKY, FROM HIS FRIEND, FRANK SINATRA.[12]

When Ehrlichman did tell Nixon about Agnew's off-the-wall idea (Nixon had long before concluded that Agnew was lazy, incompetent and dumb), he said the president "just laughed." The bicentennial job eventually went to future U.S. Republican Senator John Warner of Virginia.

Sinatra ultimately headed "Entertainers for Nixon," which did not require Senate confirmation or a background check into the singer's "thick FBI package."

President Nixon finally lured Sinatra out of retirement so that he could sing at a White House State Dinner for Italian Prime Minister Giulio Andreotti in April 1973. In introducing Sinatra, the president lavishly praised the singer. Andreotti—who had alleged Mafia links in Italy—expressed his gratitude to Nixon for inviting Sinatra: "I am going to be able to listen to him singing here. This is something which will give much prestige to me with my children."

Nixon did not keep up his contacts with Sinatra—at least not publicly—after the thirty-seventh chief executive was forced to resign over the Watergate scandal in the summer of 1974. But Sinatra proved to be Agnew's true friend and financial savior after Nixon's vice president quit the job in 1973 over bribery and tax evasion charges. Sinatra made several big loans to Agnew, including one of $200,000, so the disgraced politician could pay fines and back taxes, as well as help out with, in Agnew's words, "family expenses until I could find some way to make a living."

In Go Quietly . . . or Else, Agnew wrote, "As time went by and my business improved through my numerous trips abroad, I earned an adequate income and paid back the last of the Sinatra loans in 1978."[13]

After his resignation, Agnew faded into political obscurity and totally cut himself off from Nixon, refusing to even take any phone calls from the fallen president. Agnew did, however, maintain his strong loyalty to Sinatra. A bust of Sinatra on top of the former vice president's piano greeted visitors to Agnew's mansion in Rancho Mirage, California. In 1995, a bust of Agnew was finally installed with those of other vice presidents in the U.S. Capitol.

SEVEN

WHITE HOUSE PLOTS TO KILL JACK ANDERSON

During Richard Nixon's presidency, Jack Anderson was America's premier investigative journalist—and Nixon's most despised. In the most chilling crime contemplated by the president's men, Anderson was targeted for assassination. A strict moralist, Anderson's stated lifetime goal was to keep government honest. A devout Mormon, he viewed his reportorial undertaking as a noble summons from the Almighty.

Former Anderson legman Howard Kurtz recalls that Anderson was gentle, patient and avuncular "with the young and ambitious wannabes who rotated through his small office." He adds that Anderson's "ability to persuade people at the highest level of government to share secrets with him was uncanny, especially in an era when most journalists were deferential toward the nation's leaders and when top political columnists had cozy relationships with the high and mighty."[1]

Anderson was the last of the old-time muckrakers and, according to his biographer, Mark Feldstein, "an important transitional figure in the evolution of adversarial journalism . . ." Feldstein conceded, however, that Anderson would sometimes stoop fairly low to get a good story: "He swiped secret documents, used bugging equipment to eavesdrop on conversations, and jubilantly savaged his enemies, unconcerned with such journalistic niceties as fairness and balance."[2]

By 1972, Anderson had won both a Pulitzer Prize and the highest perch on Nixon's notorious enemies list. A bombastic self-promoter as well as an old-fashioned shoe-leather newspaperman of unquestioned accuracy, Anderson had branched out from a nationally syndicated column, "Washington Merry-Go-Round"—read by some 45 million people—into TV, radio, magazines and the lucrative lecture circuit.

His exclusives—running into the hundreds—included several that sent the volcanic Nixon up the Oval Office wall: A secret U.S. tilt away from India toward Pakistan; the CIA's clandestine use of the Mob in numerous efforts to murder Cuban leader Fidel Castro; and an under-the-table link between a Nixon administration decision to drop a government antitrust suit against ITT and a $400,000 ITT pledge to underwrite the 1972 Republican convention. After the ITT column ran, an incensed president asked No. 1 aide Bob Haldeman why he could not find someone to riffle Anderson's files. This, undoubtedly, would have required a break-in at Anderson's office.

But Nixon had an even bigger, older reason to hate Jack Anderson. He blamed the intrepid journalist, in part, for keeping him from winning his first White House bid. As the 1960 election neared, Anderson and his patron, tutor and partner, Drew Pearson—who died in 1969, leaving the column to Anderson—disclosed that, in 1956, Vice President Nixon's unscrupulous brother Donald had received a $205,000 "loan" from Dick's long-time sugar daddy, billionaire businessman Howard Hughes. Soon after the Hughes money reached Donald, the IRS—reversing a prior ruling—granted tax-exempt status to Hughes's then shady "medical institute."

Described by Nixon aide John Ehrlichman as a "florid, peach-shaped fellow given to wearing white sports jackets and colorful neckties," Donald Nixon had always been a potential embarrassment to his brother. "Don talked loudly, extravagantly and incessantly, so the Nixon campaigns always discouraged his participation," Ehrlichman wryly observed in his book, *Witness to Power*.[3]

At first, Nixon denied the Hughes loan story; but he was later forced to admit that the billionaire's bucks had indeed enriched his brother. That is, until Don blew the money on a pipe dream, a California chain of "Nixon-Burger" drive-in restaurants that quickly folded.

Richard Nixon was convinced that this particular Pearson-Anderson "Washington Merry-Go-Round" dispatch had contributed mightily to his razor-thin presidential loss to Senator John F. Kennedy.

Illustrative of Nixon's enmity toward Anderson and Pearson was the reaction of John Ehrichman, a senior 1968 Nixon campaign aide, when he learned that the two reporters would be staying at Nixon's Miami Beach hotel during the Republican convention: "'No! Of all the reporters in the world, not those two!' I yelled. Nixon would have a stroke on the very eve of his nomination; they were his deadliest foes." Ehrlichman pressured the mobbed-up Teamsters Union, which held the mortgage on the hotel, and Anderson and Pearson had to stay elsewhere.[4]

As president, Nixon was so frightened of the mischief his "poor, dumb, damn brother" Donald might blunder into—and that Jack Anderson might expose—that he bugged Don's phones and put a full-time Secret Service tail on him.

Meantime, the Central Intelligence Agency was keeping a close eye on almost all of Anderson's activities. It was also conducting "personal surveillances" of Jack's legmen, Brit Hume and Les Whitten.

In addition, Anderson was being watched and followed by agents of the FBI, whose director, Nixon crony J. Edgar Hoover, privately called the columnist a "jackal" with a mind that is "lower than the regurgitated filth of vultures."[5] When Hoover dispatched agents to stake out Anderson's house, the columnist sent several of his nine children outside to have some fun: take their pictures and let the air out of their tires. Hoover volunteered the FBI's files on Anderson to the White House, where counsel John Dean found them of absolutely no value to Anderson loathers on the premises. Sadly for them, Hoover's Anderson files turned out to be mainly old newspaper and magazine clippings.

Next, the White House secretly probed Anderson's alleged participation in a questionable Maryland land deal. The president's men came up empty. They got the same result when they tried to pin down a tip about possible shady dealings by Anderson's brother.

Dean says Nixon had full knowledge of all of the anti-Anderson maneuverings: "Colson was reporting to the President on his efforts."[6] The eventual star witness for Watergate investigators, Dean and his accusations against the president and his co-conspirators have stood the test of time. When Nixon's secret tape recordings were later released, Dean's photographic memory of events was totally confirmed. Though he was convicted of multiple felonies, the former White House counsel served only four months in a special U.S. Marshals safe house near Baltimore in return for his cooperation with prosecutors. He is now an investment banker, lecturer, and was an outspoken critic of the Iraq war.

Jack Anderson fought the administration's efforts to discredit him. He publicly charged that Colson had started a false rumor that the reporter had accepted $100,000 to write articles favorable to former Cuban dictator Fulgencio Batista. And he had one of his legman do an FBI-style ransacking of J. Edgar Hoover's garbage. A search of Hoover's refuse, however, yielded nothing of consequence—just many empty cartons of a popular antacid, indicating the FBI director suffered from gas pains.[7]

In this ugly atmosphere, the White House started plotting Anderson's slaying—one scoop Anderson was not able to break himself. That juicy story was unearthed by Watergate ace Bob Woodward. In a September 21, 1975 *Washington Post* piece, Woodward reported that an unnamed top White House aide gave Nixon's chief spy E. Howard Hunt "the order to kill Anderson."[8]

The plan allegedly involved the use of poison—one that could not be detected during an autopsy—obtained from a CIA physician. Woodward wrote that the assassination order came from a "senior official in the Nixon White House," and that it was "canceled at the last minute . . ." He added that former Watergate investigators were surprised "that such a plan could have been kept secret for so long." Hunt's former White House supervisor, Colson, claimed he'd never heard of the aborted Anderson assassination plan, Woodward elaborated.

Like Colson, E. Howard Hunt was a Brown University grad. He was handsome, literate (he had written scores of spy novels under an assumed name, and had ghost-written the autobiography of former CIA Director Allen Dulles), gun toting and take-no-prisoners—a retired spook who had worked years earlier with Vice President Nixon on the planned CIA-Mafia murder of Fidel Castro. A master of disguise, deception and disinformation, Hunt was also a close friend of CIA director Richard Helms. As a Nixon aide, Hunt got the CIA to supply him with *Mission Impossible*–like disguises—such as a red wig, a voice-altering device, and a gait-changing appliance for one of his legs.

A CIA memo that came to light in the 1970s placed Hunt in Dallas the day President John F. Kennedy was assassinated. In the mid-'80s, Hunt lost a lawsuit he brought against a newsletter for implicating him the JFK assassination.[9]

On his deathbed early in this century, Hunt confessed that he knew of plans by rogue CIA agents to assassinate Kennedy, but claimed he decided against becoming a conspirator. Hunt's son–Saint John Hunt—recently disclosed that his mother told him his dad was in Dallas "on business" on November 22, 1963.

Hunt never publicly acknowledged that Nixon White House anti–Jack Anderson efforts included murder. However, in an affidavit about a key meeting with Colson related to "dirty tricks" against Anderson, Hunt did say, "Colson seemed more than usually agitated, and I formed the impression that he had just come from a meeting with President Nixon."[10]

Furthermore, author Mark Feldstein, during an NPR interview, said that Hunt thought the president himself was behind the Anderson plot. "But what Hunt told me before his death was that he believed that Colson was acting at the behest of the president himself . . . I find it very difficult to believe that Colson and the other aides were acting without the implicit support of President Nixon. It defies logic to imagine that they would cook this up, the assassination of a journalist as prominent as Jack Anderson, unless they had the signal from above to do it."[11]

Colson was known around the White House as "the Assassin." Nixon's top assistant, Bob Haldeman, actually described him as the president's "hit man."[12] A hard-drinking, beefy, tough-talking ex-Marine captain, Colson seemed to rev up Nixon's cruelest instincts. And Nixon did the same with Colson. Even in the immediate wake of the Watergate break-in, Nixon and Colson had the abominable Anderson on their minds. In a June 20, 1972 conversation, the two men sought to minimize the seriousness of Watergate by comparing it to Anderson's award-winning story that the Nixon administration secretly tilted toward Pakistan in its war with India:

Colson: "They gave Anderson a Pulitzer Prize. In other words, stealing documents [unintelligible] for [unintelligible].

Nixon: Belonging to the government, top secret, shit . . .
did any of these people [who are criticizing the Watergate burglary] squeal about [Anderson's actions] then?
Colson: Yeah, isn't that true?
Nixon: That's my point. Did [Sen. George] McGovern,
did the [*New York*] *Times*, did the [*Washington*] *Post*
squeal about that then? Now here was an attempted
theft that failed, against a political party, not against
the government of the United States. They give Pulitzer Prizes for publishing stolen documents.

It was in this same conversation, incidentally, that the president first indicated, at least on tape, that he had known in advance of the break-in, telling Colson: "It doesn't sound like a, a
skillful job. [Unintelligible.] If we didn't know better, [we] would
have thought it was deliberately botched."[13]

G. Gordon Liddy—an articulate ex-FBI agent and defeated GOP
congressional hopeful from upstate New York—was considered
by some of his Nixon cohorts to be a wacky loose cannon. He
was a fan of Nazi propaganda films, a strong believer in racial
purity, and often packed heat—an expensive German pistol with
a silencer. In May of 1972—only weeks before the first Watergate
break-in when the listening bugs were originally planted—Liddy
used that gun to shoot out several streetlights during an aborted
pre-Watergate break-in at the Washington headquarters of Democratic presidential candidate Senator George McGovern.

When Jeb Magruder, head of the Committee to Re-Elect the
President, had an up close and personal run-in with the volatile

Liddy, Liddy threatened: "Get your hand off me or I'll kill you," Magruder recalled. But when Magruder recommended that Liddy be fired, the White House vetoed the idea. Nixon aide Gordon Strachan responded: "He may be a Hitler, but at least he's our Hitler." Nixon himself loved Liddy's loyalty, once enthusing: "He hates the other side."[14]

In his 1980 book *Will*, Liddy said that he and Hunt were assigned the White House task of "stopping" Anderson: "We examined all the alternatives and very quickly came to the conclusion the only way you're going to be able to stop him is to kill him . . . And that was the recommendation." As Liddy succinctly told Anderson in person on a subsequent TV talk show: "The rationale was to come up with a method of silencing you through killing you."[15]

Liddy said he and Hunt originally planned to poison Anderson with LSD (known more for creating colorful hallucinations than for its lethality). A CIA doctor—an expert on poisons and their antidotes—sat in on the final rub-out talks.

Those occurred in March 1972 over lunch at the swank Hay-Adams Hotel, a block from the White House. Liddy says the talks were "hypothetical," and that the murder target was not named.[16]

Liddy later admitted that the group had considered playing "aspirin roulette" with the intended victim, "in which one takes a single tablet of a deadly poison, packs it in a Bayer aspirin jar, [then] we place it in the man's medicine chest, and one day he gets that tablet and that's that."[17]

In an interview with author Mark Feldstein, Hunt said Colson had ordered Hunt and Liddy to "locate Anderson's home and examine it from the outside for vulnerabilities . . . This was high on

Chuck Colson's list of things to do," Hunt said. "That was when [we got] the idea of putting a drug-laden pill in a bottle that Anderson was taking medicine from. Liddy had an idea that by wiping poison on a man's wrist that could kill him that way." Hunt added, "The more that Colson knew about Anderson, the more resolved he was to put an end to it by whatever means. He regarded it as a protective function in terms of the president, get rid of this thorn in his side, one way or another, with hallucinogens or not."[18]

When poisoning and a fake car crash were dismissed as impractical, the Hay-Adams group settled on making Anderson's killing look like an accidental part of a random sidewalk robbery. Liddy said he handed the CIA doctor a hundred-dollar bill (from Nixon's re-election committee's intelligence fund) for the physician's consultative services.[19] After the CIA doctor left, Liddy suggested to Hunt that the Miami Cubans already recruited as leak-plugging "plumbers"—and future Watergate burglars—be assigned to kill Anderson. Liddy said Hunt had bragged to him that members of this Hunt-mentored group "had been involved in organized crime and who had, among them, killed . . . 22 men, including two who were hanged from a beam in a garage." The Cubans idolized Hunt, whom they still referred to as "Eduardo," his CIA code name during secret CIA plots against Castro and his Communist regime, including the catastrophic Bay of Pigs invasion in the early '60s. When Hunt mentioned that his Nixon White House "principal" (assumed by Liddy to be Colson) might object to using the plumbers to murder Anderson, Liddy volunteered: "If necessary, I'll do it."[20]

The Anderson assassination scheme was eventually shelved— by Nixon and Colson, according to Liddy—but Anderson went to his grave in 2005 after a long battle with Parkinson's, convinced that—as Liddy had told him—"Richard Nixon wanted me dead."[21]

Was Nixon capable of ordering a Mafia-style hit on an enemy? The answer is yes. As already mentioned, as vice president, he ran CIA-Mafia murder plots against Castro. (Attorney General Robert Kennedy later supervised these "black" operations.) He also sanctioned, if need be, the slaying of Greek shipping tycoon Aristotle Onassis, telling an aide, "If it turns out we have to kill the bastard, just don't do it on American soil."[22]

As president, Nixon gave the green light to the assassination of Chilean President Salvador Allende and once cabled a thinly veiled death threat to South Vietnamese President Nguyen van Thieu.

J. Edgar Hoover was a Nixon loyalist who seldom criticized the president. But in 1972, the FBI chief told a friendly reporter—Andrew Tully, who wrote a syndicated column called "Capital File"—on the condition his remarks would not be published until after his death, that some of Nixon's aides "don't know a goddamned thing about due process of law. They think they can get away with murder."[23]

When he and Carl Bernstein were exposing Watergate crimes left and right, *Washington Post* reporter Bob Woodward was warned by his secret FBI source, Mark Felt (aka "Deep Throat") that "your lives are in danger."

There are recordings of Nixon and his top aide, Bob Haldeman, discussing enlisting Teamsters thugs ("murderers," Haldeman called them; "guys who will knock their heads off," Nixon exulted) to assault a group of antiwar demonstrators. It is no wonder that Nixon's corrupt vice president, Spiro Agnew, feared his boss would have him bumped off if he didn't resign over a bribery scandal.

Later, George Washington University Professor Mark Feldstein, an expert on Anderson, explained why the LSD and poison ideas were discarded: "The trouble was as a Mormon and a tee-totaler, [Anderson] didn't drink alcohol, so that was out. So then they talked about making him crash in an automobile accident, but they would have had to go to the CIA and use a special car for that."

In Liddy's memory: "We discussed the doctor's suggestion, which was the use of an automobile to hit Mr. Anderson's auto-mobile when it was in a turn in the circle up near Chevy Chase. There is a way that has apparently been known by the Central Intelligence Agency that if you hit a car at just the right speed and angle, it will flip and burn and kill the occupant."

In the end, G. Gordon Liddy said he'd carry out Anderson's assassination himself by "knifing him, slitting his throat, and staging it as a mugging that would look like a Washington street crime."[24]

Who knows what bizarre turn a revived Anderson assassina-tion plot might have taken next, if Liddy and Hunt had not been put out of business—and eventually behind bars—for their lead-ership of a botched but nonfatal Watergate break-in crime in June of 1972, a black bag job the White House played down as a "third-rate burglary attempt." That break-in at the Democratic National Committee in the Watergate office building and its subsequent cover-up forced Richard Nixon to quit the presidency in disgrace in August of 1974 in order to avoid being thrown out of office. When he resigned, all but a few members of his own party had deserted him, and his public approval ratings were only in the teens—far lower than those of the recently unpopular President George W. Bush. Only a hasty pardon from his hand-picked presidential successor and close personal friend, Gerald Ford, prevented a criminal trial of, and probable jail sentence for, Nixon.

Hunt died several years ago. But Liddy and Colson are still around. Liddy, known in the talk radio trade as the "G-Man," hosts a syndicated right-wing blab fest on about 150 stations. He served the longest prison sentence of any Watergate criminal—fifty-two months—for refusing to cooperate with prosecutors. He takes pride in the fact he never "snitched."

Colson became a born-again Christian about the same time he pled guilty to the Watergate crime of defaming antiwar leader Daniel Ellsberg. He was sentenced to one to three years in prison, but was let out after seven months because of a family emergency. Nixon's "hit man" now runs a big ministry for ex-convicts and crime victims. Colson has apparently never wavered from his initial contention that he was out of the loop in the squalid conspiracy to slit the throat of the president's perceived chief villain.

Of course, Nixon and Colson—if they were indeed the puppet masters in the canceled plot—could have used the same excuse as Liddy. As the G-Man explained to Anderson during their first meeting, on ABC's *Good Morning America* in 1980: "Murder is a technical term. You call it murder because *you* think it unjustified. I would say it was justifiable homicide, given the truth of the situation."[25]

In his post-resignation years, Nixon was never quizzed about the planned hit on Anderson. If he had been, perhaps his answer would have been similar to the one he gave in his famous $1-million 1977 TV interview with David Frost. Seeking to justify his alleged violations of constitutional rights, Nixon told his British interrogator: "If the president does it, that means it is not illegal."

EIGHT

NIXON'S PLOTS AGAINST TED KENNEDY AND DANIEL ELLSBERG

In the summer of 1969, President Richard Nixon was licking his chops to discover just what had really happened to Edward Kennedy and Mary Jo Kopechne at Chappaquiddick, Massachusetts. He speedily dispatched two undercover White House investigators to the scene of the suspicious watery car crash that took the life of Kopechne, Kennedy's companion. Nixon told top aide Bob Haldeman he didn't want Kennedy to get away with anything. Haldeman wrote a diary entry saying the president believed Kennedy "was drunk, escaped from the car, let [Mary Jo] drown, said nothing until police got to him. Shows fatal flaw in his character, cheated at school [Kennedy was expelled from Harvard for cheating], ran from accident."[1]

When the senator went on TV to tell his version of what happened, Nixon privately noted many "gaps and contradictions," adding: "I could not help thinking if anyone other than a Kennedy had been involved and had given such a patently unacceptable explanation, the media and the public would not have allowed him to survive in public life."[2]

Two ex-New York cops, Jack Caulfield and Anthony Ulasewicz, posed as newspaper reporters to carry out the Nixon-ordered sleuthing in Massachusetts. They turned up nothing of consequence. Their probe took six months and cost $100,000.[3]

Kennedy pled guilty to leaving the scene of an accident and was handed a suspended sentence of two months. His driver's license was revoked for one year.

Caulfield and Ulasewicz were busy, if not all that productive, in Massachusetts. In a memo from Caulfield, released in 2009, the snooper reported to the White House that Robert Kennedy Jr. was discreetly observed going to see the car that his uncle had driven off the Chappaquiddick Bridge two weeks earlier. And, more important, Caulfield suggested a Kennedy family bodyguard could become a useful source of information for the Nixon forces.

Caulfield and Ulasewicz pressed on. They eventually rented and furnished an expensive wiretapped Manhattan apartment with the improbable aim of hiring handsome young men to seduce some of the young women who had attended the Chappaquiddick party that preceded Kennedy's fatal accident. The plan, according to Nixon aide John Dean, would result in the women volunteering "details of Kennedy's conduct in a moment of tenderness, or under fear of extortion."

Dean actually stayed in the planned undercover apartment one night when he was in New York. "I was aghast. [Dean's blind date] had one quick drink and left. The apartment looked like a Chicago whorehouse—red velvet wallpaper, black lace curtains, white Salvation Army furniture, and a fake fur rug."[4]

"Nixon was obsessed with winning the next election," says

David Kaiser, the author of several books about the Kennedys. Kaiser told the *Boston Globe* in 2010, "Teddy was consistently the candidate [Team Nixon] worried about and they wanted anything they could get on him."[5]

Previously released tapes show Nixon even contemplated bugging Senator Kennedy's phone to gather information to discredit him. And newly released FBI files display not only Nixon's keen interest in the Kennedy-Kopechne relationship, but the extent to which the Chappaquiddick crash proved irresistible for conspiracy buffs. The *Boston Globe* cites one such letter to FBI director J. Edgar Hoover. Written on the stationery of Jackson Park Baptist Church, of Kannapolis, N.C., "It raised the idea that the accident may have been an assassination plot against Kennedy that had been hushed up. Hoover's office dismissed the conspiracies with terse response letters, stating that there was no evidence in the crash of any breaking of federal laws," the newspaper reports.[6]

In April 1971, Nixon told Haldeman they should find some way to "cover Kennedy . . . I'd really like to get Kennedy taped." More than taping, what Nixon wanted most of all, according to Haldeman in *The Haldeman Diaries,* was to photograph Ted Kennedy in compromising positions, then leak the photos to the press.[7]

In June, Nixon listened with rapt attention as aide Henry Kissinger, who sometimes traveled in the same social circles as Kennedy, passed along gossip that Kennedy had now become "a total [sexual] animal."

In July, Nixon spoke to several aides about the possible need for a special $2-million "Nixon discretionary fund" to keep tabs on Kennedy and for other clandestine pursuits. On September 8, 1971, the president ordered aide John Ehrlichman to have the

IRS investigate Kennedy's taxes, and those of other prospective Democratic presidential candidates. And Nixon was given an update on surveillance that was already being carried out on Senator Kennedy.

Ehrlichman reported Kennedy was being "covered" by an unnamed informant (the Kennedy bodyguard whom Caulfield suggested could be used as an informant?) during the senator's vacations. And as Nixon's tape recorders rolled, he filled in the president on an inspection trip Ehrlichman himself had made to Chappaquiddick:

Ehrlichman: And [Kennedy] was in Hawaii on his own. He was staying at some guy's villa. And we had a guy on him every night (unclear interjection by Nixon). And he was just as nice as he could be the whole time.

Nixon: The thing to do is just watch him, because what happens to fellows like that, who have that kind of [sexual addiction] problem, is that they go for quite a while and then they go (unclear).

Ehrlichman: Yeah. Yeah. That's what I'm hoping for.

Nixon: I don't think he would break really while he was, you know, trying for the big thing. Generally, they don't. Although Jack [Kennedy] was damn careless.

Ehrlichman: This time between now and convention time may be the time to get him.

Nixon: You mean that he would be under great pressure?

Ehrlichman: He would be under pressure, but he will also be out of the limelight somewhat. Now, he was in Hawaii very much incognito. Very little staff. And played tennis, moved around, visited with people and socialized and so on. So you would expect that at a time like that you might catch him. And then he went up to Hyannis. And we've got an arrangement—

Nixon: How about [Senator Edmund] Muskie? (Unclear.) What kind of a life is he living?

Ehrlichman: Very cloistered. Very monkish.

Nixon: (Unclear.)

Ehrlichman: Yeah, big time. He's got six kids. And very ordinary (unclear). Teddy . . . I—we were over on Martha's Vineyard last week.

Nixon: Yeah—

Ehrlichman: I had never seen that site before, that Chappaquiddick-Edgartown ferry. That is a very short swim. Having seen it now, I would bet he swam it that night. It's—I don't see why—you know, they could build a bridge across there. It's a very short distance.

Nixon: Hmm.

Ehrlichman: And it's no farther than from here to the West Wing. And not a bad tide, the time we were there. So it was quite interesting. I took some pictures of it because it amazed me how short a distance it really was. But we do cover him when he goes to Hyannis.

Nixon: He will never live that down.

Ehrlichman: No. I don't think he will.

Nixon: Not that one.

Ehrlichman: I think that will be around his neck forever.[8]

In October 1971, Ehrlichman induced a chuckle in Nixon when he suggested that placards be made showing Ted Kennedy's picture and asking, "Would you ride in a car with this man?"

(Nixon's unsavory reputation had been dogged by a Democratic campaign picture-poster of the GOP candidate that asked, "Would You Buy a Used Car from this Man?")

In September 1972, Nixon's continued political fear, personal loathing, and jealously of Kennedy led him to plant a spy in Kennedy's Secret Service detail. The mole Nixon selected for the Kennedy camp was a former agent from his Nixon's vice presidential detail, Robert Newbrand, a man so loyal he told Haldeman he would do anything—even kill—for Nixon.

The president was most interested in learning about Senator Kennedy's sex life. He wanted, more than anything, stated Haldeman in *The Ends of Power*, to "catch [Kennedy] in the sack with one of his babes."[9] In a recently transcribed tape of a September 8, 1972 talk among the president and aides Bob Haldeman and Alexander Butterfield, Nixon asks whether Secret Service chief James Rowley would appoint Newbrand to head Kennedy's detail:

Haldeman: He's to assign Newbrand.

Nixon: Does he understand that he's to do that?

Butterfield: He's effectively already done it. And we have a full force assigned, forty men.

Haldeman: I told them to put a big detail on him (unclear).

Nixon: A big detail is correct. One that can cover him around the clock, every place he goes.

(Laughter obscures mixed voices.)

Nixon: Right. No, that's really true. He has got to have the same coverage that we give the others, because we're concerned about security and we will not assume the responsibility unless we're with him all the time.

Haldeman: And Amanda Burden [one of Kennedy's alleged girlfriends] can't be trusted. (Unclear.) You never know what she might do. (Unclear.)

Haldeman then assures the president that Newbrand "will do anything that I tell him to . . . He really will. And he has come to me twice and absolutely, sincerely said, 'With what you've done for me and what the president's done for me, I just want you to know, if you want someone killed, if you want anything else done, any way, any direction'":

Nixon: The thing that I (unclear) is this: We just might get lucky and catch this son of a bitch and ruin him for '76.

Haldeman: That's right.

Nixon: He doesn't know what he's really getting into. We're going to cover him, and we are not going to take "no" for an answer. He can't say "no." The Kennedys are arrogant as hell with these Secret Service. He says, "Fine," and [Newbrand] should pick the detail, too.

Toward the end of this conversation, Nixon exclaims that Newbrand's spying "[is] going to be fun," and Haldeman responds: "Newbrand will just love it."

Nixon also had a surveillance tip for Haldeman for his spy-to-be: "I want you to tell Newbrand if you will that (unclear) because he's a Catholic, sort of play it, he was for Jack Kennedy all the time. Play up to Kennedy, that 'I'm a great admirer of Jack Kennedy.' He's a member of the Holy Name Society. He wears a St. Christopher (unclear)." Haldeman laughs heartily at the president's curious advice.[10]

Despite the enthusiasm of Nixon and Haldeman, Newbrand apparently never produced anything of great value. When this particular round of Nixon's spying on Kennedy was uncovered in 1997, the *Washington Post* quoted Butterfield as saying periodic reports on Kennedy's activities were delivered to Haldeman, but that Butterfield did not think any potentially damaging information was ever dug up.[11]

Were Nixon's men more than just spying on Edward Kennedy? In 1974, William "Lefty" Gilday, a Bostonian known for his "criminal expertise," claimed to journalist Anthony Summers that he was recruited by two Nixon aides to participate in plots against certain politicians.[12] Summers, who was in touch with Gilday, says the alleged plots ranged from dirty tricks to murder:

"Those he was incited to kill, Gilday has said, included Senator Edward Kennedy and George Wallace. The aides in question are unnamed here for legal reasons, but Gilday has appeared to have knowledge of corroborating details—their nicknames, for example—and has provided reconnaissance photographs he said were taken with Kennedy's murder in view."[13]

Gilday told Summers the White House aides approached him as early as 1970. Convicted of murdering a policeman during a 1970 bank robbery in a Boston suburb, Gilday—a former minor leaguer pitcher—is currently serving a life sentence in a Shirley, Massachusetts prison.[14]

Wallace was convinced, to his dying days, that Nixon was behind a conspiracy to assassinate him.[15] Behind the scenes, the president and his men showed little sympathy for Wallace—and Nixon blamed Wallace himself for bringing on the assassination attempt:

Nixon: You know, how long did it have to be said that somebody was going to shoot Wallace? Didn't he ask for it?

Haldeman: Sure. He does, no question.[16]

In a newly released Nixon tape, Colson informs the president that anti-Kennedy efforts did indeed extend beyond surveillance: "I did things out of Boston. We did some blackmail and . . . my God, uh, uh, uh, I'll go to my grave before I ever disclose it. But, uh, we did a hell of a lot of things and never got caught . . . (E. Howard Hunt, Nixon's chief spy) ran 15 or 20 black projects in Boston, and that'll never be traced. No way."[17]

The world will never know just what Hunt and his cohorts had gathered on Kennedy. The former CIA spymaster kept his ultra-sensitive reports on Chappaquiddick and other Kennedy-related intelligence (as well as his pistol, which—when discovered—prompted Nixon aide John Dean to shout, "Holy shit!") in his White House safe, which was cleaned out after Hunt was connected to the Watergate burglary of June 1972. Those secret files were eventually turned over by presidential aides John Dean and John Ehrlichman to acting FBI Director L. Patrick Gray. They came with instructions from Dean, "These should never see the light of day." He added: "They are of a very, very, very secretive nature." Gray subsequently burned the Hunt files, he said.[18]

Was Richard Nixon capable of ordering a political enemy's assassination? That is certainly a possibility. He ran the White House in much the same way as a godfather ruled a Mafia "family." The murder of a major enemy, foreign or domestic, always seemed to be one of Nixon's first options.

Aside from pistol-packing staffers such as E. Howard Hunt,

G. Gordon Liddy, Jack Caulfield and Anthony Ulasewicz, Nixon could depend on a group of real godfathers to do his bidding. After all, he had been doing them big favors—and they had been secretly financing his political rise—ever since he was first elected to Congress in 1946.

Organized crime expert Dan Moldea has quoted an anonymous Justice Department source as saying: "The whole goddamn thing is too frightening to think about. We're talking about the president of the United States . . . a man who pardoned organized crime figures after millions were spent by the government putting them away . . . I guess the real shame is that we'll never know the full story, it'll never come out."[19]

As Nixon's White House tapes continue to be released, more of the "full story" will emerge.

Though Ted Kennedy was near the top of Nixon's long enemies list, he shared that honor with the likes of Jack Anderson and Larry O'Brien. And one brand-new name was placed among the president's leading villains in the summer of 1971—that of Daniel Ellsberg. That's when the *New York Times* published the "Pentagon Papers," a top-secret Defense Department study critical of U.S. war efforts in Vietnam. The huge report had been methodically stolen and duplicated by Ellsberg, a former Pentagon analyst who had turned against the war and leaked copies of the report to *Times* reporter Neil Sheehan.

Newly declassified tapes show Nixon first realized the seriousness of the leak during a June 13 noontime telephone call from Henry Kissinger's top deputy, Alexander Haig:

Haig: This goddamn *New York Times* expose [is] of the most highly classified documents in the war.

Nixon: Oh, that! I see! I didn't read the story. You mean that was leaked out of the Pentagon?

Haig: This is a devastating security breach of the greatest magnitude of anything I've ever seen.

By the time Nixon talked to Kissinger himself a short time later, the president was climbing the walls over the leak:

Nixon: That, Henry, that to me is just unconscionable. This is treasonable action on the part of the bastards that put it out.

Kissinger: Exactly, Mr. President.

Nixon: Doesn't it involve secure information, a lot of other things? What kind of—what kind of people would do such things?

Kissinger: It has the most—it has the highest classification, Mr. President.

Nixon: Yeah. Yeah.

Kissinger: It's treasonable! There's no question it's actionable. I'm absolutely certain that this violates all sorts of security laws.

Next on the tape, the president gives his chief foreign policy advisor permission to call Attorney General John Mitchell to determine the options for prosecuting the newspaper. In a later call the same day, Nixon tells aide John Ehrlichman, "Hell, I wouldn't prosecute the *Times*. My view is to prosecute the goddamn pricks that gave it to 'em." Nixon finally agreed to the legal route when told by Ehrlichman the Justice Department must put the *Times* on notice immediately—or forfeit the ability to prosecute them.[20]

Using "national security" as grounds, the Justice Department obtained a court injunction against further publication of the articles. For fifteen days, the *Times* was prohibited from running its stories—but Ellsberg leaked the "Pentagon Papers" to the *Washington Post* and seventeen other newspapers. The *Post* ran them while the *Times* was enjoined. On June 30, the Supreme Court found that constitutional guarantees of a free press trumped other considerations, and ruled that the *Times* was free to publish again.

On July 1, 1971, Nixon described the ruling as "unbelievable" and "stinking" in a phone chat with FBI boss J. Edgar Hoover. And he promised "to change that court." Referring to the six justices who voted 6-to-3 to permit newspapers to continue publication of material from the once-classified history of the Vietnam War, Nixon said: "You know those clowns we got on there. I'll tell you I hope I outlive the bastards." Hoover responded, "I hope you do, too."[21]

In an effort to stop Pentagon Papers–type leaks, the president set up his "Special Investigative Unit"—the infamous "plumbers." Headed by Egil "Bud" Krogh—and including G. Gordon Liddy and E. Howard Hunt—the "black bag" unit pulled its first break-in at the Los Angeles offices of Daniel Ellsberg's psychiatrist, Lewis Fielding, in September 1971. Nothing was found, but the burglars had trashed the office to make it look like they were trying to steal drugs. The plumbers next plotted to break into the psychiatrist's home, but that job was aborted by presidential aide John

Ehrlichman, according to Krogh: "I showed him the pictures [of the doctor's office]. He said, 'This is far beyond anything I approved. Shut it down.' Which I did."[22]

At the end of May 1972, a group of Liddy and Hunt–led plumbers broke into, and bugged, the Watergate offices of Democratic National Chairman Larry O'Brien. On June 17, 1972, what would become the world's most famous break-in occurred in the same offices. Its main purpose was to repair the faulty bug on O'Brien's phone. Of course, the burglars were caught red-handed by plainclothes DC cops summoned by an alert night watchman. The cops were called the Mod Squad. They drove around in unmarked clunkers and—wearing scruffy street clothes and long hair—they were not immediately noticed by the burglars' lookout in a hotel room across the street.

When Daniel Ellsberg gave himself up on June 28, 1971, he said: "I felt that as an American citizen, as a responsible citizen, I could no longer cooperate in concealing this information from the American public. I did this clearly at my own jeopardy and I am prepared to answer to all the consequences of this decision."[23] The information provided by Ellsberg was politically embarrassing to not only the Johnson and Kennedy administrations, but also to the Nixon administration. He faced punishment under the Espionage Act of 1917. Other charges including theft and conspiracy carried a total maximum sentence of 115 years.

But evidence of government misdeeds such as the Fielding burglary, wiretapping, and Nixon's secret meeting with the Ellsberg judge to offer him the directorship of the FBI, was overwhelming. The judge dismissed all the charges against Ellsberg and his accomplice, Tony Russo, on May 11, 1973. Said Federal District Judge William Matthew Byrne Jr.: "The bizarre events have incurably infected the prosecution of this case."[24]

Ellsberg and Russo contended they took and copied the papers in order to boost pressure to end the war in Vietnam. In fact, that's exactly what the release of the "Pentagon Papers" did. "In reality," the *New York Times* observed at the time, "Ellsberg and Russo were arguing in court not only constitutional issues, but their belief that the greater good required them to break some regulations to make the papers public."[25] Nixon and his men had an entirely different take, of course, and they continued to plot against the chief leaker.

In an underreported bombshell, the seventy-nine-year-old Ellsberg recently charged that those conspiracies included a plot to murder him. In an August 11, 2010 interview with The Daily Beast, Ellsberg asserted, "On May 3, 1972, a dozen CIA assets from the Bay of Pigs, Cuban émigrés, were brought up from Miami with orders to 'incapacitate me totally.' I said to the [Watergate] prosecutor, 'What does that mean? Kill me?' He said, 'It means to incapacitate you totally. But you have to understand these guys never use the word kill.' "[26] The plot alleged by Ellsberg, if there was one, was obviously never implemented.

NINE

FRANK STURGIS: NIXON PLUMBER AND SECRET CIA ASSASSIN

E. Howard Hunt was a model and an inspiration for Frank Sturgis, one of the CIA-connected Miamians selected for Hunt's undercover squad of spies and break-in artists in Richard Nixon's White House. Just three years after he was arrested as a Watergate burglar, Sturgis told Senate investigators he was much more than a common felon: he was also an actual CIA agent who would proudly do anything for the agency—even kill.

To flaunt his expertise in that department, Sturgis volunteered a grisly "How to Get Away with Murder" tutorial for the panel. He even bragged that his reputation as a hit man led the FBI to grill him as a prime suspect in the assassination of President John F. Kennedy. Did Nixon ever know that at least one of his burglars also claimed to be a CIA killer suspected of taking part in the JFK murder? It's a worthy question, but one that Nixon himself was never called on to answer. (We'll re-visit the question of Nixon's possible knowledge of Sturgis's background

at the chapter's end.) Sturgis's claims were not publicly known
until after the former president's death in 1994.

Rather than for his notoriety as a Watergate burglar—as he made
clear to the Senate committee—Sturgis preferred to be regarded
as a swashbuckling CIA assassination specialist who would gladly
bump off anyone for the agency. In fact, in his secret 1975 testimony before the Senate committee, Sturgis proudly described
himself as a "whore" who "would do anything" for the CIA.

That boast lies buried in Sturgis's lengthy, closed-door testimony to a post-Watergate investigation of alleged CIA and FBI
crimes and abuses. A bipartisan committee chaired by Senator
Frank Church, an Idaho Democrat, conducted the investigation.
Sturgis's testimony was declassified—but mostly ignored—in the
1990s.

Sturgis told the Church committee he agreed to participate in
a CIA-sponsored domestic assassination plot sometime in 1961.
He claimed not to have known the target, or exactly when a
higher-ranking CIA colleague (and also a future Watergate felon),
Bernard Barker, recruited him for the hit, which, Sturgis claims,
never came off.

His assassination skills were honed in World War II, when—as
a fearless U.S. Marine Corps "Leatherneck"—Sturgis crept behind enemy lines with lethal intent. Gaeton Fonzi, a congressional investigator who got to know Sturgis, hailed his friend's
wartime heroics:

He was shipped out to the Pacific jungles where he
volunteered for the toughest unit in the Marines, the

First Raider Battalion—the legendary Edson's Raiders. He learned how to kill silently with his bare hands. He infiltrated enemy encampments, sloshed through amphibious landings and was airdropped on commando raids.[1]

One of Sturgis's first furtive jobs for Nixon may have come more than a dozen years *before* Watergate. In 1958, Sturgis "told the Miami FBI that he once traveled to Cuba to offer Castro $100,000 for the release of some kidnapped Americans on behalf of no less a figure than Vice President Richard Nixon," according to historian David Kaiser.[2]

Sturgis is usually thought of as one of the Watergate Cubans from Miami. Yet he was of 100 percent Italian descent and was born Frank Fiorini in Norfolk, Virginia. Later he adopted the surname Sturgis from his stepfather, Ralph Sturgis. He did not even speak Spanish, but was able to communicate fairly well with his Cuban exile pals because of his fluency in Italian.

He played key roles in early CIA/Mafia plots overseen by Vice President Nixon against the life of Cuban leader Fidel Castro. As the Bay of Pigs veteran told Church committee investigators, he had also trained a number of would-be assassins for CIA plots against other foreign leaders. The committee was probably aware that Sturgis consorted with Mafia bosses.[3] His Mob activities were not deeply explored, however, because the committee's central focus was on possible law-breaking by the CIA and the FBI.

So it was as a CIA assassination authority, that Sturgis enumerated—in graphic terms—some of the methods he *might* employ on behalf of the Company. Of course, in his testimony, he never admitted to actually killing anyone. But, at about the same time, authors Alan Weberman and Michael Canfield claimed that he was not just an ordinary assassin, but in reality, a *mass* murderer.

In *Coup d'État in America*, the authors offer a photo of Sturgis in a jungle setting. Wearing an ascot and military fatigues, he poses with a rifle. One of his feet rests on a mound of dirt. The photo caption—*not* explained anywhere in the book—reads: "Sturgis, 1959, standing on a mass grave of 61 Batista supporters he had just killed. When Castro's brother, Raul, voiced doubts concerning Sturgis's loyalty and possible CIA connections, Fidel handed Sturgis a gun and commanded him to execute the Batistites as proof of his sincerity."[4]

Sturgis never disputed any part of *Coup d'État*, including the portrayal of him as a one-man firing squad. The book was published in 1975.

Despite Frank's grotesque display of fake fidelity to Fidel, Raul was correct in his suspicions about Sturgis. While one of only a few Americans to fight alongside Fidel in the mountains during the Revolution, and later a top gun in Castro's air force, Frank was, indeed, now spying on the Cuban leader for the CIA. He would later sneak back into the United States and join "Operation 40," the name of the Nixon-commanded secret CIA-Mafia schemes to eliminate Castro.

Describing himself to the Church Committee as a CIA "whore," Sturgis explained that term as flattering spook lingo for someone "who would do anything. But he has got to be motivated by patriotism. And he would do anything for his county—regardless of what it was."[5]

Sturgis's idol and ultimate CIA boss, E. Howard Hunt, had a similar attitude, once declaring: "I had always assumed, working for the CIA for so many years, that anything the White House wanted done was the law of the land."[6] And Hunt was just reflecting Nixon's own view, expressed in a post-presidential interview with David Frost, that, "When the president does it, that means it's not illegal."[7] Hunt, of course, went on to recruit, train and supervise Sturgis and Barker as part of the Nixon White House burglary team that got caught by police after breaking into Democratic headquarters at the Watergate complex in Washington on June 17, 1972.

Hunt was a perfect undercover agent: inconspicuous but articulate, personable and convincingly dishonest. His Ivy League suits usually hid a shoulder-holstered pistol.

One of Hunt's White House supervisors, Egil "Bud" Krogh, described Howard as "a short, dapper man" with a "sharp aquiline nose, light features, sandy hair, and a ready smile." Krogh observed that Hunt "could blend easily into any group without drawing undue attention to himself, a valuable characteristic for a spy."[8]

At his Church committee appearance, Sturgis recounted a time that Barker had asked him about how Hunt—fabled in Miami's Cuban exile community by one of his CIA code names, "Eduardo"—would know that the intended domestic target had, in fact, been killed. "Well," Sturgis said he replied, "there are several ways: Number one, the person would eventually be reported missing. Number two, I will cut off his right finger and give it to you . . . because there won't be no body to recover."

How would Sturgis get rid of the body? Our expert witness's answer: "I could dig a hole [in the Everglades] and put lye in it. The lye will eat up his body. I could take an airplane and fly it over the Gulf Stream and I could dump his body in the Gulf Stream weighted down. I would have to cut his stomach and his intestines so that he wouldn't float. Even weighted down, a body will float unless you cut up the insides and the intestines. Or, I says, I could go with a boat out into the Gulf Stream and use explosives in order to destroy the body completely."

Sturgis's declassified testimony has gone mostly unexamined by scholars and historians. And with justifiable reason: This burglar, spy and self-confessed killer was not a reliable witness— mostly because he had been all too willing to spread obvious disinformation for the CIA. It was Sturgis who floated the theory to the Church committee that Fidel Castro was behind the JFK assassination; that Lee Harvey Oswald had been working as an agent of Castro; and that Oswald had made a trip to Miami to try to infiltrate an anti-Castro group. And, like all CIA agents, he would surely lie under oath to protect top Company secrets. (In 1977, former CIA Director Richard Helms pleaded guilty to lying to the Church committee about the CIA's role in overthrowing President Salvador Allende in Chile.)

Nonetheless, even habitual liars sometimes tell the truth. With the benefit of new disclosures, at least some parts of Sturgis's Church committee testimony from April 3 and 4, 1975 now seem to contain at least a kernel or two of credibility.

Sturgis's pride in being grilled as a suspect the day after the JFK assassination is quite provocative. "I had FBI agents all over my house [in Miami]. They told me I was the one person they felt had the capabilities to do it. They said, 'Frank, if there's anybody capable of killing the President of the United States, you're the guy who can do it.'" Why would he implicate himself, in even a tangential way, in the Kennedy assassination? And what just did the Feds know about Sturgis that sent them scurrying to Miami to question him?

Some JFK assassination researchers are convinced that Hunt, Sturgis and Barker were in Dallas that pivotal day in U.S. history. In a deathbed "confession" to his son, that itself may have been disingenuous, Hunt apparently claimed knowledge of the Dallas plot, but that he'd refused involvement. (Although he later referred to himself as a "bench warmer" in relation to the plot.) He identified Sturgis and a number of other CIA personnel as collaborators.

In the past, Hunt and Sturgis had steadfastly claimed they were at home—in suburban Washington and Miami, respectively—when President Kennedy was killed. They both said they were watching television with their families (at about the time of day most people were at work, and soap operas were the main TV fare). But Hunt's son—Saint John Hunt—later revealed that his dad was *not* at home that day, and that his mom told him his dad was in Dallas "on business."

Like Hunt, Sturgis had only loyal family members to back up his alibi that he was at home watching television on November 22, 1963. The Rockefeller Commission—a predecessor to the Church committee—concluded: "It cannot be determined with certainty where Hunt and Sturgis actually were on the day of the assassination."[9]

At a 1985 libel trial involving Hunt's possible links to the JFK assassination, however, CIA operative Marita Lorenz—a former Castro mistress and a friend of Sturgis—placed Sturgis, as well as Hunt and Jack Ruby, at a Dallas CIA safe house the night before the assassination. The jury ruled in favor of *Spotlight*, a right-wing newsletter that had implicated Hunt in the assassination.

Hunt filed for bankruptcy protection in June 1995. He died at a Miami hospital after a long bout with pneumonia in 2007.

Watergate burglar and CIA agent Bernard "Macho" Barker was so close to "Eduardo" he was known as "Hunt's Shadow." Frank Sturgis stressed the tightness of the Hunt-Barker relationship in a *True* magazine article in August 1974:

> The Bay of Pigs, hey, was one sweet mess. I met Howard Hunt that year (1961); he was the political officer for the exile brigade. Bernard Barker was Hunt's right-hand man, his confidential clerk—his body servant really; that's how I met Barker.[10]

Sturgis later vigorously denied saying those things—which conflicted with earlier contentions by Sturgis and Hunt that they did not meet until the Watergate era. A chain-smoker, Sturgis was fifty-eight when he died of lung and kidney cancer.

As for Barker, JFK assassination witness Seymour Weitzman identified "Macho" as the man on Dallas's grassy knoll who posed as a Secret Service agent and kept people out of the area.[11] And, believe it or not, Barker was also a close friend of and neighbor of Bebe Rebozo—President Nixon's sidekick. Barker died of lung cancer and heart problems in 2009. He was ninety-two.

Will we ever know whether Frank Sturgis was telling the truth when he allegedly confessed to Marita Lorenz that "We killed Kennedy" in Dallas? Or will we ever know whether Sturgis was leveling with New York City police detective Jim Rothstein? The detective took Sturgis into custody ("We put a gun to his head") in connection with what Rothstein described as a "sanctioned" CIA murder of Lorenz. Rothstein said after he had gained Sturgis's confidence, "He did tell me that he was one of the [JFK] assassins."[12]

Gaeton Fonzi, the congressional investigator who had befriended Sturgis, well recalls an intriguing incident following Frank's introduction of Fonzi to one of Sturgis's close Miami pals. When Sturgis explained that Fonzi was with the government committee looking into the assassination of President Kennedy, Sturgis's friend quickly observed, perhaps tellingly: "Oh, you mean the guy you killed."[13]

Maybe the only way to determine "Who Killed JFK and Why?" is to set up a modern-day Church committee. The original committee found a stunning array of CIA abuses—above all, attempts to assassinate foreign leaders, including Castro. It found that the agency enlisted the aid of the Mafia in its assassination plots against the Cuban leader.

The committee took public and private testimony from hundreds of witnesses, collected huge volumes of files from federal intelligence-gathering agencies, and issued fourteen reports in 1975 and 1976. Since the passage of the JFK Assassination Records Collection Act in 1992, over 50,000 pages of Church committee records have been declassified and made available to the public.

As a result of pressure from the Church committee, President Gerald Ford issued an executive order that banned U.S.-sanctioned assassinations of foreign leaders. At least one current U.S. congressman, New Jersey Democrat Rush Holt, says it is well past time for a fresh in-depth probe of the CIA. He declares, "I think any new investigation will produce revelations that are as jaw-dropping as those that were uncovered by the Church committee."[14]

So, did President Nixon know about the backgrounds of his Watergate plumbers—including Sturgis's boasted expertise as a CIA assassin—before they were hired? Perhaps. All of the Miamians had worked, in one way or another, for Nixon's 1960 Hunt-assisted Bay of Pigs invasion plans. And at least two of the burglars were associates of Nixon's best pal, Bebe Rebozo. *The Village Voice* was the first to note, in the summer of 1973, that Rebozo had ties to "convicted Watergate conspirators Bernard Barker and Eugenio Martinez through the Barker real estate firm Ameritas. Through the firm's attorney, one Miguel Suarez, Rebozo has helped to arrange for the financing of several real estate ventures of Barker. Martinez was formerly a vice president of Keyes Realty Company, an organization which figures in the complicated history of the Key Biscayne land now owned by Nixon and Rebozo." Barker also headed "Cubans for Nixon-Agnew" in Miami.[15]

Another reason to guess that Nixon knew a thing or two about the Watergate burglars is the fact that he was a suspicious control freak who wanted to know as much as possible about everyone and everything. Especially about those he had entrusted to carry out his darkest and riskiest clandestine operations. I'll bet if Nixon didn't know about the burglars and their backgrounds from Rebozo, he would have gotten such intelligence from Hunt, who had long known and vouched for the anti-Castro Miamians. For his part, Nixon knew Hunt's background intimately, once even revealing to an aide the exact number of novels his in-house spymaster had written.

A close Nixon aide—Alexander Butterfield—has stressed that the chief executive wanted to know the smallest details of just about everything that went on in the White House. During a 1994 public appearance, Butterfield indicated that that Nixon trait convinced him the president knew in advance about the Watergate burglary: "Nothing happened that Richard Nixon didn't okay. Nothing. And it's preposterous to think that anything of the magnitude of a break-in at the Democratic National Committee headquarters didn't come from Richard Ni— Preposterous. It could not happen. I would stake my life on that."[16]

What if Democratic Party chairman Larry O'Brien had decided to pick up something he'd left at the office at the same time the burglars staged their first Watergate break-in—to plant the bugs—in late May of 1972? No watchman reported their entry that night. And no cops showed up at the crime scene. Had O'Brien dropped by, would Frank Sturgis have sneaked out of the darkness and applied one of his claimed multiple murder techniques—strangulation by bare hands, perhaps—against one of Nixon's most-hated enemies? Would Frank have cut off O'Brien's right pinky before making his body disappear? It's interesting to contemplate, too, just what the president's reaction might have been had Sturgis killed the DNC chairman. Would the president be more or less likely to cover up a murder than he would a burglary?

The head of the plumbers, Egil "Bud" Krogh, says he knew nothing about the backgrounds of Sturgis or any of his team of leak pluggers. Krogh says Howard Hunt picked all the men:

I never met Frank Sturgis. And I never knew what his real background was. Hunt was the contact with him and the Cubans, and there was no need for me to meet them. Hunt told me that he could recruit men who were very patriotic and who would carry out a national security operation without question.[17]

Krogh has credibility. He is one of many good guys who behaved in bad ways during Watergate. Like some others who got caught up in the scandal and went to jail, he was young, naïve and inexperienced in the ways of Washington. An ex-Navy officer, Bud was also patriotic and loyal. And used to carrying out orders. For his early guilty plea, forthright testimony and expressions of contrition for his role in the break-in at Daniel Ellsberg's psychiatrist's office, Krogh won the admiration of Watergate prosecutors. And he is now doing good deeds as an ethicist for the Washington-based Center for the Study of the Presidency and Congress.

TEN

NIXON'S BAY OF PIGS SECRETS

In the dark, early hours of June 17, 1972, from inside the offices of the Democratic National Committee at the Watergate office building in Washington, DC, burglar James McCord radioed an alarm to his two supervisors. Monitoring the operation from their command post in the Watergate Hotel, E. Howard Hunt and G. Gordon Liddy heard McCord's electronic whisper that he and the other four burglars might have been detected.

"Scratch it," Hunt advised. But Liddy commanded to McCord: "Let's go! Everybody's here [meaning the four burglars from Miami] . . . Go!"

"So they went . . . filed off into history," Hunt later recalled.[1]

Minutes after heeding Liddy's order, DC police nabbed McCord and the other unusually dressed burglars—who were all wearing suits and ties as well as surgical gloves. Hunt and Liddy hastily fled the scene, but were eventually tied to the crime.

These men would become the first known participants in the

nation's biggest political scandal. Two summers later, "Watergate" forced President Richard Nixon to resign in dishonor.

Aside from their attire, this was no ordinary burglary team: ex-CIA agent Hunt was Nixon's chief White House spy; ex-CIA agent McCord and ex-FBI agent Liddy were top officials of the president's 1972 campaign committee. The Miamians had CIA ties and—with Hunt as their supervisor—had been involved in planning the failed CIA-backed Bay of Pigs invasion of Cuba eleven years earlier. All of the men had been involved in previous clandestine Nixon White House operations against the president's enemies.

Hunt and Liddy had even participated in a particularly sordid affair—the planned assassination of newspaper columnist Jack Anderson, Nixon's archfoe in the media.

The plot against Anderson only came to light in 1975 when the *Washington Post* reported that—"according to reliable sources"—Hunt told associates after the Watergate break-in that he was ordered to kill the columnist in December 1971 or January 1972.[2]

President Nixon chose to be out of the country the day of the Watergate break-in. He was visiting a private island in the Bahamas owned by his old drinking buddy Robert Abplanalp, a wealthy businessman. Accompanied by Bebe Rebozo, Nixon had choppered to the tiny island from his Key Biscayne, Florida home.

Hot-tempered even under normal conditions, the chief executive went ballistic when aide Chuck Colson told him by phone that his men had been arrested at Watergate. Nixon grew so enraged he threw an ashtray against one of the walls in Abplanalp's luxurious Caribbean retreat.[3]

Knowing his presidency was seriously threatened, Nixon moved quickly to save himself. His major weapons were lies, cover-ups and blackmail.

First, he instructed his press secretary, Ron Ziegler, to inform reporters back in Florida that it was beneath the White House to even comment on a "third-rate burglary attempt."

On June 22, after returning to the White House, Nixon made his first public comment on the burglary. He flatly asserted that "the White House has had no involvement whatever" in the break-in. And he declared, with a straight face, that such an event "has no place in our electoral process or in our governmental process."

On the twenty-third, in an effort to get the CIA to stop the FBI's initial Watergate probe, Nixon tried to blackmail CIA Director Richard Helms, apparently by using his knowledge of major CIA secrets to keep the lid on Watergate.

The president wanted to scare Helms with the prospect that, under pressure, an apprehended Hunt might start blabbing to authorities about "the Bay of Pigs." That phrase, to Bob Haldeman—Nixon's most trusted aide—was secret Nixon-CIA code for one of the darkest events in our history, an event with tenuous ties to the disastrous 1961 Cuban invasion.

In a post-Watergate book, Haldeman disclosed, "It seems that in all those Nixon references to the Bay of Pigs, he was actually referring to the Kennedy assassination. (Interestingly, an investigation of the Kennedy assassination was a project I suggested when I first entered the White House. Now I felt we would be in a position to get all the facts. But Nixon turned me down.)"[4]

Watergate expert and National Public Radio correspondent Daniel Schorr independently concurs with Haldeman that Nixon's Watergate threat to the CIA about "the Bay of Pigs" was "about some deeply hidden scandal . . . an assassination or something on that order. It was supposed to involve the CIA and

President Kennedy." Schorr also says that, to this day, "Helms vows that he has no idea what dark secret Nixon was alluding to. But, whatever it was, it led Nixon into trying to enlist the CIA in an attempted obstruction of justice that became his final undoing."[5] Speculating separately, JFK assassination expert Jim Marrs—without knowing about Haldeman's revelation—asks two perceptive questions about taped "Bay of Pigs" conversations between Nixon and his most trusted adviser: Could they have been circuitously referring to the interlocking connections between CIA agents, anti-Castro Cubans, and mobsters that likely resulted in the Kennedy assassination? Did they themselves have some sort of insider knowledge of this event?[6]

Another possibility, of course, is that the "Bay of Pigs" referred to the CIA assassination plots against Fidel Castro, which were not public knowledge at the time. Both Vice President Nixon and President Kennedy backed those plans. And the CIA's Howard Hunt was an early advocate of Castro's murder and a key player in all aspects of the Bay of Pigs invasion planning. Whatever the term meant, the usually unflappable Helms came unglued when Haldeman brought it up in the wake of the Watergate burglary.

But, first, Nixon had to tutor Haldeman on just how to make the threat to Helms. During a June 23 rehearsal of Haldeman for the critical meeting with Helms later that day, the president carefully instructed his No. 1 aide on what to tell the CIA chief: "Hunt knows too damned much . . . If this gets out that this is all involved . . . it would make the CIA look bad, it's going to make Hunt look bad, and it's likely to blow the whole Bay of Pigs thing . . . which we think would be very unfortunate for both the CIA and the country . . . and for American foreign policy."[7]

At his meeting with Helms, when Nixon's emissary brought up the Bay of Pigs, according to Haldeman, the CIA chief gripped the arms of his chair, leaned forward and shouted: "The Bay of Pigs has nothing to do with this! I have no concern about the Bay of Pigs." Haldeman said he was "absolutely shocked by Helms's violent reaction" when he delivered Nixon's message.[8] Helms "yelled like a scalded cat," said Nixon aide John Ehrlichman when Haldeman mentioned the Watergate trail might lead to "the Bay of Pigs."[9] Ehrlichman sat in on the meeting.

In his book, Haldeman added that the CIA pulled off a "fantastic cover-up" that "literally erased any connection between the Kennedy assassination and the CIA."[10] Haldeman never revealed his source, but evidence points to Nixon. "Virtually nothing Nixon did was done without Haldeman's knowledge," said John Ehrlichman. "That is not to say that Haldeman approved everything Nixon said or did; but it was essential that he know, and have a chance to object, before it happened."[11]

Ehrlichman went to his grave without spilling any "Bay of Pigs" secrets, but he did write a novel about a president and a CIA chief trying to blackmail each other over a previous assassination plot that involved both men.

If Haldeman knew about the CIA's alleged involvement in the Kennedy murder, Nixon certainly did. The president would have had to tell his top aide what was truly behind his "Bay of Pigs" threat against the agency. That conclusion gains solid support from a recently released Watergate tape—from May 18, 1973—in which Nixon and Haldeman recall the "Bay of Pigs" warning Haldeman delivered to Helms the previous June.

Haldeman reminds the president that Helms said, "Oh, we have no problem with the Bay of Pigs, of anything . . . And that surprised me, because I had gotten the impression from *you* [author's emphasis] that the CIA did have some concern about the Bay of Pigs."[12] On the tape, Nixon raises no objections to the accuracy of Haldeman's memory.

Audiotapes ran on all Nixon's office and telephone conversations, so the president would not want to refer to John F. Kennedy murder secrets as "Dallas" or "the whole JFK thing." Why, logically, could the JFK assassination become known to Nixon and Helms and a few others as "the Bay of Pigs"? Perhaps because the cast of characters employed in the 1960 plan to invade Cuba at the Bay of Pigs and kill Fidel Castro and the cast of characters employed in the plan to assassinate Kennedy in 1963 were the same.

When Nixon was vice president, he and then CIA agent Hunt were principal secret planners of the invasion of Cuba at the Bay of Pigs that failed so miserably when later ordered by President Kennedy. Nixon and Hunt were key leaders of an associated—and also ill-fated—plot to assassinate Castro. For that mission, potential assassins were recruited from Mob ranks, so that if any of their activities were disclosed, organized crime could be blamed.

Helms as then director of the CIA's covert operations was a key participant in the Castro assassination plots. The plotters also enlisted the support of billionaire Howard Hughes. Like Nixon, Hughes despised the Kennedys and had strong links to both the CIA and the Mob. The mysterious and reclusive Hughes had made large, secret payoffs to Nixon and his brother Donald over most of Nixon's political career.

Fronting for Hughes, Robert Maheu approached mobsters Johnny Roselli, Sam "Mooney" Giancana and Santos Trafficante. One report says fifteen professional killers ultimately made up the "ultra-black" Castro assassination team, consistent with a typical Mafia hit, as summarized by author David Scheim: "A mob murder is usually a methodical job, performed by a coordinated team of specialists. Up to 15 gunmen, drivers, spotters, and other backup personnel, plus several cars, are used on some jobs."[13]

Maheu, a former FBI agent employed by both the CIA and Hughes, had many links with Nixon. To mention just two: In 1956, Maheu ran a Howard Hughes–bankrolled spying operation to protect Nixon against Republican "Dump Nixon" forces trying to block Nixon's renomination as Dwight Eisenhower's vice president. Also while Nixon was veep, Maheu worked for Nixon on a "dirty tricks" operation against Greek oil tycoon Aristotle Onassis.

Maheu helped the U.S. government sabotage a deal that had given Onassis a monopoly on shipping Saudi Arabian oil. As part of his mission, Maheu was reportedly even given a license—if necessary—to kill the Greek tycoon. After a meeting with Maheu about Onassis, Vice President Nixon shook Maheu's hand and whispered, "And just remember, if it turns out we have to kill the bastard don't do it on American soil."[14]

President Kennedy's former press secretary, Pierre Salinger, said Maheu told him the CIA-Mafia plots against Castro were authorized by Nixon:

> I knew Maheu well. He told me [in 1968, when Salinger was soliciting Maheu's boss, Howard Hughes, for a campaign contribution to Robert Kennedy's White

House bid] about his meetings with the Mafia. He said he had been in contact with the CIA, that the CIA had been in touch with Nixon, who had asked them to go forward with this project . . . It was Nixon who had him [Maheu] do a deal with the Mafia in Florida to kill Castro."[15]

Nixon White House counsel John Dean confirms that Maheu was "the point of contact for the CIA's effort to have the Mafia assassinate Fidel Castro in the early 1960s." Dean said he was told by fellow Nixon aide Jack Caufield that the Hughes empire "was embroiled in an internal war, with two billion dollars at stake, private eyes swarming, nerve-jangling power plays going on, and Mafia figures lurking in the wings."[16]

Longtime Mob lawyer Frank Ragano disclosed in the 1990s that the assassination plot against Castro was hatched in the summer of 1960. He reported that "Maheu's search for mob killers began with John Roselli who brought in Sam Giancana, the Chicago boss, and Santo [Trafficante] . . . The CIA operatives told Maheu he could offer $150,000 to the assassins, and that Castro's murder was a phase of a larger plan to invade Cuba and oust the Communist government." Ragano also claimed he was the unwitting messenger in a July 1963 order from Teamsters boss Jimmy Hoffa to Trafficante and Marcello for President Kennedy's murder.[17]

Sam Giancana confided to his brother, Chuck, in 1966, that the CIA had offered him $150,000 to hit Castro. "I told 'em I couldn't care less about the money. We'll take care of Castro. One way or another. I think it's my patriotic duty."[18]

Giancana said CIA Director Allen Dulles had come up with

the idea, and that two top CIA officials—Richard Bissell and Sheffield Edwards—were chosen to make the arrangements. And he said the agency made contact with him through Maheu. Giancana designated Roselli as the plan's Mafia-CIA go-between.

Of that conversation with his brother, Chuck also mentioned a number of other conspirators in the plot on Castro's life: "Mooney said he put Jack Ruby back in action supplying arms, aircraft, and munitions to exiles in Florida and Louisiana, while the former Castro Minister of Games, Frank Fiorini [also known as Frank Sturgis], joined Ruby in the smuggling venture along with a [Guy] Banister CIA associate, David Ferrie."[19]

President Kennedy was elected to office before Nixon and the other planners had time to pull off the Bay of Pigs invasion. The invasion took place on April 17, 1961 on Kennedy's watch and was a resounding failure, one for which Kennedy publicly accepted full responsibility. Fifteen hundred Cuban exiles were quickly overwhelmed by some 20,000 Cuban troops. But, convinced the CIA had set him up, Kennedy fired CIA chief Allen Dulles—an old Nixon friend—and swore he'd dismantle the agency.

Nixon, Hunt, and many CIA and exile leaders privately pinned blame for the military catastrophe on Kennedy for not providing adequate air cover. Later, Hunt publicly accused the president of "a failure of nerves."[20]

Mafia bosses, already enraged by Kennedy's anticrime crusade in this country, were upset that their lucrative gambling casinos—shut down by Castro—would not be returning to Cuba.

It is quite possible top elements of the Mob and the CIA decided to send their hired guns against Kennedy instead of Castro. Would Nixon know? After all, he and Hunt had come up with the original ideas they thought JFK later bungled. And Nixon's tight CIA and Mob contacts undoubtedly kept him completely up-to-date on major related developments. Fletcher Prouty, a former Air Force officer who regularly worked with the CIA on covert operations, has said Nixon "may very well have realized" that such a killing team "was involved" in the Kennedy murder.[21]

Though Helms reportedly exploded when Haldeman brought up the "Bay of Pigs" in connection with Watergate, he later denied knowing what Haldeman was talking about. But Helms's immediate response was to direct his deputy, Vernon Waters, to tell acting FBI Director Pat Gray the FBI investigation jeopardized covert CIA operations. Gray "dutifully carried out the order to cut back the investigation."[22] Helms's action lends weight to the probability that the subject Nixon raised with him, through Haldeman, actually dealt with something other than the 1961 CIA-backed invasion of Cuba.

Indeed, the CIA's own top-secret postmortem on the invasion—when it was finally declassified in 1998—disclosed major agency blunders and criticized the failure to inform President Kennedy that the potential for "success had been dubious." But the report contains absolutely nothing that could be interpreted as sensitive to national security.[23]

Several days before the invasion, the Miami correspondent for the *New York Times*, Tad Szulc, wrote a story about the planned landing. But, after a personal appeal from President Kennedy, senior *Times* editors toned it down. Two months later, Szulc told the Senate Foreign Relations Committee that information about the supposedly secret invasion had been available in Miami in March to any interested reporter. Kennedy later told *Times* editors, "If you had printed more about the operation, you would have saved us from a colossal mistake."[24]

. . .

Nixon's Watergate warning to Helms about the dangerous CIA secrets Hunt could tell—and the events leading up to it—deserve a closer look.

As far back in his presidency as September 18, 1971, Nixon contemplated an order to the CIA to turn over to him its complete files on the Bay of Pigs. This happened at a White House meeting of Nixon, Attorney General John Mitchell and Nixon aides Haldeman, Ehrlichman and Egil Krogh. Ehrlichman's handwritten notes have Ehrlichman telling the group: "Bay of Pigs—order to CIA—President is to have the FULL file or else—nothing withheld. President was involved in Bay of Pigs—must have the file—theory—deeply involved—must know all."[25]

The president personally followed up at a meeting with Helms on October 8, 1971. Ehrlichman sat in. His notes quote Nixon as saying, "Purpose of request for documents: must be fully advised in order to know what to duck; won't hurt Agency, nor attack predecessor."

Helms answers, "Only one president at a time; I only work for you."

Nixon then said, "Ehrlichman is my lawyer—deal with him on all this as you would me."

After Ehrlichman tells Helms he'll be making requests for more material, Helms responds: "OK, anything."[26]

Helms initially went along with the Watergate cover-up. Haldeman was able to tell the president he informed Helms that the Watergate investigation "tracks back to the Bay of Pigs . . . At that point, he got the picture. He said we'll be very happy to be helpful."[27] Helms, however, had second thoughts and was soon refusing to cooperate with Nixon's gambit. For that insubordination, he was eventually banished to be the ambassador to Iran.

That the CIA failed to obey Nixon's order is also established in a newly released Watergate tape of a May 18, 1973 conversation in which Haldeman tells Nixon: "[Helms says the CIA] has nothing to hide in the Bay of Pigs. Well, now, Ehrlichman tells me in just the last few days that isn't true. CIA was very concerned about the Bay of Pigs, and in the investigation apparently he was doing on the Bay of Pigs stuff. At some point, there is a key memo missing that the CIA or somebody has caused to disappear that impeded the effort to find out what really did happen on the Bay of Pigs."[28]

In *The Ends of Power*, Haldeman claimed the CIA cover-up of the JFK assassination included failing to tell the Warren Commission about agency assassination attempts against Fidel Castro. And he disclosed that the CIA's counterintelligence chief James Angleton phoned the FBI's Bill Sullivan to rehearse their answers to possible commission questions. Haldeman gave these samples:

Q. Was Oswald an agent of the CIA?
A. No.
Q. Does the CIA have any evidence showing that a conspiracy existed to assassinate Kennedy?
A. No.

Haldeman pointed out that Sullivan was Nixon's "highest-ranking loyal friend" at the FBI.[29]

In the early days of the Watergate cover-up, according to Ehrlichman, Nixon "knew a great many things about Hunt that I didn't know." He quotes the president as saying: "His lawyer is

Bittman . . . Do you think we could enlist him to be sure Hunt doesn't blow national secrets?"[30]

As late as March 21, 1973, Nixon was still deeply concerned about keeping Hunt quiet. He told aide John Dean that Hunt's demands for an additional $120,000 in hush money must be met. And the two men then had this exchange:

Nixon: Well, your major guy to keep under control is Hunt.

Dean: That's right.

Nixon: I think. Because, he knows . . .

Dean: He knows so much.

Nixon:. . . about a lot of other things.[31]

Nixon's blackmailing efforts even extended to former president Lyndon Johnson. A 1994 book based on Haldeman's personal diaries shows that, in January 1973, Nixon tried to coerce LBJ into using his influence with Senate Democrats to derail the Watergate investigation. Haldeman said Nixon threatened to go public with information that LBJ bugged the Nixon campaign in 1968. When Johnson heard of the threat "he got very hot and called Deke [De Loach, No. 3 man at the FBI] and said to him that if the Nixon people are going to play with this, he would release information" that would be even more damaging to Nixon.[32]

The information that President Johnson was going to release was deleted from Haldeman's dairy by the National Security Council during the Carter administration, which scrutinized it for sensitive national security material. It is the only such deletion in the entire book.

Newly declassified tapes and documents reveal, however, that

LBJ was, indeed, ready to play a huge national security card—the treason card—against Nixon's desperate Watergate gamble. The ex-president was prepared to disclose that, in 1968, for purely political reasons, presidential candidate Nixon had undermined U.S. efforts to end the Vietnam War. President Nixon dropped the blackmail plan after LBJ's counterthreat.

Nixon never publicly voiced any suspicions that CIA/Mafia assassins recruited to kill Cuban leader Fidel Castro might have murdered President John Kennedy. In fact, Nixon never admitted that as vice president he was in charge of the early Bay of Pigs invasion plan and associated CIA-Mafia plots to kill Castro. Rather, he was on record as a strong supporter of the Warren Commission's finding that the crime of the twentieth century was the work of a lone Communist nut, Lee Harvey Oswald—and that this nut was silenced by another lone nut, Jack Ruby, acting out of patriotism.

Robert Kennedy's first thoughts about who might be responsible were entirely different. In the immediate wake of his brother's assassination in Dallas, the attorney general suspected CIA-Mob involvement.

Kennedy learned the identity of Howard Hughes operative—and onetime Nixon dirty trickster—Robert Maheu when he was told about the Maheu-arranged CIA-Mafia murder conspiracy against Castro. Hughes expert Michael Drosin reports that RFK was "shocked. Not about the failed attempt to kill Castro, which he and his brother almost certainly approved in advance, but about the CIA's choice of hit men. Especially Giancana."[33] RFK knew that if the mob was involved in a political plot, it was likely with the CIA's endorsement.

Jack Newfield, producer of the 1998 Discovery Channel documentary *Robert F. Kennedy: A Memoir*, said Robert Kennedy had a firm idea about who killed his brother: "Bobby told [JFK adviser] Arthur Schlesinger he blamed 'that guy in New Orleans'— which meant [Mob boss] Carlos Marcello. Bobby was intense about prosecuting Marcello as attorney general. He deported him in 1961, indicted him when he returned, and tried him in 1963."[34]

"The Bay of Pigs" gets frequent mention on the Nixon tapes. And the term is usually employed in ways that suggest reference to the assassination. These tapes are also studded with deletions— segments deemed by government censors as too sensitive for public scrutiny. "National Security" is usually cited. Not surprisingly, such deletions often occur during discussions involving E. Howard Hunt, the Bay of Pigs and John F. Kennedy. Isn't it long past time when these censored sections of the tapes are declassified?

Meantime, more than one million JFK assassination-related CIA documents remain secret, but are supposed to be released in 2017. Let's hope that, as a result, we finally find out who killed JFK and why. And maybe these declassified records will also throw some new light on the befuddling "Bay of Pigs" code that Richard Nixon used in his very first effort to cover up the Watergate burglary.

ELEVEN

NIXON'S SPYMASTER: E. HOWARD HUNT

As President Nixon's premier spook, E. Howard Hunt was involved not only in the plot to eliminate Jack Anderson, he headed at least one other assassination scheme—a canceled overseas mission to rub out Panamanian strongman Omar Torrijos, according to *Newsweek*.[1]

From his desk in Room 16 in the Executive Office Building—where he had a "special secure phone for his personal use"[2]—Hunt planned and supervised break-ins at Daniel Ellsberg's psychiatrist's office in Los Angeles, and at Democratic National Committee headquarters in Washington, D.C. He was also involved in a plot to steal a stash of Howard Hughes's secret papers by breaking open the safe of Las Vegas newspaper publisher Hank Greenspun.[3] And he forged State Department documents to make it look as though President Kennedy approved the November 2, 1963, killing of South Vietnam's President Ngo Dinh Diem in a coup in Saigon.[4]

In late June 1971, when Nixon wanted to burglarize the

Brookings Institution—a leftist Washington think tank—to find classified documents he could use to embarrass the Johnson administration, he thought of a familiar name, a retired CIA agent now on the White House payroll, to handle the assignment.

Newly released Watergate tapes show Nixon told chief of staff Bob Haldeman to "talk to Hunt. I want the break-in. Hell, they do that. You're to break into the place, rifle the files, and bring them in."[5] Despite persistent orders from Nixon, the building was never entered.

Among many other illegal covert criminal operations Howard Hunt undertook for President Nixon, one stands out as especially seamy. In the immediate aftermath of the 1972 shooting of third-party presidential hopeful George Wallace, Hunt was dispatched to Milwaukee. His mission: to plant campaign literature from Democratic White House aspirant George McGovern at the apartment of Wallace's attacker, Arthur Bremer. By the time Hunt arrived, however, the FBI had sealed off Bremer's apartment.[6]

Following this disclosure on new Nixon tapes released in the '90s, *Newsweek* columnist Meg Greenfield stated her amazement at the blatant criminality involved in Nixon's reaction to the shooting and severe wounding of a rival—the planned scattering of pamphlets from yet another rival at the would-be assassin's home: "The president of the United States did this—the man responsible for the federal agencies investigating the heinous criminal act. In effect, he authorized tampering with the evidence and jeopardizing the case to win a political, public relations point."[7]

It was not until 2002, with the release of yet another tape, that Nixon is known to have also ordered that Bremer be falsely painted in the press as a backer of Democratic presidential hopefuls George McGovern and Edward Kennedy.

During a 1985 court case against *Spotlight*, a newsletter owned by right-wing Liberty Lobby, Hunt claimed he was libeled in an August 1978 article written by former CIA agent Victor Marchetti entitled "CIA to Admit Hunt Involvement in Kennedy Slaying."[8]

At the trial, CIA operative Marita Lorenz swore she saw Hunt in Dallas the night before the assassination. Lorenz testified that, on November 21, at a Dallas motel, she saw Hunt pay money to another agency operative: Hunt pal and future Watergate burglar Frank Sturgis. She maintained that, shortly after Hunt left, Jack Ruby showed up. Lorenz returned to her home in Miami that same night, but said Sturgis later told her what she had missed in Dallas on November 22, 1963: "We killed the President that day."[9]

Hunt co-worker Walter Kuzmuk at the CIA said he could not recall having seen Hunt at work between November 18 and sometime in December of 1963; and Joseph Trento, a reporter for the *Wilmington News & Journal*, insisted he had once seen an internal CIA memo that said, "Someday we will have to explain Hunt's presence in Dallas on November 22, 1963."[10] Hunt lost his libel case against *Spotlight*, although his presence in Dallas and involvement in the assassination has never been conclusively proven.

One of the most intriguing mysteries of the JFK assassination is the great likeness between Hunt and one of the "Three Tramps"

photographed near Dealey Plaza in the aftermath of the assassination. Hunt was a renowned master of disguise (during Watergate, the CIA gave him several appearance, and even gait-changing,
devices). Is the short hobo decked out in what appears to be a
circus clown costume Howard Hunt?

The House assassination committee—also a successor to
the Church panel—looked into the short hobo and concluded:
"Tramp C, from his battered fedora to his worn-out shoes, has
managed to achieve a sartorial effect similar to what one would
expect had he been fired from a cannon through a Salvation
Army thrift shop." The committee conceded the outfit could
have been a disguise.[11]

The biggest apparent difference between Tramp C and photos of Hunt from the Watergate era centers on the tramp's pro-
truding ears. If Tramp C *was* indeed Hunt, the answer to that
issue could reside in a statement by Teamsters/Mafia heavy-
weight Frank Sheeran in *"I Heard You Paint Houses"*: "[In 1961,
JFK assassination suspect] David Ferrie told me that the war
material [destined for the Cuban exiles] being loaded was from
the Maryland National Guard" and was to be taken to a dog
track outside Jacksonville, Florida. "He said I'd be met there by
a guy with big ears named Hunt."

Sheeran revealed, "Hunt also got some kind of operation on
his ears because the next time I saw him his ears were closer to
his head."[12]

In the Nixon White House, Hunt—often with help from his
anti-Castro group—engineered, or at least plotted, myriad "dirty
tricks" that went far beyond the criminality of Watergate. These
included the alleged plot to kill columnist Jack Anderson, a plan
that was canceled at the last minute.

. . .

Most notorious for directing Nixon's Watergate burglary, Hunt died at age eighty-eight in January 2007, in Miami. But Hunt's son—Howard St. John Hunt (known as "Saint John") of Eureka, California—is now peddling a story that his dad rejected an offer to take part in a plot by rogue CIA agents to kill President Kennedy.

In an interview with the *Los Angeles Times*, Saint John Hunt does admit to telling previous lies about his dad's whereabouts on that fateful day. He says he was instructed by Hunt in 1974 to back up an alibi for his whereabouts. "I did a lot of lying for my father in those days," St. John confessed.[13]

E. Howard Hunt's most frequently used alibi for that day was that he was at his Potomac, Maryland, home watching TV with his children. Yet, Hunt became "visibly uncomfortable" when the assassination was raised in a 2004 interview with the online magazine *Slate*. When the interviewer asked about "conspiracy theories about your being in Dallas the day JFK was killed," Hunt replied, "No comment."[14]

Saint John Hunt says his dad left him with enough juicy material about the JFK assassination to fill a book, and that he hopes to do just that. The material, Saint John says, was cut from his dad's memoir, *American Spy: My Secret History in the CIA, Watergate and Beyond*, because the elder Hunt's attorney was worried E. Howard could face perjury charges if he recanted sworn testimony.[15]

Does St. John think his planned book will reflect badly on his father? "I don't think it was terrible that he was approached [with the assassination plot] and turned them down," he told the magazine.[16]

In his memoir, E. Howard Hunt suggested that Vice President Lyndon Johnson might have headed the plot to murder JFK. Though Johnson disliked the Kennedys, especially Bobby, and profited most from President Kennedy's murder, few scholars believe LBJ was in on the conspiracy. Not long ago, the History Channel was forced to yank from its lineup, and apologize for, a program supporting that theory.

In the *Los Angeles Times* and, later, in *Rolling Stone*, Saint John said his dad definitely alleged that LBJ led the plot. *Rolling Stone* printed the names of the men Hunt allegedly told his son were the main conspirators. David Atlee Phillips was a friend of Hunt's and a CIA propaganda expert who first worked with Hunt in helping to overthrow a leftist government in Guatemala in 1954. He was the chief of covert action in Mexico City in 1963. Phillips later ran President Nixon's successful CIA-led campaign to overthrow Chilean president Salvador Allende.[17] Cord Meyer was a CIA agent and disinformation specialist. Meyer's beautiful bohemian ex-wife, Mary Pinchot Meyer, had had an affair with JFK. At age forty-three, in 1964, Mary was killed by two professionally placed bullets, fired from up close, as she strolled on a canal towpath near the Potomac River in Washington. Bill Harvey was a CIA veteran with connections to the failed CIA-backed Bay of Pigs invasion in 1961, and to Mafia godfathers Santos Trafficante and Sam Giancana. Frank Sturgis was a CIA operative and Hunt pal who once boasted that "We killed Kennedy." In 1972, Sturgis was arrested as one of Nixon's Hunt-supervised Watergate burglars. David Morales, a CIA agent who helped train Cuban exiles for the Bay of Pigs, also ran CIA-assassination programs in South America and Vietnam. In a drunken tirade in 1973, he said to his close friend Ruben Carbajal, "We took care of that son of a bitch [President Kennedy], didn't we?" Antonio Veciana was a Cuban exile and the founder of the militant CIA-backed "Alpha 66." Veciana told a Senate investigator he once saw alleged JFK assassin Lee Harvey Oswald talking with a CIA man he knew as "Maurice Bishop"—widely believed to have been David Atlee Phillips's CIA code name.[18]

In *Rolling Stone*, Saint John Hunt also said that his dad his told him there was a "French gunman" firing from the famed grassy knoll in Dealey Plaza. And he clearly recalled his mother telling him, on November 22, 1963, that his dad was on a business trip to Dallas that day.[19]

Does Saint John's tale ring true? Perhaps in that last crucial area—his dad's whereabouts on that dark day. For the most part, however, it could just be that E. Howard Hunt was practicing what was known during Watergate as a "modified limited hang out." John Ehrlichman, the Nixon aide who dealt with the CIA, coined that term. It has come to mean a reluctant partial release of information.

This is only slightly different than what is known at the CIA as a "limited hang out." Former CIA agent Victor Marchetti once defined that term as "spy jargon for a favorite and frequently used gimmick of the clandestine professionals. When their veil of secrecy is shredded and they can no longer rely on a phony cover story to misinform the public, they resort to admitting—sometimes even volunteering—some of the truth while still managing to withhold the key and damaging facts of the case."[20]

Both hangout tactics were used by Hunt many times before. Even while facing death, it seems, his old habits were hard to kick. He appears to have released to his son heaping helpings of disinformation carefully mixed with small portions of the full and true story—a mixture that would paint him in heroic and patriotic hues for the benefit of his family and his own legacy. "E. Howard Hunt Rejected Kennedy Conspirators!" That's the way he might have written the headline. Hunt was a talented writer—the author of scores of spy novels and the ghostwriter of the memoirs of CIA boss Allen Dulles.

The real E. Howard Hunt, however, was a CIA loyalist, a gun-toting spy and propaganda expert who was close to Richard Nixon, and to top CIA officials, including Dulles, Richard Helms and James Jesus Angleton. Was he still protecting such men—as well as himself? Even on his deathbed, Hunt was not likely to make a full display of what the agency calls "the family jewels." He was too much of a Company man.

It seems likelier that the old master of disinformation was now blowing a little post-mortem smoke to deflect suspicion away from the real major players behind the JFK murder.

Until his final "confession," E. Howard Hunt was destined to be remembered by history mainly as President Nixon's leading undercover operative—a former senior CIA officer who served thirty-three months in prison for his role as a leader of the Watergate burglary. Now, however, it becomes much easier to at least believe that Hunt was in Dallas on November 22, 1963, a conclusion that even the jury in the libel suit deemed plausible, in rendering their decision in favor of *Spotlight*.

What could have been the purpose of Hunt's reported "business trip" to Dallas? To stop the plot? Or to collaborate with the plotters? The following little-known links between E. Howard Hunt and the JFK assassination seem to support the second line of thinking:

In New Orleans in the early 1960s, Hunt worked out of the same office building—perhaps even the same office—as Lee Harvey Oswald. On behalf of the CIA, Hunt had set up a dummy organization called "The Cuban Revolutionary Council" at 544 Camp Street, the same address Oswald put on pro-Castro leaflets he handed out. That very building, which was close to the local offices of both the CIA and the FBI, also housed the detective agency of former FBI agent Guy Banister, who associated with leaders of the CIA, the Mafia, Cuban exile groups, and with suspected JFK assassination plotter David Ferrie. After Banister learned of the assassination, he got roaring drunk and pistol-whipped a friend. That friend, a New Orleans private eye named Jack Martin, later said Banister became angry when Martin told him about the people he saw hanging around Banister's office that summer: "There was David Ferrie . . . He practically lived there . . . [Oswald] was there, too. Sometimes he'd be meeting with Guy Banister with the door shut."[21]

Banister and all those with whom he rubbed elbows blamed JFK for the failure of the 1961 CIA-backed invasion of Cuba. They felt the president acted in a cowardly fashion in not providing adequate air cover for the exile invaders. Future president Richard Nixon said Kennedy's behavior was "near criminal."[22] All parties were keenly interested in ousting, even killing, Castro.

Then, there's the handwritten "Dear Mr. Hunt" letter. In 1975, a JFK assassination researcher in Texas received from an anonymous source a copy of a brief handwritten November 8, 1963 note to a "Mr. Hunt" purportedly from Oswald. The writer asked for "information concerding [sic] my position. I am asking only for information. I am asking that we discuss the matter fully before any steps are taken by me or anyone else. Thank you. (signed) Lee

The president's best friend, Bebe Rebozo (far left), has FBI Director J. Edgar Hoover's attention during a Key Biscayne, Florida, meeting. The man on the right is Secretary of State Bill Rogers. *The National Archives*

The president and Teamsters president, Frank Fitzsimmons, in the Oval Office. *The National Archives*

Nixon and Fitzsimmons shake hands at another Oval Office photo op. *The National Archives*

The president guides his familiar guest, Fitzsimmons to a chair at still another White House get-together. *The National Archives*

The president and Fitzsimmons at the Western White House. *The National Archives*

Nixon and Fitzsimmons confer in the San Clemente sunshine. *The National Archives*

The president and first lady attend the funeral of Nixon's longtime advisor, Murray Chotiner. *The National Archives*

Chuck Colson, Nixon's chief hatchet man. *The National Archives*

Frank Sinatra at an East End rehearsal for his performance at a White House State Dinner. *The National Archives*

The Nixons with Sinatra at the State Dinner honoring Italian Prime Minister Giulio Andreotti. *The National Archives*

Sinatra and Vice President Spiro Agnew chat at a party as an unidentified young woman looks on. *The National Archives*

Agnew partying again with Sinatra. *The National Archives*

Henry Kissinger looks at Vice President Spiro Agnew's letter of resignation, addressed to Kissinger. The photo was not released to the press at the time. Nixon told his photographer, Ollie Atkins, "This is for history." Nixon's later letter of resignation, also to Kissinger, was patterned on Agnew's. *The White House*

Harvey Oswald." The letter, which bears a Mexican postmark, was sent to assassination researcher Penn Jones. Three handwriting experts found that the writing was that of Oswald. "Concerning" was also misspelled in a letter Oswald was known to have written in 1961.[23]

Was E. Howard Hunt the Hunt addressed in the letter? It is highly likely that he was. It just so happens that Hunt was the acting CIA station chief in Mexico City at the time Oswald is supposed to have turned up there, according to Hunt's biographer. In *Compulsive Spy: The Strange Career of E. Howard Hunt*, Tad Szulc also reported that Hunt probably knew something about why the CIA destroyed its audio tapes and photos of a mystery man in Mexico City who purported to be Oswald, but who turned out not be him.[24]

What was Hunt's exact CIA role in Dallas, if he was there? Hunt expert Mark Lane believes the CIA agent was only the paymaster of the assassination team: "Miss Lorenz testified she was part of a team—a hit team of assassins—that drove from Miami to Dallas and arrived there a day before the assassination. She traveled with Frank Sturgis, among others. She met Jack Ruby in a motel in Dallas. Hunt came into the hotel room and paid off Sturgis. She saw the cash."[25] But CIA sources speculated in a Wilmington newspaper in 1978 that Hunt thought he was assigned by higher-ups to arrange the murder of Lee Harvey Oswald.[26]

Another opinion was offered by former spook Victor Marchetti—once a close associate of CIA Director Richard Helms. Marchetti was privy to most of the agency's chief secrets. His take—published in *Spotlight* just a few days before the CIA leak to the Wilmington paper—held that Hunt would be "sacrificed" to protect the agency's clandestine services: "The agency

with Hunt for having dragged it into the Nixon
:] mess and for having blackmailed it after he was ar-

ıetti said the CIA was prepared to "admit" that Hunt was
involved in Kennedy's killing. "The CIA may even go so far as to
'admit' that there were three gunmen shooting at Kennedy."[27]

Back when Nixon was vice president, he and the CIA's Hunt secretly plotted an invasion of Cuba, and favored the murder of
Castro. The CIA eventually brought the Mafia into those assassination plots.

Hunt's CIA-connected pal Bernard Barker—known as "Hunt's
Shadow" because the two men were so close—was also apparently
spotted in Dallas on November 22, 1963. Assassination witness
Seymour Weitzman identified Barker as the man on the grassy
knoll who posed as a Secret Service agent and kept people out of
the area.[28] Nine years later, under Hunt's supervision, Barker and
four other CIA men broke into the Watergate on behalf of President Nixon.

In *Mafia Kingfish: Carlos Marcello and the Assassination of
John F. Kennedy*, Mafia expert John Davis notes that Bernard
Barker "had been very much involved with the Cuban Revolutionary Council in Miami, a Cuban exiles group that was closely
linked to the Cuban Revolutionary Democratic Front in New Orleans." Davis says New Orleans Mafia godfather Carlos Marcello
supported the New Orleans group—with money funneled to the
group through his jack-of-all-trades David Ferrie. Davis adds
there are "credible links," although he doesn't spell out what those
links are, between Barker and Jack Ruby.[29]

Was Richard Nixon really in Dallas on November 22 for a PepsiCo convention, as he said, or could his presence have been some sort of signal to his friends in the Mob and the CIA and among the Cuban exiles—the eventual chief suspects of JFK assassination conspiracy theorists? Chicago Mob boss Sam Giancana proudly told relatives that, as the mastermind of the JFK assassination plot, he and Nixon had a preassassination meeting there to discuss the plot.[30]

Shouldn't some congressional committee or sharp prosecutor question Saint John Hunt under oath? After all, we're talking about the greatest unsolved political crime in American history. What kind of proof does he have to back up his claim? *The Los Angeles Times* describes as "inconclusive" the materials he produced for them. These materials apparently include a videotape of E. Howard Hunt. Why not subpoena the tape?

President Nixon's original Watergate strategy revolved around keeping Hunt from spilling secrets. Just five days after his burglars were caught in the Watergate, Nixon told aide Bob Haldeman: "Of course, this Hunt, that will uncover a lot of things. You open that scab, there's a hell of a lot of things, and we feel it would be very detrimental to have this thing go any farther."[31]

Did any of Nixon's men ever think of rubbing out E. Howard Hunt to keep him silent? Hunt's Watergate sidekick G. Gordon Liddy later confessed that such a thought did indeed cross his mind. In *Will*, Liddy said he plotted to poison Hunt while both were in the same prison. "I waited, but because the message (to kill Hunt) never came, he lives.[32]

In a sworn deposition in 1984, Liddy said E. Howard Hunt did indeed have contacts with members of organized crime. As mentioned earlier, Liddy said Hunt boasted to him that a group of CIA-connected Cuban exiles who were picked to disrupt the 1972 Democratic convention were mobbed-up and had, among them, killed twenty-two men.

The forewoman of the jury that ruled against E. Howard Hunt in the 1985 libel case, Leslie Armstrong, told reporters afterward that the jurors had faced a "very, very difficult" task because the attorney for the defense, Mark Lane, "wanted us to say our own government had killed our President. We listened to the evidence very carefully. We discussed it. We concluded that the CIA killed President Kennedy; and I call upon the United States government to do something about that."[33]

Over twenty-five years later, the government still has not done anything about that.

TWELVE

WATERGATE: WHAT SECRETS WAS NIXON SEEKING?

Early in the 1968 campaign, power-hungry, episodically nutty billionaire Howard Hughes—in a lucid moment and non-nuanced memo—stated his determination to elect a president "of our choosing . . . who will be deeply indebted, and who will recognize his indebtedness." Expressing his willingness "to go beyond all limitations on this," Hughes stressed the need for his candidate to know "the facts of political life." Leaving little doubt about his own choice, the eccentric but brilliant hermit added, "If we select Nixon, then he, I know for sure knows the facts of life."[1]

The memo suggests Hughes believed that Nixon could be bought and used. Indeed, he already knew that from previous underhanded dealings with his favorite corrupt politician. Yet one hefty post-presidential cash "bribe" or "gift" or "donation" from Hughes to Nixon might well have played a key role in the president's eventual undoing.

In fact, in the annals of disastrous U.S. political payoffs, nothing is ever likely to top Hughes's $100,000 gift to the president. That's because Nixon's subsequent paranoia over the suspected illegal contribution led, in large measure, to the Watergate burglary and its cover-up—which, of course, ultimately forced Nixon to evacuate the White House just steps ahead of an eviction notice in August 1974.

In the early years of Nixon's presidency, Hughes secretly gave Nixon the soon-to-be controversial $100,000. The money was skimmed from a Hughes gambling casino in Las Vegas, "siphoned like a sip of champagne from the Silver Slipper," according to a later account by columnist Jack Anderson.[2]

The two-installment payoff—to curry government favor for Hughes's gambling and airline businesses—was earmarked for the president's personal use. Nixon coveted the money—actively and repeatedly seeking it—after learning that his 1968 Democratic opponent, Vice President Hubert Humphrey, had received a similar under-the-table "political donation" from Hughes.[3]

Once a daring pilot, an aircraft inventor (the *Spruce Goose*), a handsome starlet-dating Hollywood producer, and a business genius, Hughes now lived alone at The Desert Inn in Las Vegas. Nixon's primary financial angel had become a ninety-pound, narcotics-addicted shut-in who refused to cut his hair, beard, fingernails or toenails. Yet he remained levelheaded enough to want the next president in his hip pocket. And he bragged to aide Robert Maheu, "Bob, remember that there is no person in the world that I can't either buy or destroy."[4]

Chief Senate Watergate Committee investigator Terry Lenzner later said if the Hughes $100,000 "had gone to a legitimate political campaign, it would have been perfectly appropriate and okay. This, however, was a bribe, in effect, through (Bebe) Rebozo to the president."[5]

Just how does one of the nation's richest men buy influence from its most powerful? In the shadows, and through middlemen—yet under swaying palms at resortlike seaside settings. Best of all, under the protective umbrella of the United States Secret Service.

On September 10, 1969, Hughes's top two lieutenants Robert Maheu and Richard Danner delivered the first $50,000 installment to Rebozo—Nixon's bosom buddy since at least 1950. The president's genial Cuban-American pal accepted a manila envelope stuffed with crisp hundred-dollar bills. The transaction took place at Rebozo's newly renovated home in the Secret Service–guarded presidential compound on Florida's Key Biscayne.

Bebe opened the envelope, shook out the bundles of cash, and then quickly counted them. After determining the promised amount was all there, Rebozo tucked the bundles back into the envelope, wrote the initials "H.H." on the envelope, and took it into another room. The three old friends then went out for a martini-soaked celebratory dinner.

On July 3, 1970, Danner alone handed Rebozo the second half of the Hughes $100,000. Another batch of hundreds had been stuffed into another manila envelope. But this time there was a new venue: Rebozo's bungalow on the grounds of the Western White House at San Clemente, California. Rebozo emptied this $50,000 installment onto his bed, counted it out, and then transferred the cash to his own handbag. Bebe took Danner on a post-transaction sightseeing stroll around the heavily guarded Nixon estate overlooking the Pacific Ocean. The two bagmen finally dropped in on the president himself for ten minutes of what was office small talk on topics other than the shady deal they'd just completed, at least according to Danner. The descriptions of these transactions come mainly from Danner's testimony to the Special Watergate Prosecution staff.[6]

In an astounding double-cross, shortly after Rebozo accepted the final payment in the $100,000 Hughes bribe, Bebe joined a White House plot to link Hughes to Larry O'Brien and the Democrats. In a White House memo uncovered in 1973 by columnist Jack Anderson, Nixon chief of staff Bob Haldeman instructs Nixon counsel John Dean to lead the plot, even though it might be "embarrassing" to Hughes. Haldeman warns Dean, however, to "keep Bebe out of it at all costs."[7]

Dated January 17, 1971, the memo urges Dean to start "an inquiry into the relationship between Larry O'Brien and Howard Hughes." Several days later, Dean files his initial finding after speaking to the president's best friend: "I discussed the matter with Bebe Rebozo who indicated that his information regarding [a retainer paid by Hughes to O'Brien] had come from Robert Maheu . . . Bebe further indicated he felt he could acquire some documentation of this fact if given a little time and that he would proceed to get any information he could."[8] Perhaps Bebe hoped to get the "documentation" through a break-in at O'Brien's Democratic Party office at the Watergate?

The lid came off the undercover Hughes payoff three years later, after Hughes fired Maheu as his right-hand man. Maheu mentioned the money in a deposition he filed as part of a $17-million suit against Hughes. At that point in 1973, with Watergate investigators breathing down his neck, Rebozo returned the $100,000 to Hughes—the very same cash originally contributed, he insisted. Rebozo's eyebrow-raising alibi is that he had kept all those bundled hundreds—undisturbed, and without the president's knowledge—all that time in a safe deposit box at his Key Biscayne bank. The Hughes money was just a campaign contribution, he claimed—a contribution he just hadn't yet gotten around to giving to any campaign.

When Watergate Committee staffers inspected the Rebozo money, however, the bills were tattered, and held together with rubber bands—not with the Las Vegas casino wrappers they came in. An extra one-hundred-dollar bill was also found. At the time, some speculated that this was actually replacement cash hastily rounded up by a wealthy Nixon friend, businessman Robert Abplanalp.

The May 6, 1974, issue of *Time*, for example, predicted Senate investigators would find that the money in Bebe's safe-deposit box was actually supplied as a cover by Abplanalp. It was an obvious leak from the probers. In addition, a preliminary report by the Senate Watergate Committee found that the Hughes funds were used illegally. Chief investigator Terry Lenzner is said to believe that "Rebozo secured the replacement cash from another millionaire friend of Nixon's, financier Robert Abplanalp, through Abplanalp's lawyer, William Griffin. In May 1973, Lenzner believes that Rebozo and Hughes Corporation executive Richard Danner, the original source of the contribution, met with Nixon, where Abplanalp provided the cash to replace the missing $100,000."[9]

Contrary to what Rebozo told Senate Watergate probers, Herb Kalmbach told the committee that Rebozo had informed him that the Hughes cash had been divided among Nixon's two brothers, Donald and Edward, and Nixon's secretary, Rose Mary Woods. Others suspect the Hughes $100,000 furnished Nixon's lavish California home.

OFFICE OF THE WHITE HOUSE PRESS SECRETARY

THE WHITE HOUSE

STATEMENT BY RONALD L. ZIEGLER
PRESS SECRETARY TO THE PRESIDENT

8:22 P.M.   EDT

     I know many of you are on deadline. I have a
brief statement to give you at this time, and following the
reading of the statement we will have an exchange of a series
of letters relating to action which President Nixon has taken
tonight.

     President Nixon has tonight discharged Archibald
Cox, the Special Prosecutor in the Watergate case. The President took this action because of Mr. Cox's refusal to comply
with instructions given Friday night through Attorney General
Richardson that he was not to seek to invoke the judicial
process further to compel production of recordings, notes or
memoranda regarding private Presidential conversations.

     Further, the office of the Watergate special prose-
cution Force has been abolished as of approximately 8:00 p.m.
tonight. Its function to investigate and prosecute those
involved in the Watergate matter will be transferred back into
the institutional framework of the Department of Justice, where
it will be carried out with thoroughness and vigor.

     In his statement Friday night, and in his decision
not to seek Supreme Court review of the Court of Appeals
decision with regard to the Watergate tapes, the President
sought to avoid a constitutional confrontation by an action
that would give the Grand Jury what it needs to proceed with
its work with the least possible intrusion of Presidential
privacy. That action taken by the President in the spirit of
accommodation that has marked American constitutional history
was accepted by responsible leaders in Congress and the country.
Mr. Cox's refusal to proceed in the same spirit of accommodation,
complete with his announced intention to defy instructions from
the President and press for further confrontation at a time of
serious world crisis, made it necessary for the President to
discharge Mr. Cox and to return to the Department of Justice
the task of prosecuting those who broke the law in connection
with Watergate.

MORE

*An old-fashioned White House press handout announcing the firing of Water-
gate Special Prosecutor Archibald Cox and the abolition of his office. The public outcry over this "Saturday Night Massacre" was so intense the president
was forced to appoint a successor to Cox.* WHITE HOUSE PRESS RELEASE.

```
                           - 2 -


        Before taking this action, the President met this
evening with Attorney General Richardson.  He met with
Attorney General Richardson at about 4:45 today for about
thirty minutes.

        The Attorney General, on hearing of the President's
decision, felt obliged to resign, since he believed the
discharge of Professor Cox to be inconsistent with the
conditions of his confirmation by the Senate.

        As Deputy Attorney General, Mr. William Ruckelshaus,
refused to carry out the President's explicit directive to
discharge Mr. Cox, he, like Mr. Cox, has been discharged of
further duties effective immediately.

        Professor Cox was notified of his discharge by the
Acting Attorney General, the Solicitor General, Robert H. Bork,
Professor of Law from Yale University.

        We have available for you now the exchange of letters
between Attorney General Richardson and the President and
the other correspondence.




                    END              (AT 8:27 P.M. EDT)
```

Investigators were at least able to trace $4,562 that Rebozo shelled out for a pair of Harry Winston diamond earrings Nixon gave wife Pat for her sixtieth birthday. And they concluded that the bribe also bought costly house upgrades—including architect's fees, an Arnold Palmer putting green, a fireplace, and a pool table at Nixon's Florida retreat.[10]

Just before Nixon's fall, former aide Chuck Colson concluded "that Bebe used that one hundred grand for himself and for the President, his family and the girls. Hughes can blow the whistle on him. . . ."[11]

For Hughes, the $100,000 was obviously intended to purchase influence on two major federal cases: In 1969, the Civil Aeronautics Board allowed Hughes to buy Air West, a small California-based passenger line. And in 1970, the Justice Department canceled an antitrust action that sought to prevent Hughes from purchasing additional Las Vegas gambling casinos.

But for Nixon, the Hughes $100,000 may have bought his political obituary. Seriously fearful that Democratic Party Chairman Larry O'Brien (then secretly on the Hughes payroll as a lobbyist/political fixer) might know about the bribe, the president prodded aides to spy on O'Brien. Nixon chief of staff Bob Haldeman said Nixon especially wanted to know just what O'Brien was doing to earn his reported $180,000-a-year retainer from Hughes. On January 14, 1971, Nixon told Haldeman, "The time is approaching when Larry O'Brien is held accountable for his retainer with Hughes."[12] O'Brien was head of the Democratic National Committee, which was housed in the Watergate office where the five burglars in business suits and blue surgical gloves were arrested on June 17, 1972. The burglars were replacing a faulty bug they had inserted into O'Brien's phone during an earlier break-in. And they were searching files and taking photos of documents.

Nixon aide Chuck Colson thought the Watergate break-in was "to get dirt on Larry O'Brien," perhaps to gather evidence that O'Brien knew about the $100,000 bribe.[13] After the burglary, Haldeman made a cryptic remark to Nixon about the intruders' keen interest in finding out about the "financial thing." Senate investigator Terry Lenzner is "absolutely certain [the bribe] was a significant part of the President's thinking that this . . .

had to be taken care of."[14] The organizer of the burglary, G. Gordon Liddy, once expressed a similar belief, saying the break-in was "to find out what O'Brien had of a derogatory nature about us, not for us to get something on him."[15]

In the mid-1970s, former top Hughes executive John Meier weighed in on the matter, saying he was "fully convinced that one big reason for the break-in wasn't to get something on [Democratic presidential candidate George] McGovern but to find out what I was telling friends of Larry O'Brien about Richard and Don Nixon and Hughes, to see if anything was going to break before the [1972] election. They knew the Nixons were Hughes's greatest asset in getting his purchase of Air West Airlines approved and that Hughes was fronting for the CIA . . ."[16]

How did the president conclude that O'Brien probably knew about the Hughes payoff to Nixon for the Air West and casino favors and might use it as a surprise election game-changer? Paranoia and natural suspiciousness might be the answer. But the president was wrong: O'Brien, it turns out, was clueless.

Years later, Robert Maheu, in effect, confirmed this. Asked whether he had told his friend O'Brien about the Hughes $100,000, Maheu responded, "Never, never. I had no reason to tell Larry. Why the hell would I tell Larry about this?"[17]

An earlier career-threatening deal with Hughes should have taught Nixon to keep a wary distance from his Golden Goose. In 1957, Hughes loaned $205,000 to Nixon's hapless brother Donald, whose chain of Nixon Burger stands was on the ropes. Disclosure of the Hughes loan, which was never repaid, badly damaged Richard in his losing runs for president in 1960, and for governor of California in 1962.

Hughes fared exceedingly better. Less than a month after his "loan" to the vice president's brother, the IRS reversed a previous decision and granted tax-exempt status to the Howard Hughes Medical Institute—a then obvious tax dodge of minor charitable merit.

The Hughes money that dogged Richard Nixon didn't seem to benefit his brother, Donald, either. Those ill-conceived burger joints quickly folded. Old Nixon friend C. Arnholt Smith never believed that the Hughes $205,000 went to Donald in the first place: "I think it was really for Richard, to help him live. He was a relatively poor man."[18] Shortly after the "loan" was delivered, Richard Nixon bought a house in Washington, reportedly putting $75,000 down before selling his old home.

In fact, veteran California reporter Frank McCullough says he was told by none other than Howard Hughes that the $205,000 "loan" was just a false story. The reclusive billionaire disclosed to McCullough: "It was for political purposes. It was a gift for [Dick], not his brother.[19]

And poor Bebe. The president's bagman was left holding the biggest bag of all. The IRS now began a detailed look into Rebozo's financial affairs, with a focus on "misappropriation of campaign contributions, acceptance of money in exchange for favors by the Justice Department, distribution of Watergate hush money, and alleged diversion of campaign funds to Nixon's brothers and personal secretary."[20]

Rebozo barely escaped prosecution. One of the IRS investigators, Andy Baruffi, later revealed, "I was assigned to review the entire case file. We had Rebozo primarily on a straight up-and-down provable false statement charge. It was a dead-bang case. I believe a deal was made with the White House to kill the investigation."[21] As for Bebe's problems with the Senate Watergate Committee, he was uncooperative, refused to deliver specified records, and—at one critical juncture in 1974—even fled the country, never to testify before the committee again.

The Watergate Committee staff devoted a whole section of its final report to the Hughes bribe, but the committee members decided against issuing it, possibly because other members of Congress were suspected of having ties with Hughes. That, it now turns out, was not just mere suspicion, it was actually true. Before Nixon quit the presidency, a Hughes employee, Michael Merhige, gave another Hughes official an earlier list of U.S politicians the CIA wanted funded through Hughes. One of the thirty-one names on the list was Congressman Gerald Ford of Michigan.[22]

The most perplexing question in the whole Nixon-Hughes saga is this: Why, after believing that the aviator's bounty had cost him two elections, did the president come back for another planeload of it? Both Terry Lenzner and Robert Maheu concur: It was plain and simple greed.

President Richard Nixon's obsession with throwing mud at Larry O'Brien—or determining just what dirt O'Brien might have on him—did not stop with the failed Watergate break-in of June 17, 1972.

In September 1972, the president again tapped his most trusted friend, Bebe Rebozo, to lead another anti-O'Brien operation: offering Justice Department leniency to Bobby Baker, a corrupt former key aide to Senator Lyndon Johnson. Baker had been sentenced to prison for larceny, fraud and tax evasion, and—upon his release—feared the Nixon justice department was behind newspaper leaks that he was under yet another investigation for apparent securities fraud. According to Baker, "I knew this leak had come from the Justice Department; and this knowledge inspired new fear; I could feel footsteps behind me and hot breath on my neck."[23]

Perhaps in exchange for dropping the investigation, the corrupt Democrat would spill gobs of negative information about O'Brien to the Nixon camp. When the president informed his top assistant, Bob Haldeman, about the deal Rebozo would soon try to arrange, Nixon pledged, "If [Baker] can help us, we will help him."[24]

In reality, though, Baker had nothing of value to give up about O'Brien—so no quid-pro-quo was ever arranged. Baker did admit, however, that he met with both Rebozo and, later, with Nixon's personal lawyer Herb Kalmbach, on the O'Brien matter. Baker's tell-all about those meetings came in a post-Watergate book that went unchallenged at the time—legally or otherwise—by Nixon, Rebozo or Kalmbach.

In *Wheeling and Dealing,* Baker disclosed that he met secretly with Bebe over breakfast at Baker's suite at the Key Biscayne Hotel, a three-minute drive from the Nixon-Rebozo enclave known as the Florida White House.

After putting his finger to his lips and turning up the volume on the hotel's TV, Rebozo sat close to his visitor from the north. At first, Bebe patiently listened to Bobby's complaints about how he was being mistreated by the Nixon Justice Department. Rebozo replied, "That's why I called you and asked you here."

According to Baker's account, Bebe soon blurted out, "What

do you know on Larry O'Brien?" Bobby replied, "Bebe, I don't really know anything on him . . . I just don't have the goods."

Nixon did not take Baker's response to Bebe as a final answer. The president subsequently dispatched Kalmbach to try out his persuasive skills on the fallen top Democratic "operator" on the Senate side of the Capitol.

Over lunch in New York, Baker reported, Kalmbach "seemed almost as desperate [as Rebozo] to uncover dirt on Larry O'Brien." And he became "morose" shortly after Baker piped up: "As I told Bebe, I just don't know a thing on the man." The president's lawyer shot back: "Well, it might be convenient for you should your memory improve."

Baker said Kalmbach's eyes "seemed to glaze over" after Baker then brought up his perceived mistreatment at the hands of certain Justice Department officials: "I had the impression he was pretending to listen, but that his mind was on a vacation in a distant place." Baker recalled Kalmbach as "a smart man . . . but he's a cold fish."

The next time Baker saw Kalmbach, it was on a TV screen. Like most of the country, Baker was tuned into the Senate Watergate hearings in the summer of 1973. And there was Kalmbach, in Baker's words, "describing himself to the Ervin Committee as a duped and innocent man."[25] Bobby Baker was sentenced to three years in federal prison for his LBJ-era crimes, but served only sixteen months.[26]

For his Nixon-era sins—mainly raising and distributing hush money for the burglars—Herb Kalmbach got off fairly easily. By promising to cooperate with prosecutors at coming Watergate trials, Kalmbach spent only 191 days in a Lompoc, California, "country club" prison that no longer exists.

The three men who dominate this tale of political corruption were all bagmen. Rebozo and Kalmbach for Nixon, of course. And Baker once collected and distributed cash-filled envelopes for one of the Senate's most powerful, crooked and richest members: Bob Kerr of Oklahoma.

Baker said Senator Kerr never carried less than $5,000 in bills in his suit pockets, and that when Kerr died, an unaccounted $2 million in cash was found in his office safe. But Richard Nixon made Bob Kerr look like a piker. While he was president, for one instance, the government spent nearly $2 million dollars alone on improvements to Nixon's vacation properties, according to the General Services Administration. After a public uproar over those expenditures, Nixon promised to donate his San Clemente estate to the American people after he and his wife died. Instead, he sold the property in 1980 and moved to New York City. And the president was hardly shy about accepting unrecorded cash from almost anyone for almost any favor he could provide in return.

In 1968, Nixon's campaign received a secret $549,000 donation from the brutal military government of Greece. Tom Pappas, a Greek-American businessman, self-admitted CIA operative and front man for the Greek junta, delivered the money in cold cash.

Through sources he still refuses to reveal, Greek journalist Elias Demetracopoulos—now an elderly man—was the first to uncover the illegal Pappas donation. And he provided this information to Democratic committee chairman Larry O'Brien.

Could Nixon's worries about just what O'Brien might know about this so-called Greek Connection have been one of the reasons for the Watergate burglary?

The funds came from the KYP, the Greek intelligence

service—an operation subsidized by the CIA. When White House tapes revealed this donation in 1997, *Salon* columnist Christopher Hitchens observed that "United States law was being broken in two outrageous ways—the supplying of campaign funds by a foreign dictatorship and the recycling of U.S. intelligence money into America's own electoral process."[27]

Back in '68, many political insiders saw Pappas as the man who persuaded Nixon to make the pro-junta Greek-American Spiro Agnew—the widely unknown Maryland governor—his vice presidential running mate.

In March 1973, Tom Pappas provided additional cash to Nixon to help pay off the Watergate defendants for their continued silence. Tapes released in 1997 show that, in return, Pappas wanted Nixon to retain U.S. Ambassador Henry Tasca in Athens.

Nixon quickly agreed to Pappas's demand, and then summoned the "Greek Bearing Gifts," as Pappas was known at the White House, to the Oval Office. There, the new tapes overhear Nixon telling Pappas: "I want you to know what I was mentioning the other night. I am aware of what you're doing to help out on some of these things that Maurie's [Nixon fund-raiser Maurice Stans] people and others are involved in. I won't say anything further, but it's very seldom you find a friend like that, believe me."[28]

Investigative reporter Seymour Hersh says a Senate investigation of a possible CIA role in the transaction was called off at the request of Secretary of State Henry Kissinger—who called Hersh's story a "slimy lie."[29]

Nixon never had the need for such deep pockets, or even an office safe. As he once jokingly bragged to an aide: "I never took a dollar. I always had someone else take it for me."[30]

Bebe served as both his bagman and his banker. And, in the case of Bobby Baker, he acted as Nixon's political fixer.

Through Rebozo, the offer of anything to a convicted man under Justice Department investigation in another case, in exchange for negative information on a Nixon enemy, sounds like a crime. Had it been known about at the time, this might well have risen to the level of an impeachable act.

Of course, Nixon was spared incarceration for any of his Watergate sins—though he apparently did fear such a fate. During the months before his August 1974 forced resignation, reliable sources say, the president told several aides, "Some of the best writing is done from prison."

President Gerald Ford erased any such prospect for Nixon just one month later—giving his fellow Republican predecessor a preemptive pardon for any and all of his White House crimes.

THIRTEEN

NIXON: VICE PRESIDENTIAL PUPPETEER

Just as Jerry Ford later helped his personal pal and political mentor Dick Nixon escape any punishment for Watergate, Nixon helped pave the way for the Michigan congressman's likely ascension to the presidency. President Nixon did this by secretly greasing the skids for Vice President Spiro Agnew—who later contended that White House pressure for his resignation included what Agnew took as a death threat.

In 1968, presidential candidate Nixon had praised Maryland Governor Spiro (Ted) Agnew—his surprise pick for a running mate—for his "tremendous brain power, great courage and un-prejudiced legal mind. He has vigor and imagination and, above all, he acts."[1] Privately, however, Nixon thought Agnew was a political bungler. In fact, in the view of Nixon's national security adviser, Henry Kissinger, Nixon—"always sensitive to being overshadowed"—may well have twice picked Agnew to be his vice president for that very reason.

Kissinger added that the president made a rather dark

comment on just why he picked the little-known governor: "[Nixon] never considered Agnew up to succeeding him. He once said, only partly facetiously, that Agnew was his insurance policy against assassination."[2]

But Nixon and Agnew never got along. By April 1969 the president was complaining about Agnew and two other high-ranking officials: Transportation Secretary George Volpe and HUD Secretary George Romney. Saying of the vice president, "He's driving me nuts," phoning him at dinner time with "Urgent!" calls, like one with the name of a friend he wanted to name to a space council. Nixon ordered Haldeman: "Just keep them [the three men] away from me."[3]

By July 20, 1971, Nixon was voicing the hope that Agnew would resign and he could name Treasury Secretary John Connally to replace him. That's when Nixon aide John Ehrlichman recalled hearing Nixon say of Connally, "I want to position him as my logical successor." In that same conversation, according to Ehrlichman, Nixon instructed him to "meet often with Connally. You woo him. And I want you and Bob [Haldeman] to meet with Connally and Bryce Harlow and figure out how the hell we can get Agnew to resign early."[4]

The Nixon-Connally hookup never occurred, of course. Agnew proved so popular with conservatives, Nixon was forced to keep him on.

Shortly after the Nixon-Agnew ticket won reelection in 1972, Nixon told top aides Bob Haldeman and John Ehrlichman that Agnew wanted the 1976 GOP nomination, "but we will not help him," recalled Ehrlichman. Ehrlichman also quoted Nixon as saying: "By any criteria he falls short. Energy? He doesn't work hard. He likes to play golf. Leadership? (Nixon laughs) Consistency? He's all over the place. He's not really a conservative, you know." When Haldeman suggests that what Agnew might need is the president's "benign neglect," the president declares: "Yes, that should be our strategy."[5]

But that strategy changed radically on June 27, 1973. That's when Attorney General Elliot Richardson told then White House Chief of Staff Alexander Haig that Agnew was under investigation for tax evasion, bribery and extortion. As a result, benign neglect morphed into outright chilliness by the president toward Agnew. Nixon left it to a deputy White House press secretary, Jerry Warren, to answer the pressing question of whether Nixon still stood by Agnew unequivocally. The best Warren could offer was that there was "no reason for the President to change his attitude about the Vice President."[6]

By August 22, when Nixon held his first press conference in five months he seemed to many Americans to be strongly supporting the beleaguered vice president:

I have noted some press speculation to the effect that I have not expressed confidence in the Vice President, and therefore, I welcome this question because I want to set the record straight. I had confidence in the integrity of the Vice President when I selected him as Vice President when very few knew him, as you may recall back in 1968—knew him nationally. My confidence in his integrity has not been shaken, and in fact, it has been strengthened by his courageous conduct and his ability—even though he is controversial at times, as I am over the past 4½ years. So I have confidence in the integrity of the Vice President and particularly in the performance of the duties that he has had as Vice President and as a candidate for Vice President.

But then came a careful presidential equivocation—and a significant downer for Team Agnew. Nixon buried in a key footnote that his confidence in Agnew's integrity extended only so far: "Now obviously the question arises as to charges that have been made about activities that occurred before he became Vice President. He would consider it improper—I would consider it improper—for me to comment on those charges, and I shall not do so."[7]

While Nixon henceforth posed in public as taking a hands-off policy toward his vice president's legal problems, he was actually a big behind-the-scenes advocate of Agnew's resignation. And he made sure two of his top aides—Haig and lawyer Fred Buzhardt—were involved in the negotiations over Agnew's fate. In a book about Agnew, reporters Jules Witcover and Richard Cohen quote an aide to Richardson as saying the White House negotiators "wanted the guy out of there. They wanted resignation without anything. They just wanted him out."[8]

On October 10, 1973, Agnew resigned in disgrace in order to stay out of jail. He pleaded no contest to cheating on his income taxes. Haig is said to have later bragged that "arranging that cop-out was one of the greatest feats of bureaucratic skill in the history of the art."[9]

In his book *Go Quietly . . . or Else*, Agnew stated that in early October Haig had made a threat "that made me fear for my life."

He said the threat came at a meeting between Haig and the vice president's military aide, General Mike Dunn. According to a Dunn memo about the meeting, Haig said if Agnew admitted guilt on the tax charge, "there would be no economic worry for debts and defense . . . no further trouble with the Federal government and no jail sentence."

The memo also quotes Haig as warning that "anything may be in the offing" once an indictment is handed down. "It can and will get nasty and dirty. Don't think that the game cannot be played from [the White House] . . . The President has a lot of power—and don't forget that."

Agnew said Haig's words "sent a chill through my body. I interpreted it as an innuendo that anything could happen to me; I might have a convenient 'accident.'" He said he had been close enough to the presidency to know the "tremendous power" it could exert:

> I knew that men in the White House, professing to speak for the president, could order the CIA to carry out missions that were very unhealthy for people who were considered enemies. Since the revelations have come out about the CIA's attempts to assassinate Fidel Castro and other foreign leaders, I realize even more than before that I might have been in great danger . . . This directive was aimed at me like a gun at my head. That is the only way I can describe it. I was told, "Go quietly or else."

Agnew pointed out that, if a decision were made to "eliminate him—through an automobile accident, a fake suicide, or whatever—the order would not have been traced back to the White House any more than the 'get Castro' orders were ever traced to their source."[10]

The vice president decided to go quietly.

About one year after Nixon's own resignation, Agnew got a telephone call from the former president. But he refused to take it. Agnew later explained that Nixon had snubbed him up until then, and he thought Nixon's call "was a little late."

Agnew did show up, however, at Nixon's 1994 funeral. And he was in a forgiving frame of mind. "I decided after 20 years of resentment to put it all aside," he said. "The last time I talked to [Nixon] was the day I resigned. He tried to call me after that several times but I didn't take the calls because at the time I felt totally abandoned. But that's all past."[11]

FOURTEEN

NIXON'S "BEST KEPT" WAR SECRET

In March 1969, President Richard Nixon launched "Operation Breakfast," the first assault in stage one of the Henry Kissinger–inspired covert carpet-bombing of defenseless and neutral Cambodia. From the start of this surreptitious venture, records were falsified to hide the attacks. Under an elaborate dual reporting system, the raids were disguised as missions against Communist forces *within* Vietnam.

Nixon ordered that any revelation of the bombings be denied. Chairman Earle Wheeler of the Joint Chiefs of Staff told his staff: "In the event press inquiries are received following the execution of the Breakfast Plan as to whether or not U.S. B-52s have struck in Cambodia, U.S. spokesman will confirm that B-52s did strike on routine missions adjacent to the Cambodian border but state that he has no details and will look into the question."[1]

In the first attack, scores of Guam-based B-52 Stratofortresses, operating in waves, dropped their payloads on suspected enemy ammunition dumps, fuel depots and troop concentrations three miles inside the Cambodian border. Initial reports indicated that North Vietnamese and Viet Cong forces there had been disabled.

On March 17, presidential aide Bob Haldeman wrote in his diary:

> Historic day. K[issinger]'s "Operation Breakfast" finally came off at 2:00 PM our time. K really excited, as is P[resident].

And on March 19, Haldeman noted:

> K's "Operation Breakfast" a great success. He came beaming in with the report, very productive. A lot more secondaries (secondary explosions) than had been expected. Confirmed early intelligence. Probably no reaction for a few days, if ever.[2]

Within a week, however, when a U.S. Special Forces ground unit was sent in for Operation Breakfast mop-up duties, it was massacred by North Vietnamese troops. A second unit was ordered to go in, "but its soldiers mutinied rather than walk headlong into the slaughter," reports historian Rob Kirkpatrick.[3]

The results of the initial raid foreshadowed the futility of the entire Cambodian air operation, dubbed "Operation Menu." The four-year clandestine campaign, illegally carried out without the consent of Congress or knowledge of the American people, succeeded, in the main, only in murdering Cambodian villagers and blasting craters out of their countryside.

The reasons the bombing failed were many, including—

according to Christopher Hitchens—the lousy aim of the behe-moth bombers: "[B-52s] fly at an altitude too high to be observed from the ground and carry immense tonnages of high explosive: they give no warning of approach and are incapable of accuracy because of their altitude and the mass of their shells."[4]

Cooler heads—Secretary of State William Rogers and Defense Secretary Melvin Laird—strongly opposed the bombings at first. Laird finally gave his reluctant approval, we now know.[5] Newly released documents and tapes also show that two senators were tipped off and sworn to secrecy about Operation Breakfast and subsequent attacks on Cambodia. Confirmation of that comes in a newly released April 24, 1970 tape of a White House con-versation between the president and Senator John Stennis of Mississippi.

Nixon assures the pro-bombing Democrat that the coming ground invasion of Cambodia would feature continued heavy bombing: "As far as American activity is concerned, the first choice is air action, including the B-52s which only you and [Democratic] Senator [Richard] Russell [of Georgia] know about. It's the best kept secret of the war!"[6]

On April 30, 1970, the president went on nationwide TV to announce the invasion—or "incursion" as he called it. "If," Nixon declared, "when the chips are down, the world's most powerful nation, the United States of America, acts like a pitiful, helpless giant, the forces of totalitarianism and anarchy will threaten free nations and free institutions throughout the world."[7]

The ground invasion of Cambodia by 31,000 American and 43,000 South Vietnamese troops took place in May and June of 1970. It, too, proved highly ineffective in rooting out Communist forces. The president was now fuming and told Kissinger he wanted to escalate the air attacks on Cambodia: "They have got to go in there and I mean really go in . . . I want everything that can fly to go in there and crack the hell out of them. There is no limitation on mileage and there is no limitation on budget. Is that clear?"[8]

Kissinger then called his top assistant, General Alexander Haig, to relay the president's latest orders: "He wants a massive bombing campaign in Cambodia. He doesn't want to hear anything. It's an order, it's to be done. Anything that flies, on anything that moves. You got that?"[9]

But the secret bombing had unforeseen consequences: It pushed Communist troops even deeper into Cambodia's interior. And the B-52s followed them, dropping even more bombs.

Nixon himself had private doubts about the effectiveness of the air raids, telling Kissinger in December 1970, "[U.S. pilots] are just farting around doing nothing . . . running goddamn milk runs in order to get the Air Medal. It's a disgraceful performance. I want gunships in there. That means armed helicopters, DC-3s, anything else that will destroy personnel that can fly. I want it done! Get them off their ass!"[10]

The secret bombing occurred between March 1969 and August 1973. An astounding three million tons of bombs were dropped on Cambodia—killing an estimated half a million villagers in the process. Allied warplanes dropped just over two million tons of bombs during all of World War II. Military historians should charge Nixon with dropping more bombs than any other U.S. president. Because of Nixon, history can also record that Cambodia leads the sad list of the world's most-bombed countries.[11]

The Nixon bombings also proved to be a major source of Cambodian political instability. General Lon Nol's coup in 1970, shortly after the American raids began, displaced Prince Norodom Sihanouk. And in 1975, racked by turmoil, the country witnessed the rise to power of Pol Pot and the Khmer Rouge—a Communist political and military organization.

Kissinger biographer Walter Isaacson contends that the Khmer Rouge proceeded to murder one million Cambodians, and he quotes Prince Sihanouk as blaming "only two men for the tragedy in Cambodia: Mr. Nixon and Dr. Kissinger. Lon Nol was nothing without them, and the Khmer Rouge was nothing without Lon Nol. They [Nixon and Kissinger] demoralized America, they lost all of Indo-China to the communists, and they created the Khmer Rouge."[12]

On May 9, 1969, the cover on the secret bombing was blown— sort of. *The New York Times* printed a front-page story by William Beecher, which accurately described Operation Breakfast. Within hours, Kissinger asked FBI chief J. Edgar Hoover to find the sources of Beecher's article.[13]

Kissinger spoke with Hoover four times on May 9, asking him to find the leakers and declaring, according to a Hoover memorandum, that the White House "will destroy whoever did this if we can find him, no matter where he is."[14]

Among the first to be tapped: Secretary of Defense Melvin Laird, Laird's top military assistant, and three NSC staffers— including Morton Halperin. No leakers were found, so Kissinger had the wiretaps extended to two more members of his own staff.[15] During the next two years, Haig regularly transmitted to the FBI the names of National Security Council staff members and reporters (including Beecher) that were to have their phones illegally bugged.[16]

Meantime, the White House was still reeling from an exclusive Beecher had filed just days earlier—a May 6 dispatch replete with details of White House deliberations on how to react to North Korea's shootdown of a U.S. Navy reconnaissance plane over the Sea of Japan. The intrepid young reporter revealed that Nixon and Kissinger had considered B-52 bombing raids against airfields in North Korea, as well as the use of nuclear weapons. But the president and his NSC chief may have wondered whether Beecher might have known something even more secret, as investigative reporter Seymour Hersh theorized:

> For Nixon and Kissinger, the May 6 Beecher account may have brought additional chills, for they could not be sure how much the *Times* reporter knew about one of the truly important secrets of the EC-121 crisis. Did he know that Nixon had become quite drunk early in the crisis?

> Nixon's drinking had yet to be perceived as a significant problem for Kissinger and his immediate staff, and the incident was quickly hushed. [Kissinger aide Morton] Halperin, for one, was not told. Larry Eagleburger [another Kissinger aide] kept a standing lunch date with an old friend that first week after the EC-121 shootdown and was obviously upset. "Here's the President of the United States, ranting and raving—drunk in the middle of the crisis," the shaken Eagleburger told his friend.[17]

While Beecher's May 9 Cambodia bombing story—which did not mention the ultrasecrecy of the operation or the fraudulent record keeping—created almost equal consternation in the White House, it gained little media, political or public attention.

Nixon's "best-kept secret" held until July 1973, when the Senate Armed Services Committee held hearings into allegations about the illegal warfare. Testimony by an ex-military officer was critical, according to *Time* magazine:

> Former Air Force Major Hal M. Knight had served as an operations officer at a radar-guidance station in Bien Hoa, South Viet Nam, in 1970. He told the committee that he and others had doctored reports to make it appear that the Cambodian missions had been flown against targets in South Viet Nam. True reports on the Strategic Air Command bombing runs out of Guam or Thailand—as many as 407 in one month—were routed directly to President Nixon, National Security Adviser Henry Kissinger and a small handful of top officials, bypassing the normally classified Pentagon record-keeping channels.[18]

As a result of the hearings, Congress ordered that all bombing in Cambodia cease effective at midnight, August 14. The cost of the bombings to American taxpayers was later estimated to be $1.5 billion.[19]

When the bombings were finally fully exposed, critics of the president's Vietnam policies charged he had kept the attacks secret to prevent further opposition to his conduct of the war.

Indeed, disclosure of the bombings at their outset undoubtedly would have ramped up antiwar feelings and led to serious debate within Congress.

In his post-Watergate years, Nixon aide John Ehrlichman conceded that point:

> I think a lot of [the secrecy] had to do with Nixon's relationship to the Congress, and there were just some things that he felt he had to do as President, that he didn't think that Congress was going to back him on, and he didn't want to create situations where the Congress repudiated him. I think those may have been such areas.[20]

Historian Ken Hughes offers an equally valid insight:

> Nixon had won the 1968 election only after publicly pledging support for Lyndon Johnson's decision to halt the bombing of North Vietnam. How would he explain that in his first months in office he had secretly started bombing another country?[21]

In a rare burst of honesty, Nixon himself confessed as much in RN—saying that at least one "reason for secrecy was the problem of domestic antiwar protest. My administration was only two months old, and I wanted to provoke as little outcry as possible at the outset."[22]

Only a few courageous congressional souls eventually stuck out their necks to protest the furtive U.S. military action. On

July 31, 1973, Representative Robert Drinan, an ultraliberal Massachusetts Democrat, and a Roman Catholic priest, introduced the first impeachment resolution—dealing not with Watergate, but Cambodia. The resolution specifically took Nixon to task for lying to Congress.

Father Drinan "marshaled a compelling case," according to Nixon biographer J. Anthony Lukas, "that Nixon had ordered some 3,700 bombing raids over Cambodia while telling Congress, "We have scrupulously observed the neutrality of Cambodia for the last five years." But Lukas described Drinan's initiative as "premature and . . . a threat to eventual impeachment."

For if the matter came to a vote in the late summer of 1973, it certainly would have been voted down by a thunderous majority, making a subsequent impeachment effort harder to mount. The White House dallied with the idea of forcing a vote on the resolution, but then decided it would only give the notion greater credence.[23]

House Democratic Leader Thomas "Tip" O'Neill later disclosed just how counterproductive his fellow Bostonian's move could have been to eventual House impeachment proceedings. "Morally," O'Neill conceded, Drinan had a "good case . . . But politically, he damn near blew it. For if Drinan's resolution had come up for a vote at the time he filed it, it would have been overwhelmingly defeated—by something like 400 to 20. After that, with most of the members already on record as having voted once against impeachment, it would have been extremely difficult to get them to change their minds later," O'Neill recalled in his memoirs.[24] Judiciary Committee Chairman Peter Rodino did not act on the Drinan resolution.[25]

. . .

In an August 20, 1973 speech in New Orleans, Nixon answered his critics: "Had we announced the air strikes, the Cambodian government would have been compelled to protest, the bombing would have to stop, and American soldiers would have paid the price . . . with their lives." Nixon did not mention the issue of the falsified bombing records, according to a *New York Times* account of the speech. Nor did he bring up, or explain, a blatant lie he'd told a nationwide TV audience when he had announced the ground invasion of Cambodia on April 30, 1970. The lie? Nixon had asserted that "American policy since [the Geneva accords of 1954] has been to scrupulously respect the neutrality of the Cambodian people."

On August 22, 1973, Nixon held his first news conference in five long months. It was held outdoors on the sun-dappled grounds adjacent to his walled San Clemente estate. All of the TV and radio networks carried the session live. Watergate was the predominant subject of the combative give-and-take. But the final question gave the president another chance to defend the secret bombing of Cambodia:

> **Question:** Mr. President, in your Cambodian invasion speech of April 1970, you reported to the American people that the United States had been strictly observing the neutrality of Cambodia. I am wondering if you, in light of what we now know, that there were fifteen months of bombing of Cambodia previous to your statement, whether you owe an apology to the American people?

Nixon: Certainly not, and certainly not to the Cambodian people, because as far as this area is concerned,
the area of approximately ten miles which was bombed
during this period, no Cambodians had been in it for
years. It was totally occupied by the North Vietnamese
Communists. They were using this area for the purpose
of attacking and killing American Marines and soldiers
by the thousands. The bombing took place against those
North Vietnamese forces in enemy-occupied territory,
and as far as the American people are concerned, I think
the American people are very thankful that the president ordered what was necessary to save the lives of their
men and shorten this war which he found when he got
here, and which he ended.

An obviously angry Nixon, perhaps upset by the bluntness of
the question, nearly ran off the stage after the senior wire service
reporter intoned the traditional, "Thank you, Mr. President."
But at least one of Nixon's key handlers seemed pleased with the
president's response to the Cambodia question . . . or at least
with what he considered the impolite manner in which it was
asked. Gerald Warren, the deputy press secretary who helped
prepare the president for possible press conference questions,
sought out the reporter afterward and, without words, shook his
hand with a sly smile.

I was that reporter. And I believe Warren might have been
saying with that silent gesture: "Hah! The old man was well prepared, and he knocked that one out of the park!" That's still de-
batable, of course. (How did so many Cambodians die from
bombings in areas "totally occupied" by North Vietnamese

troops, Mr. President?) But this was the kind of handshake no reporter worth his or her adversarial salt ever likes to get. And maybe Warren was correct; Nixon was prepped for a question on the bombing. And his answer at least *sounded* convincing. My bet, however, is that Nixon didn't expect a Cambodia question with what I thought was a pretty good zinger.

While Henry Kissinger was a co-instigator of Nixon's bombing of Cambodia, at times he actually restrained Nixon's worst bombing impulses, as new tapes demonstrate. In 1972, for example, when the two men discussed the stepped-up bombing of the North, the president declares: "I'd rather use the nuclear bomb." But Kissinger responds: "That, I think, would just be too much." Nixon, however, continues to bait, or tease. Kissinger: "The nuclear bomb. Does that bother you? I just want you to think big."[26]

Despite the efforts of Father Drinan and other antiwar lawmakers, the secret raids on Cambodia—and their cover-up— failed to make it to Nixon's official list of impeachable offenses, as drawn up by the House Judiciary Committee in 1974.[27]

For a time, Nixon seemed obsessed with bombings in all parts of Indochina. On the eve of his first visit to the Soviet Union, for example, the president was very detailed in his instructions— telling aide Alexander Haig in a May 21, 1972 memo:

> I want a relentless air attack on our targets in North Vietnam during this period . . . Concentrate on those targets [rail lines and power plants] which will have major impact on civilian morale as well as accom-

plishing our primary objective of reducing the enemy's ability to conduct the war.

In the same memo, Nixon is extremely specific—ordering 1,200 air strikes a day, with 200 sorties focusing on targets around Hanoi. He directs that the frequency of the strikes be increased to 1,300 when the U.S.S. *Saratoga*, an aircraft carrier, arrived on station.

Less than a month after this memo was sent, the bungled June 17, 1972 Watergate burglary started to distract the president from micromanaging the bombings. He would soon be engaged, almost full-time, in micromanaging his own survival in office.

On the ropes and ready to toss in the towel in that fight, however, Nixon had a really bizarre eleventh-hour bomb-related anti-impeachment move that involved—of all things—dropping a nuclear weapon on Capitol Hill.

In a March 20, 1974 telephone conversation with Secretary of State Kissinger, White House chief of staff Al Haig reported: "I was told to get the football." Kissinger asked, "What do you mean?" Haig responded: "His black nuclear bag. He is going to drop it on the Hill." Haig told Kissinger that Nixon was "just unwinding . . . don't take him too seriously."[28]

Was Nixon just joking, or was he drunk again? Both Kissinger and Haig referred to the president, behind his back, as "Our Drunk." Kissinger biographer Walter Isaacson says Nixon's booze binges had become a major concern to Kissinger's top aides:

The drinking was also a festering issue among his staff, who often listened in on the slurred late-night conversations. Kissinger used this to his advantage; he needed their support, he would tell aides, because as they alone knew, he was the one man who kept "that drunken lunatic" from doing things that would "blow up the world."[29]

Cambodia was not the only part of the war Nixon tried to hide from the public. Recently declassified tapes and documents have exploded a bombshell about how Nixon slandered a distinguished U.S. military commander in Vietnam, Air Force General John Lavelle, in order to cover up his own participation in the expanded bombing of North Vietnam.

Now buried at Arlington National Cemetery, Lavelle's decorations include the Distinguished Service Medal, Legion of Merit with three oak clusters, Air Medal with oak leaf cluster and Air Force Commendation Medal with oak leaf cluster. But in 1972, Lavelle became Nixon's fall guy for obeying what turned out to be the commander in chief's own top-secret orders to expand the bombing of North Vietnam in late 1971 and early 1972. Nixon didn't want to take the heat for that decision, unpopular with critics of the war—so Lavelle was sacrificed as the scapegoat, stripped of two of his four stars, and sacked. The decision clearly bothered Nixon. It was too late for remedial action, but the president's conscience was obviously pricked after Lavelle was hung out to dry.

Oval Office tapes released in recent years show Nixon telling Kissinger: "I don't want to hurt an innocent man . . . Frankly, Henry, I don't feel right about pushing him [Lavelle] into this thing and then, and then giving him a bad rap . . . I just don't want him to be made a goat, goddammit."[30]

Yet, Nixon refused to 'fess up that he had authorized the escalated bombings. In fact, he resorted to a bald-faced lie to hide his own guilt and finger Lavelle—telling a June 26, 1972 press conference the stepped-up assault on SAM missile sites in the north "wasn't authorized . . . It was proper for [Lavelle] to be relieved and retired."[31]

In September 1972, Lavelle led off Senate Armed Service Committee hearings prompted by the bombing controversy. He maintained that all of his actions were authorized and taken to protect the lives of airmen in his command. He said he had applied rules of engagement approved by the Joint Chiefs of Staff. The general told the senators he was just following orders and described his fate as "a catastrophic blemish on my record . . . for conscientiously doing the job I was expected to do." Lavelle also vigorously denied an associated charge that he had falsified records about the supposedly unauthorized missions.

President Nixon remained publicly silent during the hearings.

In early October 1972, the panel rejected Lavelle's nomination for retirement as a lieutenant general. The vote was 14-2. Instead, he was retired at his permanent rank of major general (two stars), and his name was dragged through the mud as a rogue officer who decided to bomb North Vietnam on his own. Lavelle never knew for sure that the bombing orders originated with Nixon.

Lavelle continued to insist on his innocence until his death at sixty-two in 1979. Not until an investigative article in *Air Force Magazine* in 2007 were General Lavelle's top rank and excellent reputation on the way to being fully restored. The article's findings were presented to Lavelle's widow, Mary Jo, then 91, and the couple's seven children. "Jack was a good man, a good husband, a good father and a good officer. I wish he was alive to hear this news," his widow said in a prepared statement.[32]

The Lavelle family chose Patrick Casey, a Pennsylvania lawyer, to try to get the Air Force to reopen the case and restore Lavelle to the rank of full general. In 2009, the Air Force Board for the Correction of Military Records endorsed the general's exoneration. President Barack Obama and top Pentagon officials have now joined the move—and General John Lavelle's long journey from scapegoat to hero next goes before the Senate for final approval.

Too bad we had to learn this of this miscarriage of justice—described by the *New York Times* in 2010 as "a cover-up, cowardice and scapegoating in the Nixon White House"—decades too late for General Lavelle to live to see his honor restored.[33]

After the *Times* ran an account of the Lavelle episode in 2010, it received a letter to the editor from former CIA Director James Woolsey, who was the general counsel of the 1972 Senate Committee that found Lavelle had exceeded his authority under the written rules of engagement:

> But we did not know that President Nixon had ordered General Lavelle, through Ambassador Ellsworth Bunker, to strike the surface-to-air missile sites at will. In my opinion, the evidence is also clear that General Lavelle neither ordered nor knew of false reporting. Mr. Nixon nonetheless publicly charged General Lavelle with exceeding his orders.

Woolsey concluded by saying "had the committee known of Mr. Nixon's action in 1972, it would have never voted to deny

General Lavelle the honor of retiring at the four-star rank he in fact held."[34]

The American Conservative weighed in with, "Great for the Lavelle family, which includes a widow and seven children who have had to live with this blemish all their lives. Bad for Richard Nixon's family, which has to face yet another embarrassing revelation about the late president."[35]

Journalist Jules Witcover has an astute reaction to Lavelle's belatedly discovered innocence. In a column in the *Daytona Beach News-Journal,* he says the case constitutes additional "documented evidence of Nixon's contempt for others and his willingness to let them take the fall for him as needed." Witcover adds that the Lavelle case provides "reminders of the perfidies, large and small, of our only resigned president." Like many Nixon junkies, Witcover observes that, with the continuing declassification and release of our thirty-seventh president's tapes and documents "more evidence of his deceptive nature keeps trickling in."[36]

Noting that the "only thing the public likes more than a good true-crime story is a good exoneration," *Newsweek* likens Lavelle to a number of other innocent "victims of justice gone wrong"— including Joan of Arc; those killed as a result of the Salem witch trials; and Alfred Dreyfus, a French Army officer wrongly accused in 1894, and later cleared, of selling military secrets to Germany.[37]

So just add the freshly revealed slandering of General John Lavelle to all the other ethical violation and crimes— past and future—that President Richard Nixon will get away with.

. . .

By August 1974, the Watergate scandal had forced Nixon's resignation. However, the Vietnam War—the first war America ever lost—did not end until April 1975, when North Vietnamese troops overran Saigon.

There had been some 20,000 U.S. combat deaths since Nixon launched Operation Breakfast, as a new president who had won the job on a pledge to "end the war and win the peace" in Vietnam.

FIFTEEN

THE WORLD'S MOST POWERFUL DRUNK

Behind President Richard Nixon's back, some top aides—including Henry Kissinger and Alexander Haig—demeaned him as "Our Drunk."

The virulently anti-Semitic Nixon was no kinder to Kissinger, calling him my "Jew boy" behind his back and occasionally to his face, as a way to humiliate him and keep him in his place.[1]

In a 2006 study by Duke University psychiatrists, Dr. Marvin Schwartz concluded: "The extensiveness of Richard Nixon's alcohol abuse was pretty remarkable and alarming, given the authority he had."[2] Nixon's fondness for alcohol secretly haunted his personal and political lives. And it only intensified as he climbed the political ladder toward the ultimate pinnacle of power—where he was seldom far from the "football," a black satchel stocked with classified plans for unleashing U.S. nuclear weapons.

Nixon's dipsomaniacal tendencies began during his undergraduate career where he gained a reputation for binge drinking. The future president guzzled plenty of gin (which eventually—when mixed with vermouth—became his drink of choice) in a San Francisco bar on his first Whittier College debate trip. In another college episode, after a few rounds of drinks with friends, Nixon got so looped he passed out. Recalled Whittier schoolmate Philip Blew, "The affair turned into a spree . . . and we, in effect, had to pour Dick into bed."[3] While bouts of heavy drinking often characterize the college experience, Nixon's penchant for liquor followed him past graduation.

As a young adult, Nixon kept his growing reliance on alcohol from his non-drinking Quaker parents. On the night of his first congressional election victory in 1946, he and other family members were at the home of Norman Chandler, the publisher of the *Los Angeles Times*. According to Mrs. Chandler, who was known as "Buff," Nixon came out in the hall after everyone had ordered milk and said, "Buff, could you get me a double bourbon? I don't want Mother and Father to see me take a drink." It was "a very small thing," Mrs. Chandler said in 1977. But "for a man that age, who'd just won an election . . . it showed a funny cheating quality that never changed through the years."[4]

Nixon's drinking followed him into the House, and then the Senate—and, next, when he served as President Dwight Eisenhower's two-term vice president.[5] During Nixon's renomination as Ike's veep nominee at the 1956 GOP convention, Bob Haldeman was disturbed by his first observation of Nixon, who was the young Haldeman's political hero. Haldeman would go on to faithfully serve Nixon in several future campaigns and, finally, in the White House, as the president's chief aide. Haldeman describes the 1956 encounter this way: "Before gray-colored draperies in a San Francisco hotel room, Dick Nixon stood among a group of Republican delegates. This was the first time I had seen

Nixon close up. I moved closer and listened in dismay. My first thought was that he had been drinking. His sentences were almost incoherent; his monologue rambled on circuitously while everyone around him looked at each other, wonderingly."

Haldeman claimed most of Nixon's slurred late-night monologues were fueled mainly by fatigue—and that Nixon couldn't drink when he was tired. "One beer would transform his speech into the rambling elocution of a Bowery wino."[6] Haldeman was not the only one troubled by Nixon's drinking. President Eisenhower himself was so concerned he sent his brother Milton on a trip with the vice president to Moscow in 1959. Before a dinner among a group of Americans, Milton reported that a "terribly upset" Nixon had "about six martinis" and soon exhibited odd behavior: "As soon as we sat down, he started going around the table to find out what everybody thinks about the speech [Nixon made on Soviet TV]. And he'd keep interrupting the person: 'Did you hear me say this? Did you hear me say this?' Then he began using abusive—well, not abusive, but vulgar swear words in this mixed company . . . He was a strange character."[7]

Following his narrow loss to Kennedy in the 1960 presidential election, Nixon went on to another election defeat—this time, in 1962, at the hands of Democratic California Governor Pat Brown. The GOP candidate also went on a roaring bender after the lopsided results were in. The next morning, the hungover and trembling loser blew a gasket and declared: "Just think what you'll be missing. You won't have Nixon to kick around anymore, gentleman, because this is my last press conference."

After that defeat, TV entertainer Jack Paar ran into Nixon on Paradise Island in the Bahamas, stating, "He was a sad, depressed man, as pathetic a national figure as I had ever seen. He was drinking heavily, and my heart went out to his family . . . Nixon would sit and brood and occasionally utter a few words of profanity . . ."[8]

Two years later, after making a speech to the 1964 Republican convention (which nominated Senator Barry Goldwater for president) in San Francisco, Nixon invited some of his closest staff to his hotel suite for food and drinks. John Ehrlichman, who did not drink, was one of the last to leave. In *Witness to Power*, he recalled being "offended" by the former vice president's behavior. "Nixon made some clumsy passes at a young woman [Editor's note: reportedly Pat Buchanan's future wife Shelley Scarney, a bright and beautiful blond assistant to Nixon's longtime secretary, Rose Mary Woods] in the group. "No one made any attempt to rescue the embarrassed girl or deflect Nixon, and he persisted. She appeared as unwilling to offend him as the rest of us, but at least she escaped the arm he had draped over her shoulder. She blushed brightly and left the suite. The rest of us soon said our good-nights and left [Bob] Haldeman to steer Nixon to bed."[9] Nixon would next address the GOP convention in 1968—again accepting the party's nomination as its presidential candidate. Defeating Hubert Humphrey in November, Nixon attained the political prize that had eluded him eight years earlier.

The constant pressures of the presidency, however, likely only increased the new president's desire to drink. Various instances throughout his administration illustrate this tendency. When the crippled *Apollo 13* splashed down safely in the Pacific Ocean at 1:07 P.M. on April 17, 1970, church bells rang out around the country—and in his Executive Office Building hideaway, Nixon got plastered. He was soon passing out cigars and telling the White House switchboard to connect him with a long list of astronauts and astronauts' wives. He asked the same question over and over again, "Isn't this a great day? Isn't this a great day?"

Nixon biographer Richard Reeves notes, "One of his calls was to Jerry Ford, the House Republican leader. Nixon was so excited that he told Ford he should call Supreme Court Justice William O. Douglas with the good news. He had forgotten that, four days before, he had persuaded Ford to publicly call for the impeachment of Douglas, the most liberal justice—as revenge for the rejection of [Nixon Supreme Court nominee Harold] Carswell. By 4:15 that afternoon, the president was drunk, falling asleep on the couch in EOB 175."[10] These sorts of drunken events would plague Nixon until the end of his administration.

In his final months, the president spent many nights zonked out on booze and Seconal sleeping pills. "He wasn't much good for anything [official business] after 6 P.M.," one White House aide conceded privately many years later. Such was obviously the case in the early evening of October 11, 1973. Passed out in bed, the president was unable to speak on the phone with Edward Heath—whose aides said the British prime minister was keen to discuss the latest details of the freshly erupted Arab-Israel War. Transcripts of Henry Kissinger's conversations released in recent years record the following exchange between the then secretary of state and his assistant, Brent Scowcroft, after Kissinger tried to converse with Nixon about the request from Heath's people:

Kissinger: "Can we tell them no? When I talked to the president, he was loaded."

Scowcroft: "Right, OK. I will say the president will not be available until first thing in the morning, but you will be this evening."

TELECON
Scowcroft/Kissinger
October 11, 1973
7:55 p.m.

K. Hello.

S. This is..., Henry. The switchboard just got a call from 10 Downing Street to inquire whether the President would be available for a call within 30 minutes from the Prime Minister. The subject would be the Middle East.

K. Can we tell them no? When I talked to the President he was loaded.

S. We could tell him the President is not available and perhaps he can call you.

K. I will be at Mr. Bradens and the President will be available tomorrow morning our time.

S. Are you coming over here at all this evening?

K. No, first thing in the morning.

S. Did you talk to ~~Schermerhorn~~ Schlosinger (?) about the F-4s scheduled for tomorrow?

K. I think two a day is fine.

S. Two a day can ....

K. Throw in another one and make it six.

S. They have in mind keeping a two a day schedule. Send two from here and two from Europe and then two from here again.

K. For an indefinite period?

S. At least through six.

K. Then tell Dinitz he is getting at least six but that we may keep it going.

S. Right, ok. I will say the President will not be available until first thing in the morning but you will be this evening.

K. In fact, I would welcome it.

S. Very good.

This transcript of a telephone conversation, released in recent years, shows that Nixon, a heavy drinker, was—in Henry Kissinger's term—"loaded" when the British prime minister was urgently trying to reach the president by telephone.
COURTESY OF NIXON LIBRARY/NATIONAL ARCHIVES.

Following President Nixon's rambling "I am not a crook" news conference at Disney World a month later, and his post-speech slapping of an airman, he flew to Key Biscayne, Florida. The president had what he described to his pilot as "a couple of good belts" on the short flight. The pilot—Colonel Ralph Albertazzie—later recalled the scene when the obviously drunk Nixon got off the plane. At the foot of the steps at Homestead Air Force Base, where a general waited to greet him for the usual exchange of salutes, Nixon bowed, according to the pilot, "from the waist, grandly, magnificently, with great flourish."[11]

Kissinger usually went along on Nixon's frequent weekend trips to Key Biscayne. While there, Henry assiduously tried to avoid contact with the president and his favorite drinking pal, Bebe Rebozo. But "Hank"—as reporters playfully privately called the German-accented intellectual who was born "Heinz"—was persuaded to go out to dinner with Nixon on one unforgettable Florida evening, according to investigative reporter Seymour Hersh:

One night in Miami, Nixon stopped an attractive woman as he left a restaurant—after having had a few drinks too many—and offered her a job in the White House. "She looks like she's built for you, Henry," the President said [to Kissinger]. [A close aide to Kissinger] learned of the encounter from a Secret Service man. "Hearing this kind of a thing made my veins hurt," the aide says. "The President of the United States, drunk in a restaurant, making crude remarks and engaging in familiarity with a strange woman in a public place—all clearly attributable to martinis . . ."

Hersh says Kissinger's aides "were convinced that they were dealing with a defective President, and Kissinger did little to reassure them."[12]

Another incident occurred on December 17, 1973, at a small White House dinner party. Sen. Barry Goldwater heard a president whose persistent blabbing made no sense and wandered aimlessly. "I became concerned," Goldwater later wrote. "I had never seen Nixon talk so much, yet so erratically—as if he were a tape with unexpected blank sections." The senator—known for his outspokenness—admonished Nixon: "Act like a president!" But nothing could stop the obviously out-of-control chief executive, who rambled on and on over dinner with what Goldwater later termed "ceaseless, chippy chatter . . . incessantly sputtering something, constantly switching subjects."

Senator Goldwater wondered to himself, "Is the president coming apart because of Watergate?" Goldwater followed up on his concern by phoning the top White House congressional lobbyist, Bryce Harlow, the next day. Harlow, who had also been at the dinner, confirmed Goldwater's suspicions: Nixon had been drunk before and during the meal.[13]

On another occasion, the president's drinking made him sound like perhaps he was speaking in religious tongues. At the staff Christmas party in the East Room in 1973, a large group gathered around the president to hear him exclaim: "Six days before Christmas and all through the house not a creature was stirring, not even the President. It might be kind of hard to do, but if you can't get enough [to drink] here, come on upstairs. We've got plenty. If you drink too much, you might go in the wrong door and surprise some girl. But if you say you were at the White House, she'll say come on in." Noting the strange comments in

[7-10-71
Item 6]

2.

- this is first time Russians have dealt to us

- it is _not_ to tell anybody — Laird, Mitchell, Connally
  etc

whenever K calls - Haig shld notify P.
from Pak — say simply it is on, off, postponed
no more info from these
use Eureka for success

ON-FILE NSC
RELEASE -
INSTRUCTIONS
APPLY-

- K to go direct to P. Tues AM
  when he lands - regardless of time

- P. laid out Mid East position to Haig
  we will take no Jewish money
  get K. out of the play - Haig handle it
  let Rabin know they have to have a
  good faith bargaining position
  no Jew can handle the Israeli thing
  Haig tell Rogers - go to brink on this - not over

- forget the Jews - they're against P-

- told Haig to go ahead on Laird to Packard

Haldeman's notes from a meeting in which Nixon ordered that no American Jew, including Henry Kissinger, is to be involved in a major way in Middle East peace talks. COURTESY OF NIXON LIBRARY/NATIONAL ARCHIVES.

The Final Days, Bob Woodward and Carl Bernstein reported, "It didn't make any sense, but [the staff] laughed anyway."[14]

On one of his final nights in the White House, Nixon acted mighty strange while drinking and praying and sobbing with Henry Kissinger in the Lincoln Sitting Room. When Henry got back to his office, the president was on the phone. As Kissinger aide Larry Eagleburger listened in, he became "shocked" at Nixon's demeanor: "The President was slurring his words. He was drunk. He was out of control . . . Eagleburger could barely make out what the President was saying. He was almost incoherent. It was pathetic. Eagleburger felt ill and hung up." But Nixon had one final request of Kissinger: "Henry, please don't ever tell anyone that I cried and that I was not strong."[15] This would be one of the last drinks Nixon had before his official departure from the White House on August 9, 1974.

Kissinger sometimes offered an excuse for his own willingness to put up with Nixon's heavy drinking, according to Kissinger expert Walter Isaacson: "When he was tired and under strain, Kissinger would say, Nixon would begin slurring his words after just one or two drinks, even if he wasn't really drunk. Still, Nixon's drinking became unsettling to Kissinger, who barely drank at all. He would poke fun at 'my drunken friend' the way people joke about things that truly scare them." Yet, Isaacson added, in NSC staff meetings, Kissinger often cited the president's drinking in an effort to curry loyalty: "Kissinger used this to his advantage; he needed their support, he would tell aides, because as they alone knew, he was the one man who kept 'that drunken lunatic' from doing things that would 'blow up the world.' "[16]

A final bit of irony deserves mention. During Nixon's presidency, Congress passed and the president signed a law to curb alcohol abuse. It was referred to as the "Hughes Act" for the pivotal role ex-alcoholic Senator Harold Hughes played in its approval. The Hughes Act identified alcohol abuse and alcoholism as major public health problems, and set up an agency to combat them.

Little did Hughes, or most anyone outside the White House, know that Nixon was drinking and also taking pills (Seconal and Dilantin) that significantly exaggerate alcohol's sometimes stupefying effects. During Nixon's long political career, Nixon gave in to his alcoholic demons, and there was almost total public ignorance of his condition.

It's sad that nobody with any influence on Nixon's behavior earlier in his life ever suggested rehab and abstinence for a man who, when three sheets to the wind, seemed mentally unstable . . . and who, as president, had the power to blow up the world. Actually, more than once, in phone calls to Kissinger, the besotted president ordered, "Nuke 'em." And even when sober, as this new tape shows, Nixon proposed the nuclear option:

Nixon: I still think we ought to take the North Vietnamese dikes out now. Will that drown people?

Kissinger: About two hundred thousand people.

Nixon: No, no, no, I'd rather use the nuclear bomb. Have you got that, Henry?

Kissinger: That, I think, would just be too much.

Nixon: The nuclear bomb, does that bother you? . . . I just want you to think big, Henry, for Christ's sakes . . . [17]

Shouldn't there be some psychological, emotional, physical and drug and alcohol tests for presidential candidates to help determine their fitness for the high-pressure life as leader of the free world? Nixon's own secret psychiatrist—Albert Hutschnecker—who began treating Nixon in the fifties, publicly proposed a mental health evaluation for prospective chief executives. Before his death in 2001, the doctor privately expressed concern over whether Nixon should have been allowed to hold high office.[18]

SIXTEEN

BATTERER IN CHIEF

Richard Nixon was certainly one of our dirtiest political fighters. But probably no other American politician actually punched, pushed, kicked, slapped, shouldered, shoved or upended as many folks who'd ignited—usually without malicious intent—his volcanic temper. The way he repeatedly behaved would land most people behind bars. Nixon's flying fists were usually dispatched as "sucker punches"—unexpected blows from out of left field when the opponent's guard was fully down. Nixon threw one such punch at a political aide—and a handicapped one at that— some fifty years ago. Had that been confirmed at the time, the newspaper headline might have read, "Vice President Assaults Crippled Campaign Consultant." But the punch, which joins myriad evidence of Nixon's violent nature, only became verified in a newly released document from the National Archives.

The incident itself took place in the fading hours of Nixon's bitterly waged, losing 1960 presidential race against Senator John Kennedy. The day before the election, Nixon put on a four-hour telethon from a Detroit studio. As airtime approached, Nixon became infuriated with TV consultant Everett Hart when Hart had declined to run a last-minute errand for the vice president. Before the aide even considered putting up his dukes, however, the short-fused Nixon let go with a haymaker to Hart's rib cage. One of the aide's arms was shriveled and he was recovering from major cardiac surgery.

On loan to the Nixon campaign from a top Madison Avenue ad agency, Hart quit on the spot and refused ever to work for Nixon again.

Muckraking newspaper columnist Drew Pearson referred to the incident in a 1968 column. He opined that Nixon's punch "could have killed" Hart, who died in 1973 after more heart surgery.[1]

Yet only now, in newly released documents, comes verification of the incident. In an October 7, 1968 "confidential" memo to chief campaign advisor Bob Haldeman, Nixon's personal secretary Rose Mary Woods reported, "As far as the [Pearson] story is concerned, it really happened." She had just talked with Hart on the phone, and he had 'fessed up to being Pearson's likely source. Woods said she was told by Hart, "RN did hit me. I was really mad because I had had a rib removed when I had had open-heart surgery and that is where he hit me—in the ribs."[2]

In the lead-up to the 1968 election, Nixon was violent toward another campaign aide—and an important and permanent one. Twenty-five-year-old Dwight Chapin, a U.S.C. grad, was the staffer in charge of the candidate's schedule. "This last role was important for Nixon, who more than most politicians needed to have his schedule tightly regimented. Disruptions and interruptions bothered him to the point of fury," writes Nixon biogra-

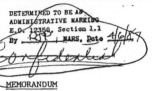
October 7, 1968

MEMORANDUM

TO: Bob Haldeman

FROM: Rose Mary Woods

     Ev Hart called the New York office for me today and I returned the call from the plane while we were in Washington, D. C.

     He said: "I wanted to call you about that thing that happened on Friday (the Pearson column). As far as the story is concerned -- it really happened.

     "About three weeks ago I talked with a fellow that I know - he is a lawyer - an acquaintance - and we got into the usual conversation about what RN is really like. You know how people ask whether in private a person who is in public life beats his wife - or drinks too much -or what-have-you. I said there is nothing like that at all. I said there are probably one or two little instances - I quoted that one incident - never thinking that it was going any further than the guy I was talking to.

     "Of course, what he or Pearson did was to take that little story and build a whole article about it.

     "I was floored by the whole thing, particularly where they said I had been approached by one of his law partners. That

A note, written in 1968, from Nixon's secretary Rose Mary Woods to Nixon campaign aide Bob Haldeman confirming that, in the 1960 campaign, an angry Nixon punched a handicapped TV advisor. COURTESY OF NIXON LIBRARY/NATIONAL ARCHIVES.

was completely wrong. What happened there -- he asked me
whether I was going to do any work for him this year. I said'
well a friend of mine was trying to arrange something with a
lawyer but I didn't think I would work this year. I will not
be because of personal reasons -- I am leaving later this
afternoon to go into the hospital for about 10 days for an
operation. But I did not tell him it was for personal reasons.
So he just mixed that all up.

"But as to the story -- RN did hit me. (Here rnw
said - who was in the studio? He said - just myself and some
newspaper men - a couple of the newspapers carried it the next
day.

"I was really mad because I had had a rib removed
when I had had open heart surgery and that is where he hit me
-- in the ribs. Ted Rogers was up in the control room watching
this thing. The Boss apologized but I was so upset and the show
was going to last four hours so I went up to Ted and said I am
going on out to Los Angeles. I flew out with Jim Bassett instead
of waiting to come with the group.

"I will tell you how upset I was about it -- the
day after the election in Los Angeles most of us were asked
to come by - I don't know but I believe we were getting little
campaign gifts or something. I didn't go in and I didn't come
back on the plane to Washington with you."

```
                        - 3 -


        At this point rmw said -- what was the name of
the lawyer? He said - "I would rather not say." rmw said --
well he probably made some money on that story. He said I don't
think he would be after money - he makes good money and he lives
at the UN PLAZA. He repeated that he had told him this three
to three and one-half weeks ago. When he saw the column he
realized that it must have been a set up.
        We talked about his going into the hospital for
a few minutes and then I said -- don't you really think you
should tell me the name of the man -- he said Freidberg.
        In case anyone else wants to talk with him -- I
don't know why -- but he will be in University Hospital for
the next ten days.
```

pher Jonathan Aitken in *Nixon: A Life*. Fury overtook Nixon in 1967, when he was less than satisfied with Chapin's work. According to Aitken: "On one occasion he was so enraged by some scheduling transgression that he threw Chapin against a wall, bruising his arm . . ."[3]

Another victim of a seething Nixon was Jim McManus, then a White House reporter for Westinghouse Broadcasting. In March of 1971, temporarily isolated from the rest of the press corps, McManus was striding along a street in Des Moines near Nixon, hoping to ask the president about a bombing carried out that day by an antiwar group in a men's room at the U.S. Capitol.

Nixon was still hot under the collar that several antiwar demonstrators had tossed snowballs his way as he left his speaking engagement in Des Moines. And to have a reporter so close to him seems to have fully sparked his notorious rage. McManus recalls the result with great clarity:

> Dick Keiser, who was chief of the Secret Service protection detail and who had been a friend of mine at Indiana University many years previously, let me move inside his protection and fall in step with Nixon on his left. I extended the mike toward his face and Nixon, a onetime Whittier College footballer, took a sidestep and slammed his shoulder hard into mine. No question that it was intentional. I tripped and started to stumble sideways. Dick Keiser, in one elegant move, put his shoulder to me on the other side and straightened me up quickly.

After McManus regained his equilibrium, and Nixon his composure, McManus was able get the president on tape denouncing the bombing as a "shocking act of violence that will outrage all Americans." McManus shared his tape with the rest of us reporters, but now discloses, "I did not mention to [Press Secretary Ron] Ziegler or any reporters about being whacked by POTUS. I considered it a small matter, and not a surprising response from Nixon." McManus also notes: "One doubts that [Nixon] ever picked on anyone whose relative status—or gender—guaranteed a counter-attack."[4]

Despite such boasts as "the tougher it gets, the cooler I get," Nixon had been known to lose it publicly on a number of other occasions. He had a nasty disposition since at least the age of seven, when he struck a smaller playmate over the head with the blunt edge of a hatchet in order to steal a jar of pollywogs.[5]

In 1952, the vice president-elect publicly slapped a woman. The incident occurred in Long Beach, California, and involved Zita Remley, a Democrat who'd helped to expose one of Nixon's 1946 political tricks: the establishment of an anonymous telephone campaign in which women called Democrats and said, "[Congressman] Jerry Voorhis [Nixon's opponent] is a communist." According to Fawn Brodie, a Nixon biographer, "In a sudden fit of rage, he walked over and slapped her. There were no cameras or newsmen to catch the happening, and Mrs. Remley, fearful of losing her job, told only a few friends."[6]

Vice President Nixon kicked an anti-Nixon demonstrator during a trip to Latin America. And during his 1960 presidential campaign Nixon got really steamed on an overly long motorcade ride. The candidate used both feet to repeatedly kick the back of the car seat occupied by his military aide, Major Don Hughes. "He wouldn't stop," remembered fellow passenger Bob Haldeman. "Thump! Thump! Thump! The seat and the hapless Hughes jolted forward jaggedly as Nixon vented his rage."[7]

In 1962, in Nixon's most famous public loss of composure, a red-eyed, trembling, hungover, and defeated California gubernatorial candidate told the press: "Gentlemen, just think what you're going to be missing. You won't have Nixon to kick around anymore, because gentlemen, this is my last press conference." On his way off the stage, he told his press secretary, Herb Klein, "I gave it to them right in the ass!"[8]

President John Kennedy led a host of political observers who thought Nixon's L.A. performance showed he had flipped his lid and probably ended his political life. In a congratulatory phone call to Governor Pat Brown—who beat Nixon by 300,000 votes—the president declared: "You reduced him to the nut house . . . That last farewell speech of his . . . it shows that he belongs on the couch." Brown agreed, saying, "This is a very peculiar fellow . . . I really think that he is psycho. He's an able man, but he's nuts!"[9]

Investigative reporter Seymour Hersh exposed three alleged Nixon wife-beating incidents—one a post-resignation attack in San Clemente that sent Pat to a nearby emergency room.[10] In the mid-'60s, clued-in Capitol Hill reporters, including yours truly, heard from several completely reliable sources that Nixon had also beat Pat when he was a member of Congress.

Even children were not immune from Nixon's hair-trigger volatility. When Nixon was running for California governor in 1962, anti-Nixon prankster Dick Tuck made up a big hand-held sign for the candidate's visit to San Francisco's Chinatown. Tuck's sign read WELCOME NIXON in English at the top. Then, the major part of it—in Chinese characters—asked HOW ABOUT THE HUGHES LOAN? Tuck got a young Chinese boy to carry the placard.

As a TV news crew and still photographers captured the scene, Nixon posed with the boy and the sign . . . until a Chinese elder exclaimed, "No! No! No!" and told Nixon the meaning of the Chinese characters. Nixon grabbed the sign out of the frightened lad's hand and then ripped it to pieces.[11]

As president, Nixon threw an ashtray against a wall when he learned of the arrests of the Watergate burglars.[12] He pushed an FBI agent against a White House wall after Bob Haldeman's office was sealed off during Watergate.[13] Nixon slapped Air Force Sgt.

Edward Kleizo at a military airfield near Disney World after telling the world, "I am not a crook."[14] And, while walking into an auditorium in New Orleans, the president grabbed Ron Ziegler by the shoulders, spun him around, and then shoved his press secretary so hard that the press immediately raised questions about Nixon's mental health and possible medication abuse.[15]

There was no press on hand to witness a mad dash-and-bump by Nixon that landed presidential aide Joe Laitin on the floor near the stairway leading to the supersecret Situation Room in the White House basement. "And just as I was about to ascend the stairway, a guy came running down the stairs two steps at a time. He had a frantic look on his face, wild-eyed, like a madman. And he bowled me over, so I kind of lost my balance. And before I could pick myself up, six athletic-looking young men leapt over me, pursuing him. I suddenly realized they were Secret Service agents, that I'd been knocked over by the President of the United States."[16]

Ron Zeigler was on the bad end of a privately raging Nixon when the president wildly and loudly demanded that North Vietnam never again be referred to as anything other than "the enemy" in press briefings. The president stressed the importance of this strange order by bursting unannounced into Ziegler's office and kicking his aide's desk. As the door closed behind Nixon, the cowering Ziegler muttered, "The Old Man's really high again."[17]

Secretary of State Henry Kissinger would later observe that Nixon's mood, since his 1972 election victory, was dominated by "sullen hostility."[18] The *New York Times* reported that during some bombing offensives against the North Vietnamese, the president was "throwing stuff against the wall." And *Times* columnist James Reston termed the bombing "war by tantrum."[19] Secretary

of Defense James Schlesinger noted that Nixon was overly hostile
and not exactly in his right mind toward the end of his reign. In a
bold and unprecedented move, the worried Schlesinger instructed
the Joint Chiefs of Staff to disregard any military order originat-
ing from the White House.[20]

What kind of vengeful thoughts might have crossed Nixon
consultant Everett Hart's mind if the 1960 victim of Nixon's
physical abuse had watched the resurrected presidential con-
tender's 1968 appearance on TV's *Rowan & Martin's Laugh-In*?
In an effort to demonstrate he was just a regular guy, the "new"
Nixon popped up on that hit show to utter its signature punch
line: "Sock it to me!"

SEVENTEEN

THREATENING TO FIRE KISSINGER, ZIEGLER: NIXON'S WAR ON THE PRESS

Presidents who don't complain about the press are rare. Barack Obama, for example, apparently doesn't find much to like about Fox News. A tiff between his White House and Fox reached a peak in October 2009, when the president's communications director Anita Dunn charged that Fox is "opinion journalism masquerading as news."[1]

No president hated the press as deeply, however, as Richard Nixon. And our thirty-seventh chief executive was an equal opportunity hater—despising not just one network or one newspaper once in a while, but bitterly ranting and scheming against almost all the news media almost all the time. Nixon's loathing of the Fourth Estate was so intense, he even raised the possibility of firing his top foreign policy advisor and his chief spokesman for not obeying his antipress orders, as newly released White House tapes reveal.[2]

On September 14, 1971, a highly agitated Nixon phoned his chief of staff, Bob Haldeman, to report that National Security

Advisor Henry Kissinger had been talking with James "Scotty" Reston of the *New York Times*:

"You're kidding!" the astonished aide replied.

"I want the goddamn staff to understand—and he [Henry] must not have understood this—that the blackout on the *Times* is total," Nixon ordered. Haldeman explained, "Well, he understood it. He stood in your office when we talked about this, and you made the point to him that he was not to see Reston; that you would not see Reston."

Nixon replied, "That's right. That's right. That's right."

Haldeman then exclaimed, "God!"

Nixon ordered, "You'd better tell Henry he must not talk to him; he's valuable. He must not talk to him, period! Under penalties of, frankly, dismissal."

Directing an obvious blast at Kissinger, Nixon added: "We cannot have our people get soft because they are trying to suck up to some of these newspaper people."

As for the prospect of a Nixon interview with Reston—which Kissinger had brought up with Nixon—the president said: "Why do I waste my time, you know, by being examined by this son of a bitch? He will never be in my office as long as I'm president! Never!" Before ending the conversation, the president reminded Haldeman that the White House press blackout extended to *Time, Newsweek,* the *Los Angeles Times* and the *Washington Post.*

The Nixon White House went on to wiretap and spy on some of the president's main foes in the press, get the IRS to audit their taxes, search for "homos" and pot smokers in the press corps and even plot the assassination of the president's most hated reporter, Jack Anderson.

The newly released tapes show that Nixon had it in for certain sports reporters, as well—even though he told more than one interviewer he would have enjoyed covering sports had he not picked politics. Back in one of the glory seasons of Washington Redskins football, Nixon privately praised coach George Allen for barring the press from practices. Allen's controversial and short-lived ban was designed to keep reporters from writing about strategy—including personnel changes.

Whether Sonny Jurgensen or Billy Kilmer would start at quarterback, for example, was a week-to-week Allen ploy to keep opponents guessing.

Nixon and Allen were both known for their paranoia, their cunning—and for their win-at-any-cost mentality. They were even known to have spied on their foes from time to time to gain an extra edge.

When the two football buffs and fellow Republicans spoke by phone on October 8, 1972, the Watergate burglary had occurred only several months before. Nixon's cover-up, however, had so far kept the scandal from spoiling what would soon be the president's landslide re-election victory.

The *Washington Post*—which had been breaking Watergate scoops almost daily since the break-in—was loudly protesting Allen's ban. And this, undoubtedly, had more than a little something to do with the president's plaudits for Allen's move.

A newly released White House tape of that Nixon-Allen chat overhears the president cautioning the coach that "those bastards," [reporters] who "would shoot their grandmother for a story," are "knifing the team and creating dissension." He advised Allen not to "confide in any of them. I'd play it pretty cool."

Nixon's angry "knifing" assertion is buried in the final

CAMP DAVID
Sunday - July 30, 1972

MEMORANDUM FOR BOB HALDEMAN

FROM THE PRESIDENT

In reading Lou Cannon's piece in the Sunday Washington Post I think we can get some guidance as to the handling of the press on campaign matters which should be followed strictly.

I do not want people who talk about the campaign to make the mistake of cutting off representatives of periodicals, TV and newspapers simply because they are generally against us. Consequently, I do not object to an article appearing from time to time, in unfriendly publications which is based on conversations with our campaign people. Having said this, however, we need some completely ironclad rules with regard to who talks to media representatives that we know are antagonistic to us.

First of all, it is vitally important that only the most intelligent and sophisticated person on our campaign staff dare to go in the ring with one of these people. Second, we should not waste time with one of them at the expense of turning down interviews with media representatives who are our friends. Third, even when our most intelligent people are meeting with people like Cannon they must constantly keep in mind that they are confronting a political enemy and that everything they say will, therefore, be used against us. I have to emphasize this over and over again because we never seem to get it across to our people no matter how many times they get burned.

The Cannon piece is the best example we can have of why these rules should be rigidly adhered to. In the first place, while we know the Washington Post is totally gainst us it is just as well to have a piece that has some favorable points in it as well as completely negative ones. Therefore, I have no objections to the fact that Cannon was given interviews by the Campaign Committee. On the other hand, it was a stupid mistake -which must never be repeated - to allow Cannon to have the run of the White House staff, the campaign staff and the National Committee staff in getting his story together. The PR types representative of each of

This newly released eyes-only Nixon political memo to Bob Haldeman shows Nixon deeply worried over GOP political missteps and eager to be his own campaign manager, even microcampaign manager. COURTESY OF NIXON LIBRARY/NATIONAL ARCHIVES.

- 2 -

these groups must have a rule that when media representatives, who
are antagonistic, come in for interviews they are treated courteously
but that only the top political man with great sophistication will be
allowed to talk to him. In addition, whenever that man talks to the
interviewer the press man should sit in on the interview so as to keep
it honest.

In that connection, incidentally, I was rather surprised to
find that we did not have a recording of Clark MacGregor's remarks
at the Press Club. It will be a very modest expense - but it is
absolutely essential that a man with a small recording device go with
him everywhere he goes so that we have a record of what he says which
he can put out in the event that we want to correct a misquotation or
get out a story that was not covered adequately. The same, I think,
should be true of Dole. As you know we have always followed this
custom with regard to my own appearances.

Now, looking at the Cannon story from both the plus and the
minus standpoints, we find a good headline - "Nixon Running Scared,"
and a good thrust insofar as there being no complacency.

From a minus standpoint, it is obvious that Cannon had the
run of the shop and in addition to talking to Haldeman in the White
House and MacGregor at the Committee to Re-Elect, Dole at the
Republican National Committee, he talked to people up and down the
line and got a number of quotes that are both inaccurate and not helpful.
I am not, of course, referring to quotes that he has from Republican
Senators and Congressmen. We have no control whatsoever over this.
What I am referring to are quotes that he obviously had to get - since
he has it in quotation marks - from people on the campaign staff.

For example, as I have often emphasized, it is a mistake
constantly to run down my previous campaigns. We should not contribute to the myth that I did not work hard enough in 1960 and 1968. The
quotation to the effect that before the election in November I had gotten
so confident that I was working on my acceptance speech, taking rests,
etc., is totally inaccurate, as you know, and very harmful.

With regard to MacGregor's own interview, I would like for
you to get together with him and Dole on one point and to have a rule
enforced throughout the balance of the campaign. He was putting out
polls from California and Texas as well as Ohio and Illinois. There was
no reason why he should not have done this since we have not indicated
in the past what our policy was in this respect. However, under

moments of a long and otherwise breezy exchange between the
chief executive and his favorite pro football coach.[3]

The two old friends reviewed the latest game, with Allen admitting that Sonny was "a little jittery in there" in the first half,

- 3 -

absolutely no circumstances are any polls whatever to be put out
showing us ahead or behind in any of the major states without my
specific approval. This is an area where well-intentioned people
will put out a poll for what they think is a good reason - in this case
to knock down complacency -- but where later on they are going to
be asked for polls in these states when they might not want to put
them out. Also, I don't want the impression to get across the country
that we are conducting our campaign on the basis of polls rather than
on the basis of principles. I want you specifically to see that this is
brought up at the next meeting where Mitchell, Dole, MacGregor, et
al, are present. Mitchell, of course, would not have made this mistake.
MacGregor made it only because of lack of experience.

Along the same line, I noted where the statement was made
that abortion was a minus issue for the President because polls showed
that a majority of women favored it. This obviously comes from the
Harper group in the Domestic Council Staff. I want you to get hold of
Ehrlichman and tell him that he is to see that absolutely no one in the
Domestic Council talks to anyone in the press without his specific
approval and then a press man from Ron's office is to be present.
Ehrlichman, of course, would not make such a stupid mistake and the
only way he can control others is to put a tight reign on them.

For example, Syndlinger ran into outraged reaction the evening
that the National Committee put out findings from their Platform
Committee poll to the effect that a majority of the members of the
Platform Committee found out that bussing was not a significant issue.
I want some discipline enforced in this respect for reasons which should
be obvious even to the most stupid of our people.

Another line which we should knock down is that there is no
grass roots support for the President and that we have to get "volunteers
one at a time." This probably comes from Sears or somebody in that
group. The question here is not whether this may be true - and I doubt
if it is in terms of getting volunteers one at a time - but it plays right
into the hands of our political enemies. I could give other examples but
I close the memorandum with this admonition: Let's quit tackling our
own ball carrier. "

and that kicker Curt Knight was "pressing." At another point,
Nixon enthused over speedy running back Larry Brown: "He
really moves!"

(Brown won the NFL's Most Valuable Player award that season. And the Redskins went to the Super Bowl, where they lost
to the Miami Dolphins 14–7.)

After the *Post*'s protests of the ban on sports reporters at practices, Coach Allen scrapped the policy and ignored couch coach Nixon's secret recommendations.

On October 14, Allen announced that all future practices would be open to the press—except for rare occasions "whenever I deem it advisable." He added: "The press has its job to do and we have ours, and while our goals may come into conflict now and then there is no reason why we cannot operate in general harmony."[4]

On November 23, in the wake of a landslide election victory, Nixon visited the Redskins practice facility in northern Virginia to give Coach Allen and his players a pep talk. He dismissed fans that booed the Skins during a November 21 loss to the Dallas Cowboys.

"A great majority of people in this town back the team," the cheerleader-in-chief remarked. "You have been good for this city."

By December 11, 1972, however, in a much darker mood, Nixon was barking more antipress orders—and he threatened another key aide, Press Secretary Ron Ziegler, with dismissal if his antipress edicts were not implemented.

The president was fuming that a *Washington Post* photographer had been allowed into the Executive Mansion to click away at a ceremony presided over by First Lady Pat Nixon.

This development particularly enraged the chief executive because it obviously broke an unwritten policy that did not allow *Post* reporters or photographers to step foot in the Executive Mansion. The apparent Nixon aim was to restrict *Post* people to the West Wing of the White House complex.

Angered over the breach of this ban, Nixon demanded that Ziegler enforce the anti-*Post* policy and remind Connie Stuart, Mrs. Nixon's press secretary, to obey it. "No reporter from the

Washington Post is ever to be in the White House again! And no photographer either. No photographer! Is that clear?" As Ziegler said, "Yes, sir," Nixon pressed his point further: "None! Ever! To be in! Now that is a total order! And if necessary, I'll fire you! Do you understand?" A chastened Ziegler responded, "I do understand."

Nixon wound up the exchange by curtly telling Ziegler: "Okay, all right, good, thank you." He displayed a similar pique by banning all reporters from his final flight on Air Force One after Watergate forced him to resign on August 9, 1974. When Nixon briefly left his cabin to visit with others on the plane, he noticed the seats usually used by the press pool were filled with Secret Service agents. "Well, it certainly smells better back here," he declared.[5]

EIGHTEEN

BACKSTAGE AT THE RESIGNATION

On August 8, 1974, while waiting to deliver his resignation speech, several critical elements of President Nixon's hidden dark side—his erratic behavior, bad temper and inability to make small talk—were on full display.

As he sat behind his desk in the Oval Office, the president got steamed at his official photographer and longtime friend Ollie Atkins for taking too many still photos ahead of the historic nationwide TV address:

"Ollie always wants to take a lot of pictures of me," the president noted. "I'm afraid he'll catch me picking my nose. But you wouldn't print that, would you, Oddie . . . ah . . . Ollie?"

After a bit of banter with the CBS-TV crew, Nixon snapped again at Atkins: "I'm not going to make the other photographers mad by giving you too many! Now that's enough!" Okay! Atkins finally stopping clicking away.

The big broadcast drew closer. Sweat was already developing on the president's upper lip and chin (he was drenched right through his suit by the end of the broadcast) when he surprisingly asked if any Secret Service agents were in the room. Agent Dick Keiser answered, "Yes." Nixon yelled: "Out!" The astonished Keiser argued that he was required to be there. The president relented, saying he was "just kidding."[1]

When the red camera light blinked on, the president looked and sounded just fine. He began:

"Good evening. This is the thirty-seventh time I have spoken to you from this office in which so many decisions have been made that shape the history of this nation. Each time I have done so to discuss with you some matters that I believe affected the national interest.

"In all the decisions I have made in my public life I have always tried to do what was best for the nation. Throughout the long and difficult period of Watergate, I have felt it was my duty to persevere; to make every possible effort to complete the term of office to which you elected me.

"In the past few days, however, it has become evident to me that I no longer have a strong enough political base in the Congress to justify continuing that effort. As long as there was such a base, I felt strongly that it was necessary to see the constitutional process through to its conclusion; that to do otherwise would be unfaithful to the spirit of that deliberately difficult process, and a dangerously destabilizing precedent for the future."

The president went on to say that, with the disappearance of his "political base," the constitutional process had been served "and there is no longer a need for the process to be prolonged." In short order, he uttered the punch line: "Therefore, I shall resign the presidency effective at noon tomorrow. Vice President Ford will be sworn in as president at that hour in this office."

The closest Nixon came to confessing to, or apologizing for, his many crimes came in these few lines: "I regret deeply any injuries that may have been done in the course of the events that led to this decision. I would say only that if some of my judgments were wrong—and some were wrong—they were made in what I believed at the time to be the best interests of the nation." The president concluded his fifteen-minute oration with a prayer: "May God's grace be with you in all the days ahead."[2]

Nixon attracted a record audience for a political speech, with an estimated 110 million viewers and 40 million listeners tuning in.

The TV network anchors were mostly complimentary, with Dan Rather even calling the speech "magisterial." Roger Mudd had a more realistic take, stating that Nixon had been evasive, and had not admitted his complicity in the Watergate cover-up.[3]

Years later, Nixon authority Stanley Kutler observed that Nixon's resignation speech—blaming Congress for depriving him of a political base—was actually "the opening salvo in his campaign for history." Indeed, Nixon—for the next twenty-five years—sought his best to downplay the criminality of his presidency and burnish his credentials as en elder statesman.

Kutler adds an ironic footnote to the resignation speech: "Six years earlier, to the day, Nixon had delivered perhaps the best speech of his career as he accepted the Republican presidential nomination. He had told the nation that he would restore respect for the law. 'Time is running out,' he said at that time, 'for the merchants of crime and corruption in American society.' "[4]

That Nixon himself was a chief merchant of crime and corruption is indisputable. And Nixon's post-presidential campaign to erase the stigma of Watergate had only minimal success.

That's because he bugged himself in the White House, and then he lost a long legal battle to keep the tapes of the bugging private. So the tapes continue be a damning indictment of his corrosive reign. As historian Barry Werth puts it, "Nixon got his freedom, but the country got the truth. Thirty years later, Nixon's guilt—spoken in his own voice, in his own words, and available on the Internet—is indelible."[5]

Nixon behaved rather oddly earlier the same evening of his resignation address when he decided to take his final walk from his hideaway office in the EOB to the Front Portico of the White House. His route would take him near the pressroom. Apparently not wanting to run into any dreaded journalists, Nixon ordered that the press be locked into the briefing room/press area during his stroll. They were.

With reporters under lock and key and unable to harass him, that last walk was uneventful for the president. But the Secret Service agent who accompanied him was forced to act like a squirrel at times—hiding behind pillars and trees in order not to tip off any reporters who might be spying out the windows of their temporary prison. The pressroom lockdown lasted about twenty minutes.

Back in the Executive Mansion, the president had one final prespeech appointment. It, too, turned into a rather bizarre scene.

The president thanked forty-six longtime congressional supporters from both parties who had gathered in the Cabinet Room. He explained that he would have preferred to fight on, but that he had to do what was best for the country.

Nixon quickly broke down in tears, however, after saying: "I just hope that you don't feel that I let you down." In *Nightmare,* Nixon expert J. Anthony Lukas reports that the president then "stumbled backward and nearly fell over a chair. Some of his friends pressed around trying to comfort him. [Barry] Goldwater hugged him. Then, with aides clearing the way, he left the room, his head bowed, his shoulders shaking."[6]

The day after his resignation speech, Richard Nixon continued his "campaign for history" when he flew off to San Clemente and told a welcoming crowd he did not intend to just sit around and soak up the Southern California sunshine. He emphasized his intention to keep working for world peace.

As noted, Nixon's assiduous post-resignation attempts to gloss over Watergate and reinvent himself as a peace-loving elder statesman met with failure. When he resigned in 1974, Nixon had a Gallup approval rating of 23 percent. By 2010, that figure had risen to only 29 percent, when Nixon was deemed by the American public as the worst modern-day president. Nixon's archenemy, John Kennedy, was considered the best—notching an 85 percent approval rating.[7]

NINETEEN

NIXON ORCHESTRATES HIS OWN PARDON

On September 8, 1974 President Gerald Ford stunned the nation by granting his crooked predecessor a preemptive blanket pardon for all of his White House crimes. He did so, Ford said, for the good of the country: "My conscience tells me it is my duty, not merely to proclaim domestic tranquility but to use every means that I have to insure it." The Ford proclamation gave "a full, free, and absolute pardon unto Richard Nixon for all offenses against the United States which he, Richard Nixon, has committed or may have committed or taken part in during the period from January 20, 1969 through August 9, 1974."[1]

That got the ex-president off the legal hook on a host of criminal activities he had ordered, led and/or covered up. The Watergate crimes alone ranged from burglary to campaign sabotage, espionage, and illegal fund-raising, and included efforts to exploit, subvert or pervert the Justice and State Departments, the CIA, the IRS, the FBI and the Secret Service, as well as a wide variety of other assaults on the U.S. Constitution and on the rules of democratic fair play. Ford also agreed to give the former president ultimate control over all his White House papers and tapes and asked Congress to give Nixon $800,000 in transitional expenses.

An outraged Congress could do nothing about the pardon. But it did move quickly to block the Ford-Nixon tape accord, and it slashed Ford's request for the transition funds to $200,000.

From exile in San Clemente, Nixon grabbed the pardon with alacrity. Though its acceptance was tantamount to an admission of guilt, Nixon nonetheless still refused to confess, saying only: "I was wrong in not acting more decisively and more forthrightly in dealing with Watergate, particularly when it reached the stage of judicial proceedings and grew from a political scandal into a national tragedy."[2]

There's no question that Ford paid an enormous political price for his action. The highly unpopular pardon helped make his presidency a national joke. After nearly losing the 1976 Republican presidential nomination to Ronald Reagan, Ford stumbled on to a general election defeat at the hands of Jimmy Carter, who promised—in sharp contrast to Nixon's behavior—never to lie to the American people.

While the pardon and the sweetness of the deal shocked most Americans, former president Nixon was not the least bit surprised. He had not only anticipated the move that would free him from possible prosecution; he had played a major hand in arranging it.

From what is now known of the secret maneuvering that went on behind the walls of the crumbling Nixon White House, it is perfectly clear that the idea of a pardon originated with Nixon, not Ford, and was broached to Ford even before Nixon stepped down. The 1974 pardon shows Nixon at his secretive, behind-the-scenes, manipulative best. And it is certainly instructive in demonstrating just how much influence he exerted over Ford.

Nixon's presidency had unraveled quickly in the summer of 1974 and, as more and more Watergaters were indicted or convicted (in the end, twenty-five Nixon Administration officials were either indicted or jailed for Watergate crimes), the mastermind of the cover-up feared his own prosecution. And for good reason.

Behind the scenes, Watergate grand jury foreman Vladimir Pregelj had written to Nixon asking for his testimony. Nixon's chief defense lawyer, James St. Clair, had quickly said no, that Nixon would only answer written questions or sit down alone with the special prosecutor—offers that were rejected by the grand jury. Years later, in 1982, ABC News would reveal that all nineteen Watergate grand jurors had voted in a straw vote to name Nixon a co-conspirator, but that Watergate special prosecutor Leon Jaworski wouldn't go along with them. Without disclosing the straw vote, Jaworski did explain, in a 1974 interview, why the president was not to be named as a full-fledged co-conspirator:

> One [hard decision] was the question of whether Nixon should be indicted. We can't talk too much about that because there is a grand jury proceeding, but you know that the grand jury named him as an un-indicted co-conspirator. Well, you must know that they probably acted on my advice. This was something that had to be weighed carefully, but why was it done? The reason was that the House Judiciary Committee was about to begin its proceedings. And this was the

proper forum to deal with a sitting president on a matter of this kind.

Jaworski painted a bleak alternative. Indicting the president, he declared, would "throw this country into a tremendous turmoil, not only domestically but internationally."[3]

In July, the House Judiciary Committee approved three articles of impeachment against Nixon—for obstruction of justice, abuse of power and contempt of Congress. In early August, what became known as the "smoking gun" tape was released. Recorded only a few days after the Watergate break-in, it caught the chief executive and his top aide, Bob Haldeman, devising a plan to block an FBI investigation of the burglary.

After two years of incrementally mounting evidence against him, this was the pièce de résistance, the evidence that backed Nixon into his final corner. At that point, the president's few remaining congressional supporters deserted him. In a strained Oval Office meeting, a Republican delegation from Capitol Hill told Nixon he would surely be impeached by the House and convicted by the Senate.

There was no telling what the grand jury might do once Nixon departed the safety of the Oval Office, and there was evidence that Nixon was aware of precisely what the grand jury was doing, because he was being clandestinely clued in on its activities. By April 1973, Nixon had manipulated the Justice Department's top Watergate investigator, Henry Petersen, into directly leaking grand jury secrets to him. Nixon twice offered the post of FBI director to Petersen while boasting to aides, "I've got Petersen on a short leash."[4]

Petersen, who was considered a man of integrity at Justice,

somehow came under the president's spell—despite his later declaration to the press, "I am not a whore" (which seemed to have the same believability as Nixon's infamous "I am not a crook.")[5]

On the very day Nixon resigned, a confidential memo to Leon Jaworski from two of his top prosecutors suggested just how close Nixon came to being indicted and prosecuted: "In our view there is clear evidence that Richard Nixon participated in a conspiracy to obstruct justice by concealing the identity" of those responsible for the scandal. The memo contained five arguments for, and five against, indicting Nixon. The No. 1 reason for an indictment was: "The principle of equal justice under the law requires that every person, no matter what his past position or office, answer to the criminal justice system for his past offenses." The top reason against indictment seemed far less compelling: that Nixon's resignation was punishment enough.[6]

Eager to avoid the risk of winding up in a federal penitentiary (even though he had once self-pityingly told Alexander Haig, "Some of the best writing is done from prison"), Nixon dispatched Haig to Vice President Ford's office on August 1—the eve of the release of "the smoking gun" tape—to raise the prospect of a pardon with Ford. The president realized the tape's contents would spark a revolt among congressional Republicans and doom his chances of survival.

Despite repeated assertions that "I'm not a quitter," the president knew a quick exit was in order. He also knew a pardon would allow him to keep his fat congressional, vice presidential and presidential pensions. He would also gain taxpayer money for an office and staff—and be provided with Secret Service protection—for the rest of his life. To stay and fight would be to face the certainty of congressional impeachment, conviction, and expulsion without any golden parachute or perks.

Haig told Ford it looked as though Nixon would soon step down, and asked whether Ford was ready to assume the presidency. Haig then raised questions about whether Nixon should pardon himself before resigning, whether others should be pardoned at the same time, or whether Ford should give Nixon a pardon if he resigned. Ford later acknowledged Haig specifically suggested "Nixon could agree to leave in return for an agreement that the new President, Gerald Ford, would pardon him."[7]

Ford aide Robert Hartmann reported in his 1980 book *Palace Politics* that, after discussing the matter with his wife, the vice president made a post-midnight phone call to Haig, saying, "They should do whatever they decided to do; it was all right with me." (Ford insists Haig initiated the call and claims he told the presidential aide, "We can't get involved in the White House decision making.")[8]

In his 1999 book *Shadow*, star *Washington Post* Watergate reporter Bob Woodward revealed that Haig also used the August 1 meeting to deliver to Ford two sheets of yellow legal paper that had been prepared by Fred Buzhardt: "The first sheet contained a handwritten summary of a president's legal authority to pardon. The second sheet was a draft pardon form that only needed Ford's signature and Nixon's name to make it legal."[9]

Former Nixon aide Clark Mollenhoff later observed that, "by any normal standard of conflict of interests," Ford should have been disqualified from even considering a pardon for his life-long friend and financial benefactor. By appointing Ford vice president, Nixon had increased Ford's salaries and pensions. Ford went from House minority leader, at $49,500 a year to $200,000 a year as president. And the pension benefits Ford gained "couldn't have been bought for a million dollars," according to Mollenhoff.[10]

Then there was the side deal—later revoked by Congress—that gave the disgraced Nixon control over all of his tapes and documents. The financial worth of such an arrangement—allowing a crook to keep self-incriminating legal evidence—is hard to estimate. But Nixon spent an estimated $10 million during a long but unsuccessful post-resignation fight to obtain the materials.[11]

Many politicians in both parties and those who followed politics suspected some sort of "Ford-Nixon deal." This included Mollenhoff, who returned to his roots as a reporter after working for Nixon. In *The Man Who Pardoned Nixon*, Mollenhoff writes: "The shock following the Nixon pardon caused members of Congress and the press to reflect back on the Nixon-Ford relationship throughout the entire Watergate affair in search for further clues to why Ford felt compelled to take such an extreme political risk for his political mentor. It had not put Watergate behind the nation but had brought it back into the full spotlight. It seemed unlikely that President Ford's compassion for Nixon was the only factor involved."[12]

In their memoirs, or in interviews with reporters, several top Nixon aides have since weighed in on the Haig-Ford discussions. Bryce Harlow found it "inconceivable" Haig was not carrying out a mission for Nixon. Charles Colson concluded that Haig had "negotiated" with Ford over the pardon. John Ehrlichman said, "I'd bet that Jerry Ford promised to pardon Richard Nixon, and that the promise was made before Nixon's resignation." And Alexander Butterfield suggested that Ford—who, as House GOP leader, had been instrumental in shutting down the initial House Watergate probe—would gladly do such a favor for Nixon: "Nixon had Ford totally under his thumb. He was a tool of the Nixon administration—like a puppy dog. They used him when they had to—wind him up and he'd go 'Arf, Arf.'"[13]

The pièce de résistance of Ford's pardon of Nixon—the ultimate irony—is that in 2001, the John F. Kennedy Library Foundation bestowed its "Profile in Courage" award on Gerald Ford for pardoning his corrupt predecessor (and the world's biggest Kennedy-hater). The Foundation said Ford met the annual award's test of being "an elected official who followed his conscience despite the political cost."[14]

The true coziness of the Nixon-Ford relationship was not known until Ford's death in late 2006. It was also not discovered until then that before being appointed VP, Ford had promised to Nixon to do "anything, under any circumstances" to aid the beleaguered president.

At that time, the *Washington Post*'s Bob Woodward disclosed that Nixon and Ford had successfully kept a big secret: They'd been tight pals—going back to their first days in Congress in the 1940s, right up until Nixon's death in 1994. Ford described himself as Nixon's "only real friend." And he put the pardon in an entirely new light: "I looked upon [Nixon] as my personal friend. And I always treasured our relationship. And I had no hesitancy about granting the pardon, because I felt that we had this relationship and that I didn't want to see my real friend have the stigma."[15] This is a far cry from the high-minded explanation Ford had publicly given in 1974, that the pardon was designed to ensure domestic tranquility and to heal the wounds of Watergate.

A telling Nixon White House tape also became public at the time of Ford's death. In a May 1, 1973 conversation, Congressman Ford is overheard consoling a self-pitying, drunk-sounding, Watergate-embattled President Nixon: "Anytime you want me to do anything, under any circumstances, you give me a call, Mr. President. We'll stand by you morning, noon and night."[16]

Robert Hartmann is convinced Haig reported to Nixon on his preresignation talks with Ford, and that "Nixon believed he had a deal."[17] And investigative reporter Seymour Hersh even contends that, shortly after the August 9 resignation, an angry Nixon telephoned the new president with a threat to disclose the deal unless Ford issued a speedy pardon.[18]

During this same period, according to the *Washington Post*, Ford got a memo from Nixon counsel Len Garment saying the ex-president's mental and physical condition could not withstand the continued threat of criminal prosecution. The memo implied that, unless he was pardoned, Nixon might kill himself. (Nixon's psychiatrist, Albert Hutschnecker, later observed that his patient was too narcissistic to commit suicide.)

A draft pardon statement accompanied Garment's memo for the new president. Written by Nixon speechwriter Ray Price, it proposed Ford say that "because, realistically speaking, there is no way that [Nixon] could be given a fair trial by an unbiased jury . . . I believe his case can be separated from those of the other Watergate defendants."[19]

Ironically, the only evidence disputing the fact that Nixon's pardon was Nixon's idea came in a newspaper story several years ago, headlined: "At First, Nixon Spurned Idea of a Pardon, Lawyer Says." Run by the *New York Times*, the story referred to an uncorroborated claim made at an academic forum in Pittsburgh by Nixon's longtime post-resignation lawyer, Jack Miller. Miller asserted that the ex-president initially didn't want Ford's pardon: "He felt that if he had done something wrong, let him be indicted and go to trial." But the lawyer said he eventually got Nixon to accept clemency by persuading him he could not get a fair trial.[20]

Nixon must have put on a pretty convincing act for Miller. But the assertion is one that even Nixon—during his lengthy post-resignation career as Revisionist in Chief—never had the audacity to press. Would one of America's most calculating and self-protective politicians—while in deep potential danger with the law—seriously consider turning down a get-out-of-jail-free card, a card he had cleverly designed and then sneaked into play from up his own sleeve? Not a chance.

For many who had watched the great "Tricky Dick" resurrect himself politically so many times in the past, the newspaper headline—coming as it did twenty-five years after the Nixon Pardon and five years after Nixon's death—was a chilling reminder that if anyone could perfect the art of spinning from the grave, it would be Richard Nixon.

TWENTY

THE POST-RESIGNATION RIBALD RACONTEUR

For most of his life, Richard Nixon was able to keep secret his dirty-minded and foul-mouthed nature. His frequent use of obscenities and crude bathroom references were not generally known until a late stage in his presidency. And, as an ex-president, he actually went public with some of his previously private vulgarities.

Under heavy pressure to release his subpoenaed Watergate tapes, Nixon first tried a trick—releasing doctored, gap-filled versions of transcripts of the tapes instead. While Nixon carefully edited the bogus transcripts to show no criminal actions, they did, however, display a sleazy atmosphere in the Oval Office and a filthy mouth on the president.

The transcripts were heavily peppered with the phrase "expletive deleted." And this didn't sit too well with Nixon supporters who had accepted his pose as a virtuous, clean-speaking gentleman. After all, Nixon was the pious pal of popular evangelist Billy Graham . . . and he was the president who brought religious services to the White House.

In retirement, however—perhaps prompted by greed— Nixon was not content to continue hiding most of his verbal indelicacies behind the expletive deleted phrase. While still waging an expensive legal battle to keep most of his presidential tapes and documents from the public—the first of these were not released until years after his 1994 death—Nixon decided to put some of his grubbiness on the record.

In 1984, Nixon was paid by former faithful aide Frank Gannon to sit down for a series of TV interviews. Gannon sold the series to CBS for $500,000, but Nixon's cut remains a closely guarded secret. (In 1977, Nixon got $1 million dollars and a 20 percent cut of the profits for his famous TV interviews with David Frost.) CBS chose not to bleep out any of Nixon's scatology. But the network did warn viewers about the crude language before the broadcasts.

In the Gannon programs, Nixon claimed President Lyndon Johnson enjoyed humiliating those for whom he had little respect by greeting them in a most unusual way: "He'd receive them while he was sitting on the toilet. He'd just love to do that sort of thing."

At another point, Nixon imitated Senator William Jenner's reaction to Averill Harriman's 1956 decision to seek the Democratic presidential nomination: "I just seen Harriman on TV. And somebody said, 'Well, what was he like, Bill? What did you think of him?' He's thin, boys, thin as piss on a rock."

In explaining the mystique of President John F. Kennedy, Nixon compared JFK with two-time Democratic loser Adlai Stevenson. He said, "I think the fact the John Kennedy very much approved of the designation that was given him by [columnist] Joe Alsop [that Kennedy] was 'a Stevenson with balls' tells us one of the reasons he had this charisma." (Privately, Nixon often falsely suggested that Stevenson was a homosexual, and one time he publicly referred to Stevenson "Sidesaddle Adlai.")

During the 1984 TV interview, the ex-president insisted that his use of four-letter words in private was not hypocritical, because, as he put it, "If I may be very direct: You don't go to the bathroom in the living room."

Nixon claimed to Gannon that, in 1952, he lectured Republican presidential candidate Dwight Eisenhower when Ike seemed indecisive about the timing of his decision on whether to keep Nixon on the GOP ticket: "And then I blew my top a bit, and I said, 'You know, there comes a time when you either have to shit or get off the pot.'"

The ex-president used the CBS forum to quote Henry Kissinger's low opinion of Hanoi's delegation to the Paris peace talks. "They're just shits, the North Vietnamese. They're just tawdry shits." As for one of his oldest and most despised enemies, the press, Nixon declared: "Now, I don't mind a microscope, but boy, when they use a proctoscope, that's going too far."[1]

Nixon's grimy performance was so extraordinary, TV's *Saturday Night Live* was quick to spoof it. In the role of the ex-president, Joe Piscopo said, "You know, during Watergate, Trisha, my daughter, I think she said it eloquently when she said, 'Daddy, you're such a dork.'"

Asked how it feels "to be the most vilified man in the country," the SNL Nixon responds, "Sensational! I love it! Let me tell you, if you lie and cheat and betray the nation's trust, people will hate you. And if they hate you, they'll want to know all about you. And if they want to know all about you, they got to pay through the nose."

Piscopo's Nixon also chews out the press for distorting his proctoscope remark: "Well, that's a lot of bull. I love it when the press uses one of those things. In fact, if you really want to look inside Richard Nixon's head, you have to use a proctoscope."[2]

Just what prompted the former president to make himself an easy target for popular comedic ridicule? Well, as Joe Piscopo correctly jested, Nixon was well aware of the nation's dark fascination with the only chief executive ever driven from office by scandal. Did Nixon promise Gannon and the network an R-rated performance in order to bring in the biggest bucks? Was Nixon hoping to convince viewers that he was a manly man who knows the inside of a locker room? Or was he just giving in, on the spur-of-the-moment, to some self-destructive impulse?

Who knows? But many close Nixon observers believe he did have a lifelong fixation with money, and on raking in as much of it, in any way he could.

Nixon had what author J. Anthony Lucas calls a "profound appreciation of the good things money could buy."[3] As chief executive, Nixon had amassed a small fortune—partly by evading or avoiding taxes through huge and highly questionable deductions. When the IRS caught up with him in April 1974, the chief executive was forced to agree to pay $432,787 in back taxes and $33,000 in interest.[4]

Chief Senate Watergate Committee investigator Sam Dash might buy into the money theory. He even thinks a monetary benefit could have been behind Nixon's decision to install his taping system. Dash says a tax accountant told the president that a law prohibiting presidents from getting tax breaks for donating their papers to museums "did not speak of tapes, just papers. And that if he put in a taping system he wouldn't have to pay taxes forever. The information that we got from insiders is that [the taping system] was to cut down on his taxes. Maybe greed is the answer."[5] Former House Speaker Thomas "Tip" O'Neill was convinced that Nixon's selfish pursuit of money was also behind his decision not to destroy his White House tapes: "I've always believed that he held on to them because he was greedy. He wanted to use them to write his memoirs, and he expected to make a fortune from them."[6]

Notes

One: Treason Wins the White House

1. Anthony Summers and Robbyn Swan, *The Arrogance of Power: The Secret World of Richard Nixon* (New York: Viking, 2000), 305, "At the end of the conversation, it was later reported 'Nixon and his friends collapsed in laughter . . .'"

2. All LBJ conversations quoted in this chapter can be listened to at the LBJ Library Web site, http://www.lbjlibrary.org.

3. See AP story in Deseret News, January 24, 1997. "Nixon Considered Blackmailing LBJ over War Policies, Tapes Show." AP says that "In his memoirs, Nixon conceded he wanted the Brookings files for leverage against Johnson administration officials at odds with his war policy."

4. Summers, *Arrogance of Power*, 385.

5. Chris Matthews, "Break In and Take It Out, You Understand?" *Chicago Tribune*, November 22, 1996.

6. G. Gordon Liddy, *Will: The Autobiography of G. Gordon Liddy* (New York: St. Martin's Press, 1980), 237.

7. John Ehrlichman, *Witness to Power: The Nixon Years* (New York: Simon and Schuster, 1982), 368.

8. Chris Matthews, "Nixon Personally Ordered Break-in," *San Francisco Chronicle*, November 21, 1996.

9. "Nixon: Arrogance of Power," History Channel, September 2000.

10. Rick Perlstein, *Nixonland: The Rise of a President and the Fracturing of America*, 1st Scribner hardcover ed. (New York: Scribner, 2008).
11. Summers, *Arrogance of Power*, 299.
12. "Anna Chennault Works to Stop Vietnam War," *Shanghai Star*, September 19, 2002, http://app1.chinadaily.com.cn/star/2002/0919/pr22-1.html.
13. This June 17, 1971 tape can be heard at the Miller Center's Web site; White House Tapes, Miller Center, whitehousetapes.net.
14. This July 1, 1971 tape can be heard at the Miller Center's Web site; White House Tapes, Miller Center, whitehousetapes.net.
15. This tape can be heard at the LBJ Library Web site, http://www.lbjlibrary.org.
16. Robert Parry, "The Significance of Nixon's 'Treason,'" Consortiumnews.com, December 9, 2008.
17. Summers, *Arrogance of Power*, 306.

Two: Ties That Bind: The Mob's President

1. Mark Feldstein, *Poisoning the Press* (New York: Farar, Straus and Giroux, 2010), 95.
2. Ibid., 100.
3. Dan E. Moldea, *The Hoffa Wars: Teamsters, Rebels, Politicians, and the Mob* (New York: Paddington Press, 1978), 104.
4. Summers, *Arrogance of Power*, 57
5. "Gambling in America: An Encyclopedia of History, Issues, and Society (Santa Barbara: ABC-CLIO, 2001), 218.
6. *Godfathers Collection: The True History of the Mafia*, The History Channel, 2003.
7. G. Robert Blakey and Richard N. Billings, *Fatal Hour* (Berkley, California: 4Shadows Books, 1992), 262.
8. Paul Hoffman, *Tiger in the Court* (Playboy Press, 1973), 81.
9. Summers, *Arrogance of Power*, 57.
10. Ibid., 128.
11. Richard Mahoney, *Sons and Brothers* (Arcade Publishing, 1999), 95.
12. Summers, *Arrogance of Power*, 127.
13. Dan E. Moldea, *The Hoffa Wars*.
14. Anthony Summers, Not in Your Lifetime (New York: McGraw-Hill, 1980).

15. Summers, *Arrogance of Power*, 114.

16. Bill Bonanno, *Bound by Honor: A Mafioso's Story* (New York: St. Martin's Press, 1999), 228.

17. Dick Russell, *The Man Who Knew Too Much* (New York: Carroll & Graf, 2003), 336.

18. Moldea, *The Hoffa Wars*, 108.

19. William C. Sullivan, *The Bureau: My Thirty Years in Hoover's FBI* (New York: W. W. Norton & Company, 1979), 53.

20. William Bastone, "Brothers 'n' the Hood," *The Village Voice*, July 30, 1996.

21. William Bastone, The Smoking Gun, http://www.thesmokinggun.com.

22. See accompanying FBI memo.

23. Jack Anderson, *Parade*.

24. Richard Reeves, *President Nixon: Alone in the White House* (New York: Simon & Schuster, 2002), 394.

25. David Scheim, *Contract on America* (Zebra, 1989), 339.

26. Bill Bonanno, *Bound by Honor*, 307.

27. http://archives.republicans.edlabor.house.gov/archives/hearings/106th/oi/teamster63099/oshoekstra.htm.

28. Summers, *Arrogance of Power*.

29. Peter Dale Scott, *Deep Politics and the Death of JFK* (University of California Press, 1996), 118.

30. Charles Rappleye and E. B. Becker, An American Mafioso: The Johnny Roselli Story (Doubleday, 1991), 225–226.

31. Ibid., 226.

32. Richard Reeves, *President Nixon: Alone in the White House*, 266.

33. David Scheim, *Contract on America*, 304.

34. Chris Rojek, *Frank Sinatra* (Polity, 2004), 93.

35. John Lahr, *Show and Tell: New Yorker Profiles* (University of California Press, 2002), 63.

36. Ronald Goldfarb, *Perfect Villains, Imperfect Heroes* (Capital Books, 2002), 43.

37. Time, Volume 118, Part 1, 192.

38. Gus Russo, *Supermob* (Bloomsbury USA, 2006), 376.

39. Watergate and the White House, July–December 1973, Facts on File.

40. Moldea, *Hoffa Wars*, 319.

41. *Time* magazine, December 25, 1972, "Prison: Life Can Be Fun."

42. *Life* magazine, March 24, 1972; *New York Times,* April 5, 1998, obituary, "John Alessio, 87, Businessman and California Political Force."

43. The National Archives believes the tape was probably erased by mistake by Secret Service overseers of Nixon's taping system. But an Archives spokesman acknowledges that Nixon, or someone else, might possibly have tampered with the Nixon-Trertotola tape.

44. *Detroit Free Press,* Dec. 4, 2002.

45. Ibid.

46. Dan Moldea, *The Hoffa Wars,* 402

47. Neff, *Mobbed Up,* 191.

48. Jeff Gerth, "Richard Nixon and Organized Crime," *Penthouse,* July 1974.

49. Moldea, *Hoffa Wars,* 451.

50. Summers, Arrogance of Power, 399.

51. Neff, *Mobbed Up,* 193.

52. Ibid., 182.

53. Waldron, *Ultimate Sacrifice.*

54. Charles Colson, White House Memo.

55. Moldea, *Hoffa Wars,* 31.

56. Ibid., 315.

Three: Nixon's Favorite Godfather: Carlos Marcello

1. John Davis, Mafia Kingfish, 405–407.

2. Tim Reid and Tom Baldwin, *The London Sunday Times,* June 27, 2007, "Secret Papers Show How the CIA Hired the Mafia to Hit Castro," These papers are known as "the family jewels."

3. In 1993, the PBS TV program *Frontline* showed a group photo—taken in 1955—of sixteen men and boys on a picnic. Ferrie and Oswald are at opposite ends of the group.

4. Richard Mahoney, *Sons and Brothers,* 229.

5. John Davis, *The Kennedys: Dynasty and Disaster,* 570.

6. *Encyclopedia of the Kennedy Assassination,* 245.

7. *Who's Who in the JFK Assassination, An A-to-Z Encyclopedia,* 134

8. *Encyclopedia of the Kennedy Assassination,* 225.

9. Ibid., 225–226.

10. Michael Benson, *The Encyclopedia of the JFK Assassination,* Facts On File Library of American History (New York: Facts On File, 2002), 148.

11. Anthony Summers, *Not in Your Lifetime* (New York: Marlowe & Co., 1998), 365.

12. Ibid., 364.

13. David M. Sheim, *Contract on America: The Mafia Murder of President John F. Kennedy* (New York: Shapolsky Publishers Inc., 1988), 229.

14. Thomas Jones, "Carlos Marcello: Big Daddy in the Big Easy," Trutv.com.

15. Gore Vidal, "Drugs: Case for Legalizing Marijuana," *The New York Times*, September 26, 1970.

16. David Kaiser, *The Road to Dallas: The Assassination of John F. Kennedy* (Belknap Publishers, 2008), 411.

17. To quote from the committee's report: "Scientific acoustical evidence establishes a high probability that two gunmen fired at President John F. Kennedy. Other scientific evidence does not preclude the possibility of two gunmen firing at the President. Scientific evidence negates some specific conspiracy allegations. The committee believes, on the basis of the evidence available to it, that President John F. Kennedy was probably assassinated as a result of a conspiracy. The committee is unable to identify the other gunman or the extent of the conspiracy"; Spartacus Education Web, http://www.spartacus.schoolnet.co.uk.

18. Blakely's views are in *Fatal Hour*, Bonanno's in *Bound by Honor*; G. Robert Blakey and Richard N. Billings, *Fatal Hour: The Assassination of President Kennedy by Organized Crime* (New York: Berkley Books, 1992); Bill Bonnano, *Bound by Honor: A Mafioso's Story*, 1st ed. (New York: St. Martin's Press, 1999).

19. In 2003, based on new evidence indicating CIA withholding of key information, Blakey wrote a scathing letter about CIA obstruction of the HSCA inquiry: "I now no longer believe anything the Agency told the committee any further than I can obtain substantial corroboration for it from outside the Agency for its veracity."; "House Select Committee on Assassinations." Mary Ferrell Foundation, http://www.maryferrell.org/wiki/index.php/HSCA.

20. H. R. Haldeman and Joseph DiMona, *The Ends of Power* (New York: Times Books, 1978), 39.

21. That expression was used by Chicago godfather Sam Giancana, according to *Conspiracy in Camelot*, by Jerome Kroth, 185.

22. Ron Goldfarb, "Tying the Mafia to the Slaying of JFK," SFGate.com, February 26, 2006.

Four: Mobster in the White House: Bebe Rebozo

1. Anthony Summers and Robbyn Swan, *The Arrogance of Power: The Secret World of Richard Nixon* (New York: Viking, 2000), 112.
2. Ibid., 112.
3. Summers, *Arrogance of Power*, 114.
4. Ibid., 114.
5. Ibid., 114. According to Mafia expert Dan Moldea the phrase "take a hot stove" likely means someone who "would be willing to steal anything."
6. Ibid., 107.
7. Ibid., 111.
8. Jeff Gerth, "Richard M. Nixon and Organized Crime," in *Government by Gunplay*, ed. Sid Blumenthal and Harvey Yazjiian (New York: New American Library, Signet, 1976), 130–151.
9. Jeff Gerth, "Richard Nixon and Organized Crime," *Penthouse* magazine, July 1974.
10. According to JFK assassination expert A. J. Weberman, Nodule x13, ajweberman.com/nodulex13.pdf.
11. Ibid., 101.
12. Marvin Miller and Art Kunkin, *The Breaking of a President* (Los Angeles: Therapy Productions, 1974).
13. John Ehrlichman, *Witness to Power: The Nixon Years* (New York: Simon and Schuster, 1982), 51.
14. Roger Morris, "Perspective on Cambodia," *Los Angeles Times*, November 8, 1991; Morris was monitoring the president's "drunken phone call" from Camp David to Kissinger, whose reaction was, "Our Peerless leader has flipped out."
15. Arthur Schlesinger, *Robert Kennedy and His Times* (New York: Ballantine Books, 1996), 262.
16. Michael Woodiwiss, *Organized Crime and American Power: A History* (Toronto; Buffalo: University of Toronto Press, 2001), 266.
17. John Dean speculated that Haig might have tucked such information away for possible later use against the president. "To my knowledge, Al Haig has never commented on his actions in calling for this investigation. But it took little imagination . . . to appreciate that a man who would institute a secret criminal investigation against the President would have little trouble being the instrument of his ruin." (At the time, Dean thought Haig might

have been "Deep Throat," the then mysterious source for *Washington Post* Watergate reporter Bob Woodward); *Washington Star*, December 5, 1976, in John Dean, *Lost Honor* (New York: Stratford Press, 1982), 341.

Five: Nixon's Sexuality

1. Anthony Summers and Robbyn Swan, *The Arrogance of Power: The Secret World of Richard Nixon* (New York: Viking, 2000), 100.
2. Frank Gannon, "The Good Dog Richard Affair," *The American Spectator*, December 1981.
3. Summers, 104.
4. Ibid., 105.
5. Ibid.
6. Ibid., 36.
7. Bonnie Angelo, telephone conversation with author, 2010.
8. Jim McManus, e-mail message to author, 2010.
9. Roger Gittines, e-mail message to author 2010.
10. J. Anthony Lukas, *Nightmare: The Underside of the Nixon Years* (Athens, Ohio: Ohio University Press, 1999), 363.
11. John Ehrlichman, *Witness to Power: The Nixon Years* (New York: Simon and Schuster, 1982), 50.
12. David Abrahamsen, *Nixon vs. Nixon: An Emotional Tragedy*, 1st ed. (New York: Farrar, Straus and Giroux, 1977).
13. James Reston Jr., *The Conviction of Richard Nixon: The Untold Story of the Frost/Nixon Interviews*, 1st ed. (New York: Harmony Books, 2007), 57.
14. Summers, 103.
15. Ibid., 58–59.
16. From a May 13, 1971, conversation among President Richard Nixon, John Ehrlichman and Bob Haldeman. http://www.youtube.com/watch?v=TivVcFSBVSM.
17. Hersh, in a February 6, 1998 appearance before Neiman fellows; "Two Stories Seymour Hersh Never Wrote," *Neiman Reports*, Spring 1998, http://www.nieman.harvard.edu/reports.aspx.
18. Eli S. Chasen, *President Nixon's Psychiatric Profile: A Psychodynamic-Genetic Interpretation* (New York: P. H. Wyden, 1973).
19. Fawn M. Brodie, *Richard Nixon: The Shaping of His Character* (New York: W.W. Norton and Company, 1981), 466.

20. Seymour Hersh, "Kissinger and Nixon in the White House," *The Atlantic Monthly*, 249, No. 5 (1982).

21. Muriel Dobbin, telephone conversation with author, 2010.

22. Frank McCullough, telephone conversation with author, 2010.

23. Summers, *The Arrogance of Power*, 233.

24. Lester David, *The Lonely Lady of San Clemente: The Story of Pat Nixon*, 1st ed. (New York: Crowell, 1978), 186.

25. Sid Davis, telephone conversation with author, 2010.

26. Michael John Sullivan, *Presidential Passions: The Love Affairs of America's Presidents* (S.P.I. Books, 1994), 114.

27. Bonnie Angelo, *First Families: The Impact of the White House on Their Lives*, 1st ed. (New York: Morrow, 2005), 288.

28. Vamik D. Volkan, Norman Itzkowitz, and Andrew W. Dod, *Richard Nixon: A Psychobiography* (New York: Columbia University Press, 1997), 49.

29. David, *The Lonely Lady*, 188.

30. Bob Woodward and Carl Bernstein, *The Final Days*, 2nd ed. (New York: Simon and Schuster, 1994).

31. Jimmy Breslin, "How the Good Guys Finally Won," 114–115.

32. Ronald Kessler, *Inside the White House: The Hidden Lives of the Modern Presidents and the Secrets of the World's Most Powerful Institution* (New York: Pocket Books, 1995), 38.

33. John Dean in *The Rehnquist Choice: The Untold Story of Nixon Appointment That Redefined the Supreme Court*, according to *Time* magazine, "William Rehnquist: 1924–2005, September 4, 2005.

34. Summers, 159.

35. Sally Denton, *The Pink Lady: The Many Lives of Helen Gahagan Douglas*, 1st U.S. ed. (New York: Bloomsbury Press, 2009), 158.

36. James David Barber, *The Presidential Character: Predicting Performance in the White House* (Englewood Cliffs, N.J.: Prentice-Hall, 1977), 349–350.

37. Brodie, *The Shaping of His Character*.

38. Rick Perlstein, *Nixonland: The Rise of a President and the Fracturing of America*, 1st Scribner hardcover ed. (New York: Scribner, 2008), 64.

39. Brodie, *The Shaping of His Character*.

Six: Nixon's Wooing of Frank Sinatra

1. Anthony Summers and Robbyn Swan, *Sinatra: The Life* (New York: Knopf, 2005), 148.
2. Summers, *Sinatra*, 344.
3. Kitty Kelley, *His Way: The Unauthorized Biography of Frank Sinatra* (Toronto; New York: Bantam Books, 1986), 32.
4. Ronald Kessler, *The Sins of the Father: Joseph P. Kennedy and the Dynasty He Founded* (New York: Warner Books, 1996), 376.
5. Summers, *Sinatra*, 278.
6. Robert W. Welkos, "Daughter Blows Lid off of Meyer Lansky's Mafia Secrets," Hollywoodnews.com, May 20, 2010.
7. Summers, *Sinatra*, 295.
8. This phone conversation between the president and his daughter, on September 15, 1972, can be heard at the Miller Center Web site; White House Tapes, Miller Center, millercenter.org.
9. Summers, *Sinatra*, 351.
10. All of these new tapes and documents can be accessed at the Nixon Library's Web site; "New Releases," The Nixon Library, http://www.nixon library.gov.
11. John Ehrlichman, *Witness to Power: The Nixon Years* (New York: Simon & Schuster, 1982), 134.
12. Anthony Bruno, "Frank Sinatra and the Mob," TrueTV.com, http://www .truetv.com.
13. Spiro T. Agnew, *Go Quietly . . . or Else* (New York: Morrow, 1980).

Seven: White House Plots to Kill Jack Anderson

1. Howard Kurtz, "Jack Anderson, Gentleman with a Rake," *Washington Post*, Decmber 18, 2005.
2. Mark Feldstein, "The Last Muckraker," *Washington Post*, July 28, 2004.
3. John Ehrlichman, *Witness to Power: The Nixon Years* (New York: Simon & Schuster, 1982), 148.
4. Ibid., 25.
5. Pete Yost and Lara Jakes Jordan, "FBI Searched Long, Hard for Jack Anderson Sources," *USA Today*, October 11, 2008.
6. John Dean, *Blind Ambition: The White House Years* (New York: Simon & Schuster, 1976), 56.

7. Jack Anderson and Daryl Gibson, *Peace, War, and Politics: An Eyewitness Account*, 1st ed. (New York: Forge, 1999), 169.

8. "Hunt Told Associates of Anderson of Orders to Kill Jack Anderson," Bob Woodward, *Washington Post*, September 21, 1975.

9. Mark Lane, *Plausible Denial: Was the CIA Involved in the Assassination of JFK?* (New York: Thunder's Mouth Press, 1991), 129–132; Victor Marchetti, "CIA to Admit Hunt Involved in Kennedy Slaying," *Spotlight*, August 14, 1978.

10. Carol J. Williams, "Two of E. Howard Hunt's Sons Say He Knew of Rogue CIA Agents' Plan to Kill President Kennedy in 1963," *Los Angeles Times*, March 20, 2007; " 'This is Probably the Last Interview I'll Do': An Interview with Saint John Hunt on His Father & The JFK Assassination," Waking the Midnight Sun, http://cadeveo.wordpress.com.

11. Mark Feldstein, interview by National Public Radio, September 30, 2010, http://www.npr.org/templates/story/story.php?storyId=130192940.

12. Haldeman, *The Ends of Power*, 5.

13. Mark Feldstein, interview by National Public Radio, *All Things Considered*, August 3, 2004.

14. James Reston Jr., *The Conviction of Richard Nixon: The Untold Story of the Frost/Nixon Interviews*, 1st ed. (New York: Harmony Books, 2007), 46.

15. Fred Emery, *Watergate: The Corruption of American Politics and the Fall of Richard Nixon* (New York: Times Books, 1994), 99.

16. G. Gordon Liddy, *Will: The Autobiography of G. Gordon Liddy*, 3rd. ed. (New York: St. Martin's Press, 1997), 207.

17. Ibid., 288.

18. Mark Feldstein, *Poisoning the Press: Richard Nixon, Jack Anderson, and the Rise of Washington's Scandal Culture*, 1st ed. (New York: Farrar, Straus and Giroux, 2010), 282.

19. Jim Hougan, *Secret Agenda: Watergate, Deep Throat, and the CIA*, 1st ed. (New York: Random House, 1984), 93.

20. Liddy, *Will*, 292.

21. Anderson, *Peace, War and Politics*, 17.

22. Anthony Summers, and Robbyn Swan, *The Arrogance of Power: The Secret World of Richard Nixon* (New York: Viking, 2000), 196.

23. Anthony Summers, *Official and Confidential: The Secret Life of J. Edgar Hoover* (New York: G.P. Putnam's Sons, 1993), 409.

24. Feldstein, *Poisoning the Press*, 287.

25. Liddy was repeating a justification for bumping of Anderson that he had used before, in a January 1977 interview with *Playboy*: "[It was] not murder, but justifiable homicide, since murder is a legal term for a specific type of homicide that by its very definition is unjustifiable . . . [But] Anderson is one of those mutant strains of columnist who are half-legitimate, because he passes off biased interpretations and selective information as straight reporting. At one point, Anderson's systematic leaking of top-secret information rendered the effective conduct of American foreign policy virtually impossible . . ."

Eight: Nixon's Plots Against Ted Kennedy and Daniel Ellsberg

1. H. R. Haldeman, *The Haldeman Diaries: Inside the Nixon White House* (New York: G.P. Putnam's, 1994), 72.
2. Christopher Matthews. *Kennedy & Nixon: The Rivalry That Shaped Postwar America* (New York: Simon & Schuster, 1996), 280.
3. John W. Dean, *Blind Ambition: The White House Years* (New York: Simon and Schuster, 1976), 78.
4. "Nixon aides pressed FBI on Kopechne," *Boston Globe*, June 14, 2010.
5. "Was Mary Jo in Greece at the Same Time as Ted Kennedy?" *Boston Globe*.
6. Haldeman, *The Haldeman Diaries*.
7. Nixon Tapes Transcript, September 8, 1971, Miller Center, whitehouse tapes.net/transcript/nixon/274-044.
8. Nixon Tapes Transcript, September 7, 1972, Miller Center, whitehouse tapes.net/ transcript/nixon/772-015-0.
9. "Nixon: The Portrait Painted by His Close Aide," *Lakeland Ledger* [Florida], February 19, 1978.
10. George Lardner, "Nixon Ordered Spy Placed in Sen. Kennedy's Secret Service Detail," *Washington Post*, February 8, 1997.
11. "Crime: The Radical Bank Job," *Time*, October 5, 1970.
12. Anthony Summers, and Robbyn Swan, *The Arrogance of Power: The Secret World of Richard Nixon* (New York: Viking, 2000), 406.
13. Ibid.
14. In his only season of play, 1952, the twenty-five-year-old Gilday won thirteen and lost nine with the Bluefield, West Virginia Blue-Grays of the Class D Appalachian League, according to baseball-reference.com.
15. Summers, *Arrogance of Power*, 406.

16. "Covering Up the Coverup?" by Lucian Trescott, August 9, 1973. http://
    blogs.villiagevoice.com/runningscared/2011/05/dick#nixons#bud.php.
17. Summers, 407.
18. Louis Patrick Gray and Ed Gray, *In Nixon's Web: A Year in the Crosshairs
    of Watergate*, 1st ed. (New York: Henry Holt and Co., 2008), 138–139.
19. Dan E. Moldea, *The Hoffa Wars: Teamsters, Rebels, Politicians, and the Mob*
    (New York: Paddington Press, distributed by Grosset & Dunlap, 1978), 352.
20. The National Archives recently released Nixon's conversations with
    Haig, Kissinger and Ehrlichman. They can be heard at the Web sites of
    the Nixon Library, The Miller Center, or Nixontapes.org. The Miller Cen-
    ter has prepared a transcript: White House Tapes, Miller Center, http://
    whitehousetapes.net/transcript/nixon/005-059.
21. Walter Pincus, "Nixon, Hoover Bashed Justices in '71 Phone Call,"
    Washington Post, September 28, 2007, http://www.washingtonpost.com/
    wp-dyn/content/article/2007/09/27/AR2007092701947.html.
22. Robin Lindley, "Egil Krogh's Lesson Learned," *Washington Law & Poli-
    tics*, http://www.lawandpolitics.com/washington/Egil-Kroghs-Lessons
    -Learned/0ca80bdc-6a6f-102a-ab50-000e0c6dcf76.html.
23. "The Pentagon Papers," 1971 in Review, UPI, 1971, http://www.upi.com/
    Audio/Year_in_Review/Events-of-1971/The-Pentagon-Papers/
    12295509436546-7/.
24. "Judge William Byrne; Ended Trial over Pentagon Papers," *Washington
    Post*, January 15, 2006, http://www.washingtonpost.com/wp-dyn/content/
    article/2006/01/14/AR2006011401165.html.
25. "Pentagon Papers Charges Are Dismissed," *New York Times*, On This
    Day, May 12, 1973, http://www.nytimes.com/learning/general/onthis
    day/big/0511.html.
26. Daniel Ellsberg, "Assange Is in Some Danger," The Daily Beast, June 10,
    2010, http://www.thedailybeast.com/articles/2010/06/11/daniel-ellsberg
    -wikileaks-julian-assange-in-danger.html.

Nine: Frank Sturgis: Nixon Plumber and Secret CIA Assassin

1. Gaeton Fonzi, *The Last Investigation* (Ipswich, Mass.: Mary Ferrell Foundation Press, 2008), 76.
2. David E. Kaiser, *The Road to Dallas: The Assassination of John F. Kennedy*
   (Cambridge, Mass.: Belknap Press of Harvard University Press, 2008), 30.

3. According to a memo sent by L. Patrick Gray, Director of the FBI, to H. R. Haldeman in 1972: "Sources in Miami say he [Sturgis] is now associated with organized crime activities." In his book, *Assassination of JFK* (1977), Bernard Fensterwald claims that Sturgis was heavily involved with the Mafia, particularly with the criminal activities of Santos Trafficante and Meyer Lansky in Florida. (These citations are found on the Education Forum Web site.) In *Mafia Kingfish*, Mob expert John Davis reports that both Sturgis and Barker "were closely associated with organized crime, and especially with associates of [New Orleans boss] Carlos Marcello's, Meyer Lansky and Santos Trafficante." In *Ultimate Sacrifice* by Lamar Waldron with Thom Hartman, Sturgis is described as a "bag man" for Trafficante; John H. Davis, *Mafia Kingfish: Carlos Marcello and the Assassination of John F. Kennedy* (New York: McGraw-Hill, 1989), 402; Lamar Waldron and Thom Hartmann, *Ultimate Sacrifice: John and Robert Kennedy, the Plan for a Coup in Cuba, and the Murder of JFK* (Berkeley, Calif.: Counterpoint: Distributed by Publishers Group West, 2008), 342.

4. Michael Canfield and Alan J. Weberman, *Coup d'État in America: The CIA and the Assassination of John F. Kennedy* (New York: Third Press, 1975), 221.

5. "Confession of Howard Hunt," Mary Ferrell Foundation. http://www.maryferrell.org/wiki/index.php/Confession_of_Howard_Hunt.

6. "The Last Confessions of E. Howard Hunt," *Rolling Stone*, April 2, 2007.

7. Stanley Kutler, *The Wars of Watergate: The Last Crisis of Richard Nixon* (New York: Knopf, 1990), 614; Professor Kutler notes that nearly three-quarters of the viewing audience believed he had been guilty of an obstruction of justice, as nearly as many thought he had lied during the Frost interviews themselves.

8. Egil Krogh and Matthew D. Krogh, *Integrity: Good People, Bad Choices, and Life Lessons from the White House*, 1st ed. (New York: Public Affairs, 2007), 39.

9. Fonzi, *The Last Investigation*, 76.

10. Fonzi, *The Last Investigation*, 78.

11. Michael Benson, *The Encyclopedia of the JFK Assassination*, Facts On File Library of American History (New York: Facts On File, 2002), 23.

12. Jim Rothstein, broadcast interview with Greg Szymanksi, *Investigative Journal*, January 15, 2007. http://www.youtube.com/watch?v=P7cFqDjPluo.

13. Fonzi, *The Last Investigation*, 82.
14. "U.S. Rep. Holt Heads Campaign to Probe CIA Practices," *The Star-Ledger*, July 15, 2009.
15. Lucian Truscott, "Covering Up the Cover-up?" *The Village Voice*, August 9, 1973.
16. Butterfield made the remarks at a Watergate panel discussion in Washington, D.C. that was televised by C-SPAN on July 25, 1994. Author Fred Emery also attended the event. Emery said that when Butterfield made the remark that Nixon must have known about Watergate in advance, Nixon's White House lawyer, Len Garment, told Emery, "He's right you know. I believe that." Fred Emery, *Watergate: The Corruption of American Politics and the Fall of Richard Nixon* (New York: Times Books, 1994).
17. Egil Krogh, e-mail message to author, 2011.

Ten: Nixon's Bay of Pigs Secrets

1. Hunt offered his recollections in a 1992 interview with CBS.
2. *The Washington Post*, September 21, 1975.
3. C. W. Colson, *Born Again* (Grand Rapids, Mich.: Chosen Books, 2008), 78.
4. H. R. Haldeman, *The Ends of Power* (New York: Times Books, 1978), 39.
5. Schorr makes the statement in a book companion to Oliver Stone's movie of the same name; Oliver Stone and E. Hamburg, *Nixon: An Oliver Stone Film* (New York: Hyperion, 1995), 10.
6. Jim Marrs, *Crossfire* (New York: Carroll & Graf Publishers, 1989), 273.
7. The June 23 conversations are from the "smoking gun" Watergate tape, originally made public on August 5, 1974. They can also be found in Stanley Kutler's *Abuse of Power*; Stanley I. Kutler, *Abuse of Power* (New York: Simon & Schuster, 1997), 67.
8. Haldeman, *The Ends of Power*, 38.
9. The Ehrlichman novel, *The Company*, features a president named "Monckton"—an obvious play on "The Mad Monk," Ehrlichman's favorite nickname for the erratic and reclusive Nixon; John Ehrlichman, *Witness to Power: The Nixon Years* (New York: Simon & Schuster, 1982), 318.
10. Haldeman, *The Ends of Power*, 39.
11. Ehrlichman, *Witness to Power*, 59.

12. Kutler, *Abuse of Power*, 528.

13. David Scheim, *Contract on America: The Mafia Murder of President John F. Kennedy* (New York: Shapolsky Publishers, 1988).

14. Maheu made the comments in a 1992 interview with Anthony Summers; Anthony Summers and Robbyn Swan, *The Arrogance of Power: The Secret World of Richard Nixon* (New York: Viking, 2000), 196.

15. Salinger made the disclosure during a 1977 interview with Summers; Summers, *Arrogance of Power*, 196–197.

16. John Dean, *Blind Ambition: The White House Years* (New York: Simon and Schuster, 1976), 66–67.

17. Frank Ragano and Selwyn Raab, *Mob Lawyer* (Toronto: Scribners, 1994).

18. Sam Giancana and Chuck Giancana, *Double Cross: The Explosive, Inside Story of the Mobster Who Controlled America* (New York: Warner Books, 1992).

19. Ibid.

20. E. Howard Hunt, *Give Us This Day* (New Rochelle, N.Y.: Arlington House, 1973).

21. L. Fletcher Prouty, *The Secret Team: The CIA and Its Allies in Control of the United States and the World* (Englewood Cliffs, N.J.: Prentice-Hall, 1973).

22. *Wars of Watergate*, 220.

23. A Freedom of Information Act request resulted in the release of the secret CIA report, written in the wake of the failed invasion. *New York Times*, February 22, 1998.

24. "Obituaries," *Washington Post*, May 22, 2005.

25. Robert Morrow, *First Hand Knowledge: How I Participated in the CIA-Mafia Murder of President Kennedy* (New York: SPI Books, 1992), 293.

26. J. Anthony Lukas, *Nightmare: The Underside of the Nixon Years* (New York: Viking Press, 1976), 232–233.

27. Haldeman, *The Ends of Power*, 38.

28. Kutler, *Arrogance of Power*, 258.

29. Haldeman, *The Ends of Power*, 39–40.

30. John Ehrlichman, *Witness to Power*, 232.

31. Woodward and Bernstein, *The Final Days*, 91.

32. Haldeman, *The Haldeman Diaries*, 567.

33. Michael Drosnin, *Citizen Hughes*, 259.

34. Newfield made the comment in a 2001 interview with *Parade* magazine.

Eleven: Nixon's Spymaster: E. Howard Hunt

1. John Dean, *Lost Honor* (New York: Stratford Press, 1982), 342–343; On June 18, 1973, *Newsweek* reported a "White House–concocted" plan to murder Torrijos. The magazine said Hunt had his team in Mexico before the plot was scrubbed. *Newsweek* credited the information to Dean—who, in *Lost Honor*, claimed he'd never heard of the planned hit. Dean theorizes, however, that the story "had apparently been planted by someone who feared that I knew about it and would be testifying to such knowledge publicly; in leaking it the White House was trying to soften the impact of its discovery." In *Operation Condor*, Daniel Brandt says "Hunt recruited Cuban exiles in 1972 to 'waste' Omar Torrijos in Panama, ostensibly because he protected heroin traffickers, but really because of his position on the Panama Canal," according to Spartacus Education Web.

2. Egil "Bud" Krogh and Matthew D. Krogh, *Integrity: Good People, Bad Choices, and Life Lessons from the White House*, 1st ed. (New York: Public Affairs, 2007), 46.

3. Charles Higham, *Howard Hughes: The Secret Life*, 274.

4. James Warren, "Nixon Tapes Illuminate Squeeze on CIA to Smear JFK," *Chicago Tribune*, December 31, 2000.

5. H. Lowell Brown, *High Crimes and Misdemeanors in Presidential Impeachment*, 1st ed. (New York: Palgrave Macmillan, 2010), 202.

6. United Press International from *Deseret News*, December 7, 1992, "Report on Tapes Says Nixon Hoped to link Gunman to McGovern." http://www.desertnews.com/article/263120/REPORT-ON-TAPES-SAYS-NIXON-HOPED-TO-LINK-GUNMAN-TO-MCGOVERN.html.

7. Meg Greenfield, "Memorial Frenzy," *Newsweek*, June 30, 1997.

8. The entire *Spotlight* article of August 14, 1978, "CIA to Admit Hunt Involvement in Kennedy Slaying" has been published in *Plausible Denial*; Mark Lane, *Plausible Denial: Was the CIA Involved in the Assassination of JFK?* 1st pub. ed. (Emeryville, Calif.: Thunder's Mouth Press, 1992), 129–132.

9. Michael Benson, *The Encyclopedia of the JFK Assassination*, Facts On File Library of American History (New York: Facts On File, 2002), 141.

10. Joseph Trento, "Was Howard Hunt in Dallas the Day JFK Died?" *Wilmington Sunday News Journal*, August 20, 1978; Lane, *Plausible Denial*, 152–155.

11. Report of the House Select Committee on Assassinations, Volume 6, Section 5, Analyses; Section 674.

12. Charles Brandt, *"I Heard You Paint Houses": Frank "the Irishman" Sheeran and the Inside Story of the Mafia, the Teamsters, and the Last Ride of Jimmy Hoffa* (Hanover, N.H.: Steerforth Press, 2004), 129.

13. "Watergate Plotter May Have a Last Tale," *Los Angeles Times*, March 20, 2007.

14. Ibid.

15. A.L. Bardach, "Scavenger Hunt: E. Howard Hunt talks about Guatemala, the Bay of Pigs, and What Really Happened to Che," *Slate*, October 6, 2004.

16. Ibid.

17. "The Last Confessions of E. Howard Hunt," *Rolling Stone*, April 5, 2007.

18. The backgrounds of these men are spotlighted, alphabetically, in *Encyclopedia of the JFK Assassination*; Benson, *Encyclopedia*.

19. "The Last Confessions of E. Howard Hunt," *Rolling Stone*, April 5, 2007.

20. Trento, "Was Howard Hunt in Dallas the Day JFK Died?"; Lane, *Plausible Denial*, 129.

21. Benson, *Encyclopedia* 22–23.

22. Christopher Matthews, *Kennedy & Nixon: The Rivalry That Shaped Postwar America* (New York: Simon & Schuster, 1996), 200.

23. Jim Marrs, *Crossfire: The Plot That Killed Kennedy* (New York: Carroll & Graf Publishers, 1989), 200.

24. Tad Szulc, *Compulsive Spy: The Strange Career of E. Howard Hunt* (New York: Viking Press, 1974).

25. Trento, "Was Howard Hunt in Dallas the Day JFK Died?"

26. Lane was interviewed by *Spotlight*; "Who Killed JFK: A Special Report," *Spotlight*, March, 1992.

27. Victor Marchetti, "CIA to Admit Hunt Involvement in Kennedy Slaying," *Spotlight*, August 14, 1978.

28. Benson, *Encyclopedia*, 23.

29. John H. Davis, *Mafia Kingfish: Carlos Marcello and the Assassination of John F. Kennedy* (New York: McGraw-Hill, 1989), 410.

30. Chuck Giancana and Sam Giancana, *Double Cross: The Explosive, Inside Story of the Mobster Who Controlled America* (New York: Warner Books, 1992).

31. This is on the famous "smoking gun" tape of June 23, 1972. Its release in 1974 was hard proof that Nixon had directed the Watergate cover-up from the start. A transcript of this tape can be found at: watergate.info/tapes/72-06-23_smoking-gun.shtml.
32. "Liddy Was Ready to Kill Hunt Over Watergate," (UPI), *The Hour*, Norwalk, Connecticut, April 12, 1980.
33. "Who Killed JFK?" *Spotlight*, March 1992.

Twelve: Watergate: What Secrets Was Nixon Seeking?

1. Peter H. Brown and Pat H. Broeske, *Howard Hughes: The Untold Story* (New York: Dutton, 1996), 362.
2. Jack Anderson, Daryl Gibson, *Peace, War, and Politics: An Eyewitness Account*, 1st ed. (New York: Forge, 1999), 218.
3. Michael Drosnin, *Citizen Hughes*, 237. "Within two weeks [of Humphrey's nomination for president in 1968, Robert] Maheu met privately with the vice president. The deal was struck. Before the campaign was over, Hubert Humphrey would receive $100,000—half of it in secret cash—from Howard Hughes.
4. "Watergate: The Aviator Connection," *60 Minutes*, CBS, http://www.cbs news.com/stories/2005/02/24/60minutes/main676414.shtml.
5. Ibid.
6. "Hughes-Rebozo Investigation," *National Archives*, http://www.archives .gov/research/investigations/watergate/hughes-investigation.html.
7. Anderson, *War, Peace and Politics*, 221.
8. "Hughes-Rebozo Investigation."
9. History Commons, http://www.historycommons.org/entity.jsp?entity= richard_danner_1[.
10. Both the Watergate Special Prosecutor and the Senate Watergate Committee investigated this matter. A chief Senate investigator, Terry Lanzner, later concluded on "60 Minutes" in 2005 that the money was, indeed, a bribe—as reported by the *Las Vegas Sun*, February 28, 2005, "Hughes Bribe of Nixon Alleged."
11. Jack Anderson, "Why Nixon Fears the CIA," *Oelwein Daily Register*, July 16, 1974.
12. Robert Jackson and Paul Houston, "Further Release of Tapes Shows a Beleaguered President," *Los Angeles Times*, May 29, 1987.

13. Michael Drosnin and Howard Hughes, *Citizen Hughes*, 1st ed. (New York: Holt, Rinehart and Winston, 1985).

14. "The Aviator and the President," *60 Minutes*, CBS, February 27, 2005; "Watergate: 'Aviator' Connection?" CBS News, http://www.cbsnews.com/stories/2005/02/24/60minutes/main676414.shtml.

15. G. Gordon Liddy, *Will: The Autobiography of G. Gordon Liddy* (New York: St. Martin's Press, 1980), 237.

16. Larry DuBois and Laurence Gonzales, "The Puppet and the Puppetmasters," *Playboy*, September 1976; "The Aviator and the President," Feb. 27, 2005.

17. "Watergate: 'Aviator' Connection?"

18. Summers, 157.

19. Frank McCullough phone conversation with author, December 2010.

20. "Bebe Rebozo," Spartacus Educational, http://www.spartacus.schoolnet.co.uk/JFKrebozo.htm.

21. Anthony Summers and Robbyn Swan, *The Arrogance of Power: The Secret World of Richard Nixon* (New York: Viking, 2000), 109.

22. DuBois, "The Puppet and the Puppetmasters."

23. *Wheeling and Dealing*, 346.

24. Kutler, *The Wars of Watergate*, 196.

25. Baker's recollections of his meetings with Rebozo and Kalmbach can be found in *Wheeling and Dealing*; Robert Gene Baker and Larry L. King, *Wheeling and Dealing: Confessions of a Capitol Hill Operator*, 1st ed. (New York: Norton, 1978), 249–256.

26. Spartacus Educational, http://www.spartacus.schoolnet.co.uk/

27. Christopher Hitchens, "Dick the Greek," *Salon*, November 10, 1977, http://www.salon.com/col/hitc/1997/11/nc_10hitc2.html.

28. Stanley I. Kutler, *Abuse of Power: The New Nixon Tapes* (New York: Free Press, 1997), 206.

29. Seymour Hersh, *The Price of Power: Kissinger in the Nixon White House*, 1st ed. (New York: Summit Books, 1983).

30. "Alexander Haig Dies at 85," *New York Times*, February 20, 2010.

Thirteen: Nixon: Vice Presidential Puppeteer

1. "Spiro T. Agnew, Former Vice President, Dies at 77," *New York Times*, September 18, 1996.

2. Stanley I. Kutler, *The Wars of Watergate: The Last Crisis of Richard Nixon*, 1st ed. (New York: Knopf, 1990), 392.

3. Richard Reeves, *President Nixon: Alone in the White House* (New York: Simon & Schuster, 2001), 71.

4. John Ehrlichman, *Witness to Power: The Nixon Years* (New York: Simon & Schuster, 1982), 234–235.

5. Ibid., 120–121.

6. "The Nation, Out of the Past: The Agnew Case," *Time*, August, 20, 1973.

7. The transcript of this presidential news conference from August 22, 1973 in San Clemente, California can be accessed at The American Presidency Project Web site; "The President's News Conference," The American Presidency Project, http://www.presidency.ucsb.edu/ws/index.php?pid=3937.

8. Richard M. Cohen and Jules Witcover, *A Heartbeat Away: The Investigation and Resignation of Vice President Spiro T. Agnew* (New York: Viking Press, 1974), 272.

9. Roger Morris, *Haig: The General's Progress*, 1st ed. (New York: Playboy Press, 1982), 240.

10. All of the Agnew quotes are from his book *Go Quietly . . . or Else*; Spiro T. Agnew, *Go Quietly . . . or Else*, 1st ed. (New York: Morrow, 1980).

11. "Spiro T. Agnew, Former Vice President, Dies at 77," *New York Times*, September 18, 1996.

Fourteen: Nixon's "Best Kept" War Secret

1. William Shawcross, "Sideshow," 22.

2. H. R. Haldeman, *The Haldeman Diaries: Inside the Nixon White House* (New York: G.P. Putnam's, 1994), 40.

3. Rob Kirkpatrick, *1969: The Year Everything Changed* (New York: Skyhorse Publishing, 2009), 8.

4. Christopher Hitchens, *The Trial of Henry Kissinger* (London: Verso, 2002), 35.

5. Seymour M. Hersh, *The Price of Power: Kissinger in the Nixon White House*, 1st ed. (New York: Summit Books, 1983).

6. Transcripts, Nixontapes.org. http://nixontapes.org/transcripts.html.

7. Robert Dallek, *Nixon and Kissinger: Partners in Power* (New York: HarperCollins, 2007), 199.

8. Nigel Hamilton, *American Caesars: Lives of the Presidents from Franklin D. Roosevelt to George W. Bush* (New Haven & London: Yale University Press, 2010).

9. Elizabeth Becker, "Kissinger Tapes Describe Crisis, War, and Stark Photos of Abuse," *The New York Times*, May 24, 2004.

10. Michael Dobbs, "Haig Said Nixon Joked of Nuking Hill," *The Washington Post*, May 27, 2004.

11. Taylor Owen and Ben Kiernan, "Bombs Over Cambodia," Yale University Web site www.yale.edu.cgp.walrus_CambodiaBombing_Oct06 .pdf.

12. Richard Reeves, *President Nixon: Alone in the White House* (New York: Simon and Schuster: 2002), 208.

13. Walter Isaacson, *Kissinger: A Biography* (New York: Simon & Schuster, 1992).

14. Seymour Hersh, "Kissinger and Nixon in the White House," *The Atlantic Monthly*, 249, no. 5 (1982).

15. Rick Perlstein, *Nixonland: The Rise of a President and the Fracturing of America* (New York: Scribner, 2008).

16. "This Day in History: May 9th 1969," The History Channel, http://www .history.com.

17. Hersh, "Kissinger and Nixon in the White House."

18. "Defense: Bombing Coverup," *Time*, July 30, 1973.

19. "The Air Force, the Courts and the Controversial Bombing of Cambodia," AirPower Information Services, http://airpower.com.

20. "Interview with John Ehrlichman," *The National Security Archive*, The George Washington University, http://www.gwu.edu/~nsarchiv/cold war/ interviews/episode-13/ehrlichman4.html.

21. Kenneth J. Hughes, Jr., "How Paranoid was Nixon?" History News Network, http://hnn.us/articles/41698.html.

22. Hersh, *The Price of Power*.

23. J. Anthony Lukas, *Nightmare: The Underside of the Nixon Years* (Athens, Ohio: Ohio University Press, 1999), 472.

24. Mark Feeney, "Rev. Drinan, First Priest Elected as Voting Member of Congress, Dies," *Boston Globe*, January 28, 2007, http://www.boston .com/news/globe/obituaries/articles/2007/01/28/rev_drinan_first_ priest_elected_as_voting_member_of_congress_dies.

25. Douglas Martin, "Robert Drinan Dies at 86; Pioneer as Lawmaker Priest," *New York Times*, January 30, 2007, http://www.nytimes.com/2007/01/30/obituaries/30drinan.html?_r=1&scp=1&sq=Peter+Rodino+&st=nyt.

26. "Nixon Had Notion to Use Nuclear Bomb in Vietnam," Associated Press, *USA Today*, February 28, 2002.

27. Douglas Martin, "Robert Drinan Dies at 86; Pioneer as Lawmaker Priest."

28. Michael Dobbs, "Haig Said Nixon Joked of Nuking Hill: Transcripts of Phone Talks Are Released by Archives," *Washington Post*, May 27, 2004, http://www.washingtonpost.com/wp-dyn/content/article/2004/05/27/AR2005040311188.html.

29. Isaacson, *Kissinger: A Biography*, 263.

30. Craig Whitlock, "Honor Restored for General Blamed after Nixon Denied Authorizing Vietnam Bombing," *Washington Post*, August 5, 2010.

31. Ibid.

32. "Two Stars for Lavelle," *Air Force Magazine*, August 11, 2010, http://www.airforce-magazine.com/Features/personnel/Pages/box081110lavelle.aspx.

33. "Correction: The Lavelle Case," *New York Times*, editorial, August 7, 2010, http://www.nytimes.com/2010/08/08/opinion/08sun3.html.

34. R. James Woolsey, "A General's Demotion," *New York Times*, editorial, August 28, 2010, http://www.nytimes.com/2010/08/29/opinion/l29lavelle.html.

35. "Nixon's Vietnam Scapegoat Finally Gets Justice," *The American Conservative*, August 5, 2010, http://www.amconmag.com/blog/2010/08/05/nixons-vietnam-scapegoat-finally-gets-justice.

36. Jules Witcover, "Nixon Disgraced an Innocent Man," *Daytona Beach News-Journal*, August 8, 2010.

37. "Famous People Falsely Accused, Then Exonerated," *Newsweek*, August 19, 2010, http://www.newsweek.com/photo/2010/08/19/famous-people-falsely-accused-then-exonerated.html.

Fifteen: The World's Most Powerful Drunk

1. Robert Dallek, *Nixon and Kissinger*, 93.

2. Haley Hoffman, "Forty-nine Percent of Presidents Suffered Mental Illness in Duke Study," *The Chronicle*, February 23, 2006.

3. Fawn M. Brodie, *Richard Nixon: The Shaping of His Character* (New York: W.W. Norton and Company, 1981), 167.

4. Dennis McDougal, *Privileged Son: Otis Chandler and the Rise and Fall of the LA Times Dynasty*, 178.

5. Anthony Summers and Robbyn Swan, *The Arrogance of Power: The Secret World of Richard Nixon* (New York: Viking, 2000), 43.

6. H. R. Haldeman and Joseph DiMona, *The Ends of Power* (New York: Times Books, 1978), 45.

7. Anthony Summers and Robbyn Swan, *The Arrogance of Power: The Secret World of Richard Nixon* (New York: Viking, 2000), 172.

8. Ibid., 240.

9. John Ehrlichman, *Witness to Power: The Nixon Years* (New York: Simon and Schuster, 1982), 21.

10. Richard Reeves, *President Nixon: Alone in the White House* (New York: Simon & Schuster, 2001), 192.

11. *The Arrogance of Power*, 462.

12. Seymour Hersh, "Kissinger and Nixon in the White House," *The Atlantic*, May 1982.

13. Stephen Ambrose, *Nixon* (New York: Simon and Schuster, 1987), 285.

14. Bob Woodward and Carl Bernstein, *The Final Days*, 2nd ed. (New York: Simon and Schuster, 1994), 102.

15. Ibid, 424.

16. Walter Isaacson, *Kissinger: A Biography* (New York: Simon & Schuster, 1992), 263.

17. *New York Times*, "Nixon Proposed Using A-Bomb In Vietnam War," March 1, 2002.

18. *The Arrogance of Power*, xv.

Sixteen: Batterer in Chief

1. Jack Anderson and Drew Pearson, "Dirty Fighter," *The Washington Merry-go-Round*, October 4, 1968.

2. Memorandum from Rose Mary Woods to Bob Haldeman, October 7, 1968, nixon.archives.gov/virtuallibrary/documents/donated/100768_woods.pdf.

3. Jonathan Aitken, *Nixon: A Life* (London: Weidenfeld and Nicolson, 1993).

4. Jim McManus, e-mail correspondence with author, 2010.

5. The playmate's name is Gerald Shaw, and the interview is from the Oral History Program, California State University, Fullerton. References to the incident can also be found in *All the Presidents' Women*, by John Berecz, 107; and *Nixon's Shadow*, by David Greenberg, 245.

6. David Greenberg, *Nixon's Shadow: The History of an Image* (New York: W.W. Norton, 2003), 245.

7. Fawn McKay Brodie, *Richard Nixon: The Shaping of His Character* (Cambridge, Mass.: Harvard University Press, 1983).

8. Gary Wills, *Lead Time: A Journalist's Education* (New York: Penguin Books, 1984), 113.

9. White House Tapes, Miller Center, http://whitehousetapes.net/transcript/kennedy/dictabelt-06a2.

10. Seymour Hersh, "Two Stories Seymour Hersh Never Wrote," *Neiman Reports*, Spring, 1998: http://www.nieman.harvard.edu/reports/article/102486/Two-Stories-Seymour-Hersh-Never-Wrote.aspx.

11. Christopher Matthews, *Kennedy & Nixon: The Rivalry That Shaped Postwar America* (New York: Simon & Schuster, 1996), 215.

12. Colson, *Born Again*, 78.

13. from Richard Reeves, *Alone in the White House* (April 30, 1973): "Walking to the Oval Office, he passed an FBI agent guarding the door of Haldeman's office, then realized the man was there to prevent records from being destroyed or taken away. He turned, came back, and shoved the FBI man against the wall. 'What the hell is this?' said the president. 'These men are not criminals.'"

14. Witnessed by the author.

15. Witnessed by the author.

16. Anthony Summers and Robbyn Swan, *The Arrogance of Power: The Secret World of Richard Nixon* (New York: Viking, 2000), 478.

17. William Henry Chafe, *The Unfinished Journey: America Since World War II* (New York: Oxford University Press, 1986), 414.

18. Tom Wells, *The War Within: America's Battle over Vietnam* (Berkeley, Calif.: University of California Press, 1994), 562.

19. Richard Reeves, *President Nixon: Alone in the White House* (New York: Simon & Schuster, 2001), 554.

20. Christopher Hitchens, "Let Me Say This About That," *New York Times, Books*, October 8, 2000.

Seventeen: Threatening to Fire Kissinger, Ziegler: Nixon's War on the Press

1. "Calling 'Em Out, The White House Takes on the Press," *TIME*, October 8, 2009, http://www.time.com/time/politics/article/0,8599,1929058,00.html.

2. All the new tapes included in this chapter can be listened to at The Miller Centers Web site; White House Tapes, Miller Center, millercenter.org.

3. This conversation is on a tape released in recent years by the National Archives. It can be heard on C-SPAN's online collection of presidential tapes; "History of the Nixon White House Tapes," C-SPAN, http://legacy.c-span.org/apa/nixon.asp?Code=APA.

4. *Washington Post*, October 15, 1972.

5. Helen Thomas, *Front Row at the White House: My Life and Times* (New York: Scribner, 1999), 192.

Eighteen: Backstage at the Resignation

1. The author has a personal recording of Nixon's prespeech comments.

2. "President Nixon's Resignation Speeech," *Presidential Linls*, PBS, http://www.pbs.org/newshour/character/links/nixon_speech.html.

3. Stephen E. Ambrose, *Nixon*, 3 vols. (New York: Simon and Schuster, 1987), 437.

4. Stanley I. Kutler, *The Wars of Watergate: The Last Crisis of Richard Nixon*, 1st ed. (New York: Knopf, 1990), 549.

5. Barry Werth, *31 Days: The Crisis That Gave Us the Government We Have Today*, 1st ed. (New York: Nan A. Talese/Doubleday, 2006), 343.

6. J. Anthony Lukas, *Nightmare: The Underside of the Nixon Years* (New York: Viking Press, 1976), 567.

7. Lydia Saad, "Kennedy Still Highest Rated Modern Day President, Nixon Lowest," *Gallup*, December 6, 2010, http://www.gallup.com/poll/145064/kennedy-highest-rated-modern-president-nixon-lowest.aspx.

Ninteen: Nixon Orchestrates His Own Pardon

1. "Remarks on Signing a Proclamation Granting Pardon to Richard Nixon," The Ford Library, http://www.fordlibrarymuseum.gov/library/speeches/740060.asp.

2. "Nixon's Response," Watergate.info, http://watergate.info/ford/pardon.shtml.

3. Leon Jaworski, "He Knew Nixon Was Lying but Couldn't Say It," *People* magazine, December 30, 1974.

4. Jonathan Shell, *Time of Illusion*, 316; "Watergate Notes: An Impromptu Offer," *Time* magazine, June 10, 1974.

5. MRPopCulture.com, Week of May 1, 1974, www.mrpopculture.com.

6. The entire memo can be found at Super70s.com; "Post Resignation Memo to Special Prosecutor," Super70s, http://www.super70s.com/super70s/News/Special-Reports/Watergate/740809_Jaworski_Memo.asp.

7. Bob Woodward, *Shadow: Five Presidents and the Legacy of Watergate* (New York: Simon & Schuster, 1999), 6.

8. Robert Trowbridge Hartmann, *Palace Politics: An Inside Account of the Ford Years* (New York: McGraw-Hill, 1980).

9. Woodward, *Shadow*, 7.

10. Clark R. Mollenhoff, *The Man Who Pardoned Nixon* (New York: St. Martin's Press, 1976).

11. The estimate comes from Professor Stanley Kutler, author of *The Wars of Watergate*, who sued to keep the tapes from Nixon—and won; Stanley I. Kutler, *The Wars of Watergate: The Last Crisis of Richard Nixon* (New York: Norton, 1992).

12. Mollenhoff, *Man Who Pardoned*.

13. Seymour Hersh, "The Pardon" from *The Price of Power*, *The Atlantic*, August 1983, http://www.theatlantic.com/magazine/archive/1983/08/the-pardon/5571/.

14. "Award Announcement," May 21, 2001, the John F. Kennedy Library, http://www.jfklibrary.org.

15. "Friendship Played a Role in Ford's Pardon of Nixon," *Good Morning America*, ABC News, http://abcnews.go.com/GMA/Politics/story?id=2758590&page=1.

16. Bob Woodward, "Ford, Nixon Sustained Friendship for Decades," *Washington Post,* December 29, 2006, http://www.washingtonpost.com/wp-dyn/content/article/2006/12/28/AR2006122801247.html.

17. Hartmann, *Palace Politics*.

18. Seymour Hersh, "The Pardon."

19. Barry Werth, "The Pardon," *Smithsonian Magazine*, February 2007, http://www.smithsonianmag.com/people-places/ford.html?c=y&page=2.

20. Adam Clymer, "At First Nixon Spurned Idea of Pardon, Lawyer Says," *New York Times*, November 13, 1999.

Twenty: The Post-Resignation Ribald Raconteur

1. "Nixon/Gannon Interviews," University of Georgia Library, http://www.libs.uga.edu/media/collections/nixon.
2. *Saturday Night Live*, NBC.
3. Lukas, Nightmare, 356.
4. Ibid., 358. Deductions disallowed by IRS included $6,750 for family Christmas cards and $5,391.43 for Tricia Nixon's 1969 masked ball."
5. Dash made the comments at a Watergate panel discussion in Washington, D.C. in August 1994. The discussion was broadcast by C-SPAN.
6. Tip O'Neill, "Nixon Played Hardball: O'Neill Believes Greed Kept Embattled President From Destroying Watergate Tapes," *Broward Sun-Sentinel*, op-ed, September 14, 1987.

Bibliography

Abrahamsen, David, M.D. *Nixon vs. Nixon*. New York: Farrar, Straus & Giroux, 1997.

Agnew, Spiro. *Go Quietly . . . Or Else*. New York: William Morrow, 1980.

Anson, Robert Sam. *Exile*. New York: Simon and Schuster, 1984.

Belli, Melvin. *Dallas Justice*. New York: David McKay Company, Inc., 1964.

Benson, Michael, ed. *Encyclopedia of the JFK Assassination*. New York: Facts On File, 2002.

———— *Who's Who in the JFK Assassination: An A-to-Z Encyclopedia*. New York: Citadel Press, 2003.

Ben-Veniste, Richard, and George Frampton, Jr. *Stonewall*. New York: Simon & Schuster, 1977.

Bernstein, Carl, and Bob Woodward. *All the President's Men*. New York: Simon & Schuster, 1974.

———— *The Final Days*. New York: Simon & Schuster, 1976.

Blakey, Robert, and Richard Billings. *The Plot to Kill the President*. New York: New York Times Books, 1981.

Brodie, Fawn M. *Richard Nixon*. New York: W. W. Norton, 1981.

Canfield, Michael, with Alan J. Weiberman. *Coup d'État in America*. New York: Third Press, 1975.

Colson, Charles. *Born Again*. New York: Bantam, 1976.

Crouse, Timothy. *The Boys on the Bus*. New York: Ballantine, 1973.

Davis, John H. *Mafia Kingfish*. New York: Signet, 1989.

Dean, John. *Blind Ambition*. New York: Simon & Schuster, 1976.

DeFrank, Thomas. *Write It When I'm Gone*. New York: G.P. Putnam's Sons, 2007.

—— *Lost Honor*. Los Angeles: Stratford Press, 1982.

DiEugenio, James, and Linda Pease, ed. *The Assassinations: Probe Magazine on JFK, MLK, RFK and Malcolm X*. Port Townsend, Wash.: Feral House, 2003.

Drosin, Michael. *Citizen Hughes*. New York: Bantam, 1985.

Ehrlichman, John. *Witness to Power*. New York: Pocket Books, 1982.

Emery, Fred. *Watergate: The Corruption of American Politics and the Fall of Richard Nixon*. New York: Times Books, 1994.

Flammonde, Paris. *The Kennedy Conspiracy: An Un-commissioned Report on the Jim Garrison Investigation*. New York: Meredith, 1969.

Fonzi, Gaeton. *The Last Investigation*. New York: Thunder's Mouth Press, 1993.

L. Ford, Gerald. *Foreward, A Presidential Legacy and the Warren Commission*. Nashville, Tenn.: Flatsigned Press, 2007.

Gray III, Patrick L. *In Nixon's Web*. New York: Times Books, 2008.

Haldeman, H. R., with Joseph Di Mona. *The Ends of Power*. New York: Times Book Co., 1978.

—— *The Haldeman Diaries*. New York: Putnam, 1994.

Hartmann, Robert. *Palace Politics*. New York: McGraw-Hill, 1980.

Higham, Charles. *Howard Hughes: The Secret Life*. New York: Putnam, 1993.

Hunt, E. Howard. *Give Us This Day*. New York: Arlington House, 1973.

Kantor, Seth. *Who Was Jack Ruby?* New York: Everest House, 1978.

Kessler, Ronald. *Inside the White House*. New York: Pocket Books, 1993.

Kissinger, Henry. *Years of Upheaval*. Boston: Little, Brown, 1982.

Kuntz, Tom and Phil, ed. *The Sinatra Files*. New York: Three Rivers Press, 2000.

Hinckle, Warren, and William Turner. *Deadly Secrets*. New York: Thunder's Mouth Press, 1992.

Hurt, Henry. *Reasonable Doubt*. New York: Holt, Rinehart and Winston, 1985.

Kutler, Stanley. *Abuse of Power: The New Nixon Tapes*. New York: The Free Press, 1997.

—— *The Wars of Watergate*. New York: Alfred A. Knopf, 1990.

La Fontaine, Ray and Mary. *Oswald Talked: The New Evidence in the JFK Assassination*. Gretna, LA: Pelican Publishing, 1996.

Lane, Mark. *Plausible Denial*. New York: Thunder's Mouth Press, 1992.

———— *Rush to Judgment*. New York: Holt, Rinehart and Winston, 1996.

Livingstone, Harrison Edward. *High Treason 2*. New York: Carroll & Graf, 1992.

Mailer, Norman. *Oswald's Tale: An American Mystery*. New York: Random House, 1995.

Mankiewicz, Frank. *Perfectly Clear, Nixon from Whittier to Watergate*. New York: Quadrangle, 1973.

Marrs, Jim. *Crossfire*. New York: Carroll & Graf, 1989.

Matthews, Christopher. *Kennedy and Nixon*. New York: Simon & Schuster, 1986.

Moldea, Dan E. *The Hoffa Wars*. New York: Paddington Press, 1978.

Mollenhoff, Clark R. *The Man Who Pardoned Nixon*. New York: Giniger, in association with St. Martin's Press, 1976.

Morris, Roger. *Richard Milhous Nixon*. New York: Henry Holt, 1990.

———— *Haig: The General's Progress*. Chicago: Playboy Press, 1982.

Morrow, Robert. *First Hand Knowledge*. New York: S.P.I. Books, 1992.

Newman, John. *Oswald and the CIA*. New York: Carroll & Graf, 1995.

Nixon, Richard. *RN: The Memoirs of Richard Nixon*. New York: Simon & Schuster, 1978.

Oudes, Bruce, ed. *From: The President*. New York: Harper & Row, 1989.

Perlstein, Rick. *Nixonland*. New York: Scribner, 2008.

Prouty, L. Fletcher. *The Secret Team*. Englewood Cliffs, N.J.: Prentice-Hall, 1973.

Ragano, Frank, and Selwyb Raab. *Mob Lawyer*. New York: Charles Scribner's Sons, 1994.

Reeves, Richard. *President Nixon: Alone in the White House*. New York: Simon & Schuster, 2001.

Reston, James Jr. *The Conviction of Richard Nixon*. Harmony Books, 2007.

Russell, Dick. *The Man Who Knew Too Much*. New York: Carroll & Graf, 1992.

Russo, Gus. *Live by the Sword*. Baltimore: Bancroft Press, 1998.

Scheim, David. *Contract on America: The Mafia Murders of John and Robert Kennedy*. New York: Shapolsky Books, 1988.

Schorr, Daniel. *Clearing the Air*. Boston: Houghton Mifflin, 1977.

Sullivan, William. *The Bureau*. New York: W.W. Norton, 1979.

Summers, Anthony. *The Arrogance of Power*. New York: Viking, 2000.

———— *Not in Your Lifetime*. New York: Marlowe & Company, 1998.

Witcover, Jules. *The Resurrection of Richard Nixon*. New York: G. P. Putnam's Sons, 1970.

—— *Very Strange Bedfellows*. New York, Public Affairs, 2007.

—— and Richard Cohen. *A Heartbeat Away*. New York: Viking, 1974.

Woodward, Bob. *Shadow*. New York: Simon & Schuster, 1999.

Official Tapes

Richard Nixon's White House tapes are housed at the National Archives in College Park, Maryland. Copies will soon be trucked to the Nixon Library in Yorba Linda, California, now that that facility is controlled by the National Archives.

Cited conversations on the Watergate tapes released in the 1970s are from transcripts made by the Senate Watergate Committee, the House Judiciary Committee, or the Watergate Special Prosecution Force.

Most cited conversations on tapes made public in the mid-1990s were transcribed at the National Archives under the direction of historian Stanley Kutler. They are found in his 1997 book *Abuse of Power*.

Some of these tapes and even newer ones are available on the Internet at the Web sites of C-SPAN, the Nixon Library, the Miller Center at the University of Virginia, and at Luke Nichter's nixontapes.org. For the purpose of this book, all "new" tapes are those released since 1997.

Nixon strongly fought the release of all tapes right up until his death in 1994. But a lawsuit filed by Kutler and the advocacy group Public Citizen led to a 1996 settlement with the Nixon estate that brought the new tapes to light. They are still being released, in small batches, on an irregular basis.

Index

About the Author

The author and the president in China. WHITE HOUSE PHOTO.

Don Fulsom covered the White House during five presidential administrations and served as UPI's radio bureau chief in Washington for seven years, anchoring scores of live, on-the-scene radio broadcasts for major news events, including President Kennedy's funeral and President Nixon's arrival in Peking.

Fulsom is an adjunct professor of government at American

University, where he teaches courses on the presidency and Watergate.

The author has written about Nixon for *The Washington Post*, the *Chicago Tribune, Esquire, Los Angeles Times, Regardie's* (a now-defunct Washington political and business magazine), and *Crime Magazine.*

In 1999, when UPI closed its radio operation and Fulsom cleaned out his White House booth, the independent *White House Weekly* described him as "one of the best White House correspondents when it came to grilling press secretaries. His questions were tough, intelligent, and always delivered with gentlemanly professionalism. At the daily White House press briefings, reporters can be divided into those who sit back and quietly drink in the scene and those who consistently engage administration officials in the great game of eliciting newsworthy information. Fulsom was always in the latter group."